GW00649432

Guide to Birds of the Falkland Islands

SARA BERRY

Guide to Birds of the Falkland Islands

Robin W Woods

Illustrated by Franklin Coombs

Anthony Nelson

© 1988 Robin W Woods
First published 1988 by Anthony Nelson Ltd
PO Box 9, Oswestry, Shropshire SY1 1 1BY, England

ISBN 0 904614 22 0

All rights reserved. No part of this book may
be reproduced, stored in a retrieval system, or
transmitted in any form or by any means, electronic,
mechanical, photocopying or otherwise, without
the permission of the publisher.

Designed by Alan Bartram
Filmset and printed by BAS Printers Limited,
Over Wallop, Hampshire.

Contents

List of plates

Preface

The events of early 1982 brought the Falkland Islands to the notice of many people who were not previously aware of their existence. Thousands more have visited the islands and interest in conservation of the natural habitat and the wildlife, has increased tremendously. As a result, several more species have been added to the list of birds by residents and visitors who have included several experienced birdwatchers.

This book provides a comprehensive guide to the identification of all 185 species known to have been recorded on the Falkland Islands or within the 200 mile zone of surface water surrounding the archipelago. Twenty-one colour plates by Franklin Coombs illustrate all breeding species and most of the non-breeding visitors and vagrants. Short notes on field identification are given opposite the plates and birds not illustrated are listed. Identification notes are cross-referenced to the main text, where full details on each species are provided. Several birds that have not yet been recorded are mentioned in the text where separation from similar species is difficult. A Checklist is provided with a number and a coded summary for the status of each species.

The book can be used merely as a field guide, by reference to the plates and checking with the full descriptions in the text. For those who wish to learn more about the environment, the Introduction gives a comprehensive description of many factors that affect the birds of the Falkland Islands and a historical summary of ornithological and conservation activity. An explanation of scientific classification and general notes on distribution of breeding birds and the occurrence of vagrants, complete the Introduction.

Preceding the field guide are notes on abbreviations used and a diagram showing the plumage of a bird. The headings describing breeding and non-breeding species are explained.

As the Introduction shows, ornithological work in the Falklands has been sporadic and basic information on most species is barely recorded. It is hoped that this book will be useful for the accurate identification of all breeding species and most non-breeders, thus allowing birdwatchers to increase the published knowledge of these fascinating birds.

Acknowledgements

Many people in the Falkland Islands and other countries have contributed to this Guide, through their published work in books and journals or by reporting observations to me, to the Falkland Islands Trust in Stanley or to the Royal Naval and Army Bird Watching Societies. My thanks are due to them all, especially to Shane Wolsey of the F I Trust, who has done much recently for bird watching in the Falklands, encouraged other people and given time to collecting records.

I am particularly indebted to Dr Franklin Coombs who took great care in painting the colour plates over several years and willingly made additions.

The value of this book has been enhanced significantly by the vast number of sightings made and records submitted by Dr Bill Bourne and Bill Curtis. I thank them both for supplying records of several species identified for the first time in Falkland waters and for enabling me to make far more realistic statements about seabird occurrences.

I am grateful to my publisher Tony Nelson for his interest and encouragement and for his continuing enthusiasm about all aspects of the Falkland Islands.

ROBIN W WOODS
November 1987

Introduction

The Falkland Islands lie in the South Atlantic on an extension of the Patagonian Continental Shelf, between latitudes 51°S and 53°S and longitudes 57°30′W and 61°30′W. They are centred about 500km (350 miles) northeast of the nearest point of South America, Cape San Diego on Tierra del Fuego, about 1000km (625 miles) north of Elephant Island, the nearest of the South Shetlands group and about 1450km (900 miles) west of South Georgia. East and West Falkland, the main islands, are separated by Falkland Sound. There are now known to be 778 much smaller islands (Woods 1986). Of these, 291 are around the northern, eastern and southern coasts of East Falkland, 58 in Falkland Sound and 397 off the northern, western and southern coasts of West Falkland; 32 are in lakes or ponds. The total land area is about 12,200 square kilometres (4700 square miles).

West Falkland is generally more hilly than East Falkland and has a northern range of low mountains running east to west and another range, the Hornby Mountains, running parallel to Falkland Sound. The highest peak on West Falkland is Mount Adam (700m, 2297 feet). On East Falkland, north of Choiseul Sound which almost bisects the island, the land rises gently from sea level to the Wickham Heights, which reach 450m to 600m (1,500 to 2,000 feet) and stretch east to west from Stanley, the capital and only town, to San Carlos settlement. Mount Usborne (705m, 2,312 feet) north of Darwin settlement, is the highest peak on East Falkland. Outcrops of rock occur on most ridges and hilltops and form the higher parts of the mountains. Red-backed Hawk, Crested Caracara and Peregrine Falcon are typical birds of these crags. Lafonia, the southern part of East Falkland, is an area of remarkably low, undulating land, rarely rising above 60m (200 feet).

Stone-runs are an impressive feature of the Falkland uplands. They occur extensively on hillsides and along valleys and are formed from accumulations of large angular boulders, often several metres across and sometimes weighing more than 50 tonnes. It is not known how they were formed although several theories have been advanced. Stone-runs appear completely barren, apart from growths of lichens, but low shrubs gradually spread over the edges and the many available cavities provide ideal nesting sites for one passerine species, the Dark-faced Ground-tyrant.

The coastline is deeply indented with many sheltered harbours. Extensive beaches of near-white sand occur on the northern and eastern coasts of both main islands, sometimes with adjoining lagoons or ponds. Two-banded Plover and Magellanic Oystercatcher are typical of this habitat throughout the year. Rocky points, headlands and boulder-strewn beaches are also regular coastal features where Kelp Geese, Blackish Oystercatchers and Night Herons may be found. The western coasts of West Falkland and its offlying islands are rugged with some cliffs rising to 370m (1,200 feet) meeting the full force of the South Atlantic swell and westerly gales.

Throughout the Falklands, peat soils are widespread with deposits up to 5m (16½ feet) thick, though peat formed from tussac grass has developed over the past 12,000 years to a depth of 13m (42½ feet) on Beauchêne Island, south of East Falkland (Smith & Prince 1985). Peat formed from woody shrubs and grass has been the main source of fuel since settlement began and, behind Stanley, much of the Common is scarred by peat cuttings. Drainage is usually poor because the peat overlies clay and the ground is often waterlogged for long periods in winter. Tracks between settlements begin to dry out in September, allowing easier overland travel by four-wheel drive vehicles and motorcycles during the following summer months.

There are numerous ponds ranging in size from a few square metres to 250 hectares (618 acres), particularly in the centre of West Falkland, in Lafonia, the northeast of East Falkland and south of the Wickham Heights. All ponds are acidic and those in peat with steep sides and peat bottoms lack submergent and fringe plants. Ponds with sand or clay bottoms sometimes have rich growths of plants and where banks are sloping, they are very attractive to ducks and grebes (Weller 1972). The uplands are drained by many streams and small rivers but none is navigable for any appreciable distance.

There is little cultivated land. Most houses in Stanley and the settlements have large gardens in order to grow vegetables, particularly root crops and potatoes. There are planted windbreaks of European gorse or the native 'Box', a few plantations of Monterey Cypress and various pines and some other deciduous trees where they have been protected from grazing animals. Some settlements have small fields where oats are grown for fodder.

The Falkland landscape has made very different impressions on visitors. Pernety (1771), one of the original settlers with de Bougainville's French expedition was impressed that, 'In the quarter of the island which we saw, the land everywhere presents a very agreeable aspect.' In contrast, others who were stationed there and two eminent scientists described the islands in very unflattering words which have prejudiced many people over the past two centuries. McBride (1767) made comments such as, 'ranges of craggy barren mountains . . . in the valleys between them are swamps and large ponds of water. The ground where it is dry, is shallow and poor. They are totally destitute of wood, and produce nothing but wild celery and sorrel; and that to be had only in the summer months.' Clayton (1774) described them as, 'mountainous, boggy, rocky and every where barren . . . overspread with a tufty long round bladed sour grass.' Joseph Hooker (1847) remarked that, 'The uniform plains and undulating hills of the Falkland Islands betoken at first sight a country of little interest for the botanist; and a closer inspection proves this to be, to a certain extent, the case.' Charles Darwin (1845) also painted a very unattractive picture: 'An undulating land, with a desolate and wretched aspect, is everywhere covered by a peaty soil and wiry grass, of one monotonous brown colour. Here and there a peak or ridge of grey quartz rock breaks through the smooth surface . . . The country is uniformly the same undulating moorland; the surface being covered by light brown withered grass and a few very small shrubs, all springing out of an elastic peaty soil.'

Before Hooker's visit, G T Whitington published material (1840) based on his own experiences and those of Lieutenant Smith, Governor at Port Louis from 1834 to 1838. He aimed to encourge settlers and his remarks are still relevant. 'The appearance of the Islands, upon entering Berkley Sound is at first sight rather unfavourable, arising principally from the rocky mountains then visible, with the absence of wood, which gives the country a dreary and barren aspect; from these appearances I have little doubt that, in remote periods, casual observers were deterred from exploring the country, and gave those deplorable accounts of these islands, which despite numerous authentic testimonials, and recent accurate information, continue, even in the minds of well-informed persons, and proves how difficult it is to remove preconceived prejudices of long standing.'

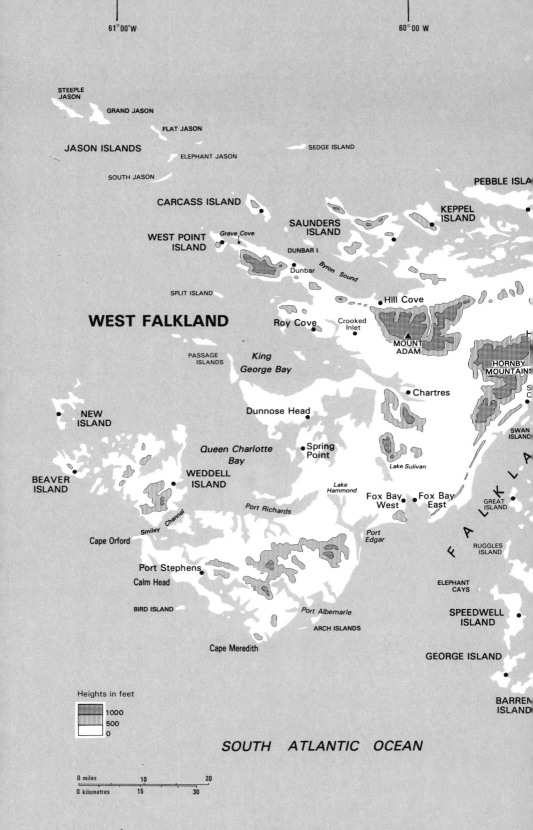

61°00'W   60°00 W

STEEPLE JASON

GRAND JASON

FLAT JASON

JASON ISLANDS   SEDGE ISLAND

ELEPHANT JASON

SOUTH JASON

PEBBLE ISLA

CARCASS ISLAND   KEPPEL ISLAND

SAUNDERS ISLAND

WEST POINT ISLAND   *Grave Cove*

DUNBAR I.

Byron Sound

Dunbar

SPLIT ISLAND

Hill Cove

WEST FALKLAND   Roy Cove   Crooked Inlet

▲ MOUNT ADAM

HORNBY MOUNTAINS

PASSAGE ISLANDS   *King George Bay*

Chartres

NEW ISLAND   Dunnose Head

SWAN ISLAND

Queen Charlotte Bay   Spring Point

BEAVER ISLAND   WEDDELL ISLAND   *Lake Sulivan*

Lake Hammond

Fox Bay West Fox Bay East

GREAT ISLAND

Smiley Channel   *Port Richards*

Cape Orford   Port Edgar   RUGGLES ISLAND

Port Stephens

Calm Head   ELEPHANT CAYS

BIRD ISLAND   *Port Albemarle*   SPEEDWELL ISLAND

ARCH ISLANDS

Cape Meredith   GEORGE ISLAND

Heights in feet

1000
500
0

BARREN ISLAND

SOUTH ATLANTIC OCEAN

0 miles   10   20
0 kilometres 15   30

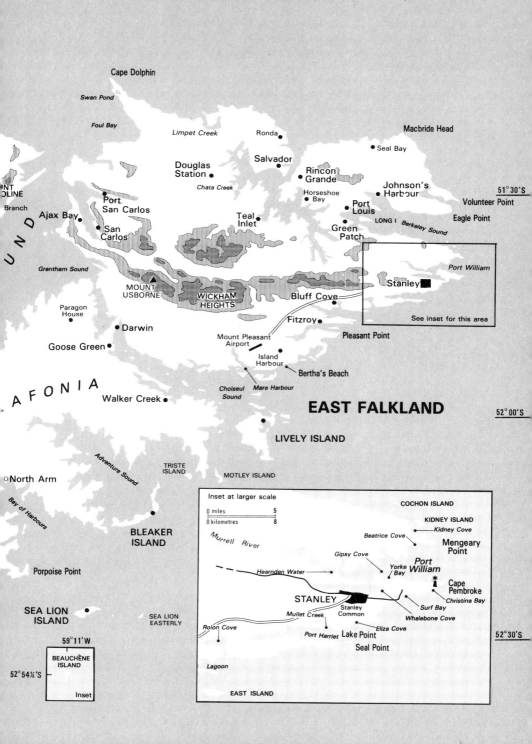

SOUTH ATLANTIC OCEAN

59°00'W
58°00'W
51°00'S

Cape Dolphin

Swan Pond

Foul Bay

Limpet Creek
Ronda

Macbride Head

Salvador
Seal Bay

Douglas
Station
Rincon
Grande
Johnson's
Harbour

Chata Creek
Horseshoe
Bay
51°30'S
Volunteer Point

NT
OLINE
Port
San Carlos
Port
Louis
Eagle Point

Branch
Ajax Bay
Teal
Inlet
LONG I *Berkeley Sound*

San
Carlos
Green
Patch

Grantham Sound
Stanley
Port William

MOUNT
USBORNE
WICKHAM
HEIGHTS
Bluff Cove
See inset for this area

*Paragon
House*
Fitzroy
Pleasant Point

Darwin
Mount Pleasant
Airport

Goose Green
Island
Harbour

Bertha's Beach

*Choiseul
Sound*
Mare Harbour
EAST FALKLAND
52°00'S

AFONIA
Walker Creek

LIVELY ISLAND

Adventure Sound
TRISTE
ISLAND
MOTLEY ISLAND

North Arm

Bay of Harbours
BLEAKER
ISLAND

Porpoise Point

SEA LION
ISLAND
SEA LION
EASTERLY

59°11'W

BEAUCHÊNE
ISLAND

52°54½'S

Inset

Inset at larger scale

0 miles _____ 5
0 kilometres _____ 8

COCHON ISLAND

KIDNEY ISLAND

Murrell   River
Beatrice Cove
Kidney Cove
Mengeary
Point

Gipsy Cove
*Yorke
Bay*
Port
William

Hearnden Water
Cape
Pembroke

STANLEY
Christina Bay

Mullet Creek
Stanley
Common
Surf Bay

Rolon Cove
Whalebone Cove

Port Harriet
Eliza Cove

Lagoon
Lake Point
Seal Point

EAST ISLAND
52°30'S

Hooker and Darwin spent little time in and around the islands. People who live for longer periods or settle are much more enthusiastic about the islands, often finding that the land appears bleak due to the absence of native trees but white sand-beaches, brilliant green grass around ponds or the smaller offshore islands covered with tussac grass, contrast pleasantly with the windswept uplands. The wide expanses of rolling straw-coloured grassland, mottled with dark patches of diddle-dee and grey rock outcrops have an attraction of their own and the atmosphere is so clear that it is often possible to see vast distances. The silence of the camp, broken only by cries of animals and birds and the thunder of surf, the solitude and the strong, cool winds all combine to give a sense of exhilaration and freedom.

Climate

The climate of the Falkland Islands is cool with a small temperature range, high winds, much variability from day to day and little change between seasons, except in day-length which varies seasonally as in southern Britain. As Maling (1960) commented, these are all characteristic features of temperate oceanic climates. Falkland weather is dominated by westerly winds, associated with the usual track of depressions through Drake Passage south of the islands. Westerly gales occurring during spring and autumn migration periods often carry landbirds eastwards from Tierra del Fuego or Patagonia to the Falklands. Calm periods are rare and occur more frequently in winter. Average wind speed is about 15 knots (17mph); strong winds are frequent and gale force winds (34 knots/39mph or more) occur on about four days a month. The persistent wind often makes air temperatures feel lower than they are due to the chilling effect, but this is partly alleviated by the clarity of the air and brilliance of the sunlight.

Average monthly temperatures vary between 9°C (49°F) in January and 2°C (36°F) in July. The average annual temperature is about 6°C (43°F). Humidity is generally high due to the oceanic situation and there are few completely cloudless days. Average annual precipitation at Stanley, one of the wetter places and where all the above meteorological information was obtained, is about 610mm (24ins). September and October are usually the drier months, when camp tracks dry out making travel overland easier, gardens can be planted and peat can be cut. Most rain tends to fall in the summer months of December and January, often as heavy showers of rain, hail or sleet, with clouds developing rapidly after brilliant sunny mornings.

The climate has been much maligned by some writers. It is true that often in winter it can be depressingly dull and damp, or bitterly cold with southerly gales but there are calm frosty days and in spring and summer, there are many days of bright sunshine with a brisk drying wind which are very enjoyable. The sudden changes in weather are an annoying feature for farmers and birdwatchers alike. Where transport by small boats is essential, a period of strong winds or gales for several days can be very frustrating. The clear air is a bonus however, and the relative tameness of many species makes bird photography a rewarding pastime.

The cool and equable climate has affected the breeding birds in several ways, first described by Pettingill (1960a) and summarized below.

1. Apart from seabirds, most species have long breeding seasons or start nesting

early in spring because there is no marked change in temperature between seasons.

2. Persistent strong winds have so limited the amount of plant cover for landbirds that only nine native passerine species occur. Persistent wind and lack of tall vegetation have both led to a shortage of flying insects. The small number of these species and low density of their populations, is almost certainly due to a paucity of both cover and flying insects. Islands covered with dense tussac grass are an exception, as will be explained later. Settlements with planted trees and shrubs support higher densities of some passerines than the surrounding land.

3. The cool climate and consequent shortage of food cause several Falkland species to lay smaller clutches of eggs than similar species on the South American mainland.

4. The body-size of at least six Falkland races of passerines is greater than that of the equivalent South American mainland form. Larger birds have less difficulty in maintaining body-heat than small birds because their surface area per unit of weight is less.

5. The lack of severe weather allows most breeding species to survive the Falkland winter. Species which could migrate are probably deterred by the prevailing westerly winds though there are at least three landbirds for which there is some evidence of migration.

Falkland seas

The seas around the Falkland Islands and their marine life, have a great influence on the resident birds. The Falkland Islands are in the Southern Cold-Temperate zone of surface water, which has here a surface temperature rarely exceeding 10°C (50°F). The cool Cape Horn Current divides southwest of the Falklands and two branches sweep around the islands as the Falkland Current to rejoin south of Uruguay. This current penetrates northwards to Rio de Janeiro (23°S), while the influence of the warm Brazil Current extends southwards to about 40°S. Where these two currents meet, and in the areas of upwelling water off the continental shelf north of the Falklands, marine life is abundant. Lobster-krill (*Munida* species) occur in huge red shoals off the coasts of Patagonia, Tierra del Fuego and the Falklands. Three species of squid, the Argentine Shortfin (*Illex argentinus*), the Patagonian (*Loligo gahi*) and a smaller species, *Teuthowenia*, occur in vast numbers in Falkland waters. Lobster-krill, Patagonian Squid, *Teuthowenia* and euphausian shrimps are taken by several seabirds, including the Black-browed Albatross, Sooty and Great Shearwaters, Rockhopper Penguin and the Imperial Shag. Gulls and both species of shags feed on lobster-krill when shoals are close to shore.

Extensive beds of Giant Kelp (*Macrocystis* and *Lessonia*) species are found in sheltered waters around all Falkland coasts between about six and 20 fathoms deep. They support many crustaceans and fish which provide food for the Steamer Ducks, Rock Shag, three species of gulls and the South American Tern.

Since the Falklands were settled, several forms of hunting have been carried out in Falkland waters. During the late eighteenth and the nineteenth centuries, Elephant Seals and Fur Seals were hunted almost to extermination for their oil and skins respectively. Penguins were killed in hundreds of thousands on land and tried out for oil until about 1871; whales were hunted in the early nineteenth century and, briefly from a base at New Island, between 1908 and 1915. Offshore waters, mainly to the east of the Falklands, have attracted foreign deep-water vessels during the past 25 years and are now being fished heavily, particularly for squid and for some fin fish such as Blue Whiting and Hake. The effect of these activities on Falkland seabirds is not known in detail, though it is obvious that penguin numbers were continually reduced until penguin-oiling ceased. The offal discharged by several hundred fishing vessels has probably benefitted scavenging birds such as albatrosses, some petrels and gulls. In contrast, intensive squid fishing may have reduced available food for several species.

Natural vegetation

The natural vegetation of the Falkland Islands consists of grasses, shrubs which rarely reach 2m (6 feet) in height and various low plants. Only 163 species of native flowering plants and ferns have been recorded in the Falklands with at least another 90 introduced species (Moore 1968). There are no native trees, probably because the Falklands have been isolated from South America since the Ice Age, acid peat blanketed much of the surface and stopped soil development and mycorrhizal fungi that aid tree growth were largely absent.

Most of the Falkland Islands surface is covered by plant associations known as oceanic heath. White grass *Cortaderia pilosa* is dominant on damper ground with associated rushes, sedges and mosses where underlying peat is saturated. This 'Soft camp' is inhabited by a few bird species, including the Grass Wren and Common Snipe. On ridges or where the subsoil is better drained, a resinous dwarf shrub known as Diddle-dee *Empetrum rubrum*, ferns and white grass occur with other low shrubby plants, forming what is known as 'Hard camp'. Typical birds are the Rufous-chested Dotterel, Falkland Pipit and the Long-tailed Meadowlark. In stream valleys, bordering ponds and around settlements, better quality grassland occurs, often dominated by introduced species such as Yorkshire Fog *Holcus lanatus* with Pigvine *Gunnera magellanica*, a creeping plant that produces berries which are important as food for the Falkland Thrush and the Black-throated Finch. At higher altitudes above about 600m (2000 feet) and on lower stony slopes, large cushion plants such as Balsam-bog *Bolax gummifera* occur on otherwise bare ground.

On coastal cliffs of West Falkland and adjacent islands native 'Box' *Hebe elliptica* grows where it is inaccessible to sheep. The shrub Fachine *Chiliotrichum diffusum* borders streams and rivers throughout the Falklands. Sandy areas above high water mark often have dense growths of grey-green Sand Cabbage *Senecio candicans*, which are bright with many small yellow flowers in summer. The tallest and most spectacular native plant, the giant Tussac (tussock grass) *Poa flabellata* is discussed separately because it is of singular importance to Falkland birds.

Two grasses introduced about 1923 (Hubbard 1937) to stabilize drifting sand dunes, Marram *Ammophila arenaria* and Lyme-grass *Elymus arenarius*, are now common in low-lying coastal regions. Many species of trees and shrubs have been introduced in attempts to provide shelter for gardens. The first efforts were made by McBride (1767) who brought 'large quantities' of fir seed with him in 1766, which germinated but soon withered. Ross and Hooker tried another way in 1842, when they brought 700 young trees of several species from Cape Horn. In 1848, many plants were sent out from the Royal Botanic Gardens at Kew. Little is known of their fate except for that of Gorse *Ulex europeaus*, which flourished and apparently led to the development of dense gorse livestock barriers at most settlements and in Stanley. In the late nineteenth century, Robert Blake of Hill Cove succeeded in establishing a plantation of Austrian Pine *Pinus nigra*, Scots Pine *P. sylvestris*, a spruce, probably Sitka *Picea sitchensis* and Antarctic Beech *Nothofagus betuloides*. In the 1950s these trees started to grow vigorously and in 1982 they had reached 18m (60 feet) in a dense plantation. Several others have succeeded as isolated trees or windbreaks, the most common being Monterey Cypress *Cupressus macrocarpa* which has grown to at least 9m (30 feet) at Stanley.

Stewart (1982) reviewed tree introductions and concluded that most early attempts failed through lack of knowledge, absence of experienced foresters and insufficient local interest. He advocated the establishment of a tree nursery and eventual planting of several trees and shrubs, mainly from Chile, in small woodland areas and shelterbelts as part of the rural development programme.

An exciting new project at Many Branch on West Falkland may have far-reaching effects on habitats for landbirds. A tree nursery was started in 1986, with help from the F I Development Corporation, after Tim Miller had visited England to study tree growing. He has cultivated thousands of seeds or cuttings of many deciduous and evergreen trees and shrubs in a sheltered garden. In early 1987, 3000 trees and shrubs were imported and 1000 were sold very quickly in Stanley (Spafford 1987). If this project is successful, it is probable that some passerines inhabiting Tierra del Fuego will colonise the Falklands; the Rufous-collared Sparrow could be the first.

Tussac Grass

Tussac Grass *Poa flabellata* is one of several species of tussock-forming grass that occurs in maritime grassland on sub-Antarctic islands. It is also found on Gough Island, South Georgia, Staten Island, Diego Ramirez and islands south of Tierra del Fuego. All species are extremely vulnerable to grazing and damage by fire and are notable as having evolved only in those parts of the world with very few or no native herbivorous mammals (Wace 1960).

Tussac can grow to at least 3.5m (11½ feet), forms dense monospecific stands and is very long-lived. Smith and Prince (1985) obtained a radiocarbon date from the pedestal of a large healthy plant on Beauchêne Island of about 300 years. A mature tussac plant produces a fibrous pedestal (tussac-bog) 1–1.5m (3–5 feet) high from the crown of which spring the flower stems and thousands of long leaves that remain green for about two years. Foliage that has died eventually folds down, remains attached to the base and forms a skirt projecting around the pedestal. Tussac leaves are tough but, fortunately, do not have sharp or serrated edges. Nevertheless, adjacent plants in mature tussac grassland are so close together that skirts interlace completely and are inseparable. Below mature tussac, the heavily shaded ground remains damp throughout the year and becomes carpeted with dead and decomposing leaf litter in which no other flowering plants can establish themselves. Tussac grows best on coastal slopes where Magellanic Penguins, shearwaters and diving petrels burrow and aerate the underlying tussac peat and provide fertilizers from excreta. Tussac also occurs up to at least 220m

(720 feet) above sea level but most commonly grows as a coastal fringe, formerly very abundant and, according to mid-nineteenth century accounts, up to 800m (880 yards) in breadth.

In 1842, J D Hooker (later Sir Joseph Hooker) was assistant naturalist on the Antarctic Expedition led by James Clark Ross, which spent six months at Port Louis before proceeding south for the third time. Hooker (1847) was the first person to describe tussac in detail and to realise its importance as fodder, green or dry, for cattle, horses and pigs. He described tussac-covered land as a labyrinth and noted the great amount present, but remarked that it did not occur on all coasts as Lieutenant Governor Robert Moody had stated (1842). Through their respective fathers Sir William Hooker and Colonel Moody, Hooker and Moody reported to the Geographical Society in November 1842. This apparently led many owners of barren peat-bogs in the British Isles to believe that they could plant tussac and produce vast quantities, more than sufficient for all their cattle. It seems however, that landowners did not appreciate that tussac had to be two or three years old before it was able to yield significant amounts of fodder for cutting (Huxley 1918).

Hooker was so taken by the use of tussac as forage that he under-estimated its importance to the native fauna. He mentioned a sparrow-sized bird, possibly the Siskin, that ate the seeds for one month a year, one small insect that ate leaves, penguins and petrels that burrowed beneath tussac (though they also burrowed where no tussac existed) and sea-lions that cowered beneath the foliage while being equally suited to using rocks elsewhere. His comment that tussac could have remained unknown and unprized, 'if cattle had not been introduced into its locality by man, so that man thus became, first the injurer and then the protector and propagator of the existence of this noble grass', was only partly true. Events since 1842 have not included wholesale protection and propagation of tussac.

The French had introduced cattle at Port Louis and when Hooker reached East Falkland 78 years later, there were about 30,000 feral cattle roaming the country. He commented that tussac had been greatly reduced by uncontrolled grazing and believed that it would have been exterminated if people had not returned, realised its importance and dispersed it to other countries. Unfortunately his efforts did little to protect the tussac remaining in the Falklands. When Carl Skottsberg, a Swedish botanist, visited the Falklands 60 years later, in 1901–02 and 1907–09, he stated (1913) that the once widely spread tussac was then occupying very restricted areas such as small, unstocked islands and hardly occurred on coasts of the main islands. He noted tussac remnants on pebble beaches but none on sandy beaches and wondered whether tussac had ever occupied most of the coastline.

On the larger islands, almost all of the original tussac grassland has been destroyed by over-grazing. Many small islands were fired intentionally in the late eighteenth and nineteenth centuries by sealers trying to evict seals or were burnt out accidentally. Long Island in Berkeley Sound was deliberately fired by de Bougainville, leader of the first settlers in 1764. Pernety (1771) tried to stop this destruction but was unsuccessful; 'M de B imagined, that by destroying this useless herbage he was doing a piece of service, as it would save trouble whenever these lands were cleared.' Hundreds of Magellanic Penguins burrowed on Long Island, originally called Penguin Island by the French but renamed Burnt Island after the fire. Pernety also warned de Bougainville about the dangers of firing the long, coarse grass on East Falkland near their settlement at Port Louis. Unfortunately, 'He paid no regard to my remonstrances; and set fire that very evening to several parts of the continent.'

On East and West Falkland, tussac is now restricted to a few points and peninsulas where it is protected from sheep. The subdivision of large farms since 1982 and the new owners' intentions of grazing offshore tussac islands led to concern being expressed by F I Government in 1986 that more tussac would be lost. A baseline photogrammetric survey of tussac was therefore commissioned, using the complete cover of air photographs taken by Hunting Aerosurveys in 1956 for the 1961–62 Overseas Surveys Directorate maps. A sample of 1983 air photographs taken by the Royal Air Force will give a comparison and some information on the rate of loss. Ian Strange's paper (in preparation) on visits to many islands over the past 25 years should add further information. These surveys have been jointly sponsored by the Falkland Islands Government and a member of the Falkland Islands Foundation. Preliminary results from photogrammetric work showed that 74% of approximately 11,000ha (27,170 acres) of tussac remaining in 1956 was on 316 of the 780 islands in the archipelago. 198 (63%) of these were of 5ha (12.3 acres) or less in area, 103 (32.6%) were between 5.1 and 40ha and only 15 (4.7%) were of 40ha (99 acres) or more.

Since Hooker's time, visiting botanists and agricultural advisers, including Skottsberg, Munro (1924), William Davies (1939) and Tom Davies et al (1971), have commented on the value of tussac for livestock and have regretted its loss from almost all East and West Falkland coasts. The probable effects of this loss of habitat on Falkland birds were not considered until a preliminary ecological study of Kidney Island off East Falkland was carried out between 1958 and 1963 (Woods 1970a). On this island of only 32ha (80 acres) at least 5,000 pairs of 28 bird species were breeding. Further field work was carried out in 1983 on Kidney, Carcass and West Point Islands (Woods 1985). Sample censuses of nine breeding passerine species were made in fenced tussac paddocks re-established by farmers since the 1890s, on West Point and Carcass Islands and in dense tussac on Kidney Island. Results showed that areas of mixed dense tussac and heathland supported up to eight passerines while dense tussac held only five passerines. Population densities were equally high in dense tussac on Kidney Island and in a mosaic of tussac and heathland on Carcass Island. Mosaic tussac/heathland on West Point Island held seven breeding species but, due almost certainly to the presence of feral cats, rats and mice, population density was only a sixth of that on Carcass Island. On Kidney Island, by chance, and on Carcass Island, largely due to the conservationist policies of owners since sheep farming began, there were no introduced mammalian predators. On both islands many other bird species occupied nesting habitats above, on or below ground level. In the Carcass Island census plot, it was estimated that at least nine species including Magellanic Penguins, geese, ducks and two waders had a total population density as high as that of the passerines.

It is of great significance that Dyke paddock on Carcass Island, in which the census plot was situated, had become bare ground by the 1920s through overgrazing and subsequent loss of topsoil by wind erosion. Jason Hansen, the owner at that time, had seen the results of replanting fenced tussac paddocks on West

Point. He started fencing and replanting several coastal paddocks from 1927, and in 1934 Dyke paddock was still being replanted (Bertrand 1968). Fifty years growth of re-established tussac has therefore re-created habitat for almost 20 bird species. Apart from the Magellanic Penguin and possibly the Tussac-bird, none of these species could have occupied the bare, eroded slopes.

Changes in vegetation

Changes in vegetation have altered the appearance of the land since the first recorded sighting 300 years ago and settlement nearly a century later. Unrestricted grazing by cattle from 1764 to the 1870s on East Falkland, from 1838 on West Falkland and by sheep from 1852, has also altered the inland vegetation and led to a great reduction in some grasses and shrubs.

The resemblance of coastal tussac to low palm trees was mentioned by Hooker but there are few detailed descriptions of the inland flora. Pernety (1771) provided a picture that is very different from that which confronts a visitor today. At a distance, Pernety thought East Falkland looked dry and parched but on landing, he found it covered with vegetation a foot or more high that reached to the tops of hills and through which he had great difficulty in walking. A century later, one of the early settlers, H Felton (Woods 1975), described the northern camp of West Falkland as covered in dense grass and wild celery, often difficult to get through. In the summer of 1871, according to Felton, the camp was burnt to the soil from Chartres to Port Purvis, a distance of about 50km (30 miles); it took 15 years before there was a semblance of recovery, apparently because sheep pulled out the grass as it started to grow, making the camp look like a hayfield.

Before sheep farming began, cattle had grazed East Falkland for almost a century and West Falkland for about 30 years. Within half a century, the sheep population increased rapidly, reaching a peak of over 800,000 by 1898. Numbers fell by about 20% during the first quarter of the twentieth century because the best pasture had been overgrazed. An associated and long established farming practice is the deliberate firing of dead white grass leaves in late winter or early spring, so that sheep can graze the more nutritious young green shoots. This management technique continues, and although several grassland specialists have condemned the practice, it remains controversial. Fires are generally unsupervised, strong winds are a feature of the climate, and there is no legislation to control the timing of grass-burning. Fires are left to die out and may continue for months in a dry season when diddle-dee on hard camp has caught fire and burnt deep into the peat. Roots of other plants are destroyed leading to destruction of the topsoil and serious erosion by wind and rain. Therefore any short-term benefits to farmers seem to be heavily outweighed by the detrimental effects.

It is certain that the introduction of livestock in a country that had no native herbivorous mammals and the use of grass-burning to clear areas of 'useless' vegetation, have changed the distribution and numbers of Falkland landbirds considerably. A change in vegetation that has had a local and beneficial effect on bird populations is the development of windbreaks, shrubs and trees at settlements and in Stanley. Although there are many early general observations, there are no accurate records of bird populations before grazing animals and other mammals associated with human colonisation were introduced. Evidence from recent bird population census work on Kidney, Carcass and West Point Islands suggest that passerine birds were far more numerous before grazing started and predators were introduced (Woods 1985).

Falkland birds: classification and distribution

Birds constitute the class Aves in the animal kingdom and the birds of a definable geographic area are described as the avifauna. The Falkland Islands avifauna includes rather few breeding species, some of which are present in very large numbers concentrated around the coasts and on some smaller offshore islands.

Order, family, genus and species are terms used in biological classification.

An *Order* consists of a number of families considered to have certain general affinities.

A *family* comprises few or many genera (plural of genus) with several recognizable similarities that separate them from other families.

A *genus* is a group of species considered to be closely related and with many basic characteristics in common.

A *species* is regarded as a biological unit, and is characterized by inherent reproductive isolation, *ie* two species inhabiting the same area do not normally interbreed.

A species may be sub-divided into geographical races (*subspecies*) that have certain recognizable differences. The Upland Goose *Chloephaga picta* for example, occurs in the Falklands, southern Chile and southern Argentina. The *Falkland Island* Upland Goose is larger than the continental bird and the male is always white-breasted. The Falkland Island Upland Goose is therefore described as a local race and given the additional subspecific name *leucoptera*. Its full scientific name is *Chloephaga picta leucoptera*.

Table 1 on page 24 summarizes the classification of 61 known breeding species, including two introduced species, the Domestic Goose and the House Sparrow. Two species, have been added to the list of Falkland breeding birds since 1975. One is the Domestic Goose, now well established in free-flying populations at several settlements. The second is the Chilean Swallow which bred, apparently for the first time, at Port Stephens settlement in the 1983/84 season. Eight possible breeding species were omitted from Table 1: Northern Giant Petrel, Black-bellied Storm-Petrel, Coscoroba Swan, Mallard, American Kestrel, Cordilleran Snipe, Least Seedsnipe and Barn Owl. They have either been claimed as breeding species without good evidence or been suspected of breeding in the past.

This table differs slightly from that shown in the 1975 book because some reclassification has been suggested by taxonomists. It shows that Falkland breeding birds are representatives of 12 orders and 29 families. Only 18 species are true landbirds while 43 species depend on a salt or fresh water environment for food or refuge. It can therefore be inferred that the Falklands provide generally poor habitats for landbirds and good habitats for waterbirds. The most abundant family (Anatidae) has a swan, four sheldgeese, one true goose and eight ducks, reflecting the presence of grassland rather than woodland, a very long and varied coastline with many

Table 1. Classification of Falkland Islands breeding birds

Order	Family	Genera	Species
SPHENISCIFORMES	Spheniscidae – Penguins	4	5
PODICIPEDIFORMES	Podicipedidae – Grebes	1	2
PROCELLARIIFORMES	Diomedeidae – Albatrosses	1	1
	Procellariidae – Petrels and Shearwaters	4	6
	Hydrobatidae – Storm-petrels	2	2
	Pelecanoididae – Diving Petrels	1	1
PELECANIFORMES	Phalacrocoracidae – Shags/Cormorants	1	2
CICONIIFORMES	Ardeidae – Herons	1	1
ANSERIFORMES	Anatidae – Sheldgeese, Swans and Ducks	6	14
CATHARTIFORMES	Cathartidae – New World Vultures	1	1
ACCIPITRIFORMES	Accipitridae – Hawks	1	1
FALCONIFORMES	Falconidae – Caracaras and Falcons	3	3
CHARADRIIFORMES	Haematopodidae – Oystercatchers	1	2
	Charadriidae – Plovers	1	2
	Scolopacidae – Sandpipers and Snipes	1	1
	Stercorariidae – Skuas	1	1
	Laridae – Gulls	1	3
	Sternidae – Terns	1	1
STRIGIFORMES	Strigidae – Owls	1	1
PASSERIFORMES	Furnariidae – Ovenbirds	1	1
	Tyrannidae – Tyrant-flycatchers	1	1
	Hirundinidae – Swallows	1	1
	Motacillidae – Pipits	1	1
	Troglodytidae – Wrens	2	2
	Turdidae – Thrushes	1	1
	Passeridae – Sparrows	1	1
	Fringillidae – Finches	1	1
	Emberizidae – Buntings	1	1
	Icteridae – American Orioles	1	1

sheltered bays and abundant inland pools and lakes in some parts. Second in abundance are the tubenosed Procellariiformes with an albatross, six petrels or shearwaters, two storm-petrels and one diving petrel. Their presence indicates abundant marine organisms in Falkland waters and the availability of suitable coastal nesting sites, especially coasts with dense tussac grass. Penguins are well represented (five species) and three species are particularly numerous, again due to the presence of suitable food offshore and coastal sites on which to breed.

Only nine species in the order Passeriformes have been able to adapt to the windy and exposed habitats, that lack native trees. All native passerines are representatives of southern South American species and most of them have been isolated from the original populations long enough to develop slight differences which allow them to be classed as geographic races/subspecies. It is probable that they established Falkland populations as glaciation decreased during the Holocene period of the last 10,000 years.

About 22 species occur as regular *non-breeding migrants*. Most of these are seabirds, breeding at Antarctic and sub-Antarctic islands, which pass the Falklands on migration. Three species are North American waders that spend their non-breeding season in South America. The Whimbrel has only recently achieved this status in the Falklands, possibly because the North American breeding population has increased.

The largest group on the Falkland list is composed of vagrants from South America and the Antarctic. About 100 species have been identified to date. Fifteen species have been recorded for the first time within the past five years, clearly reflecting the presence of more experienced observers since 1982. Increased fishing activity offshore may have led to the appearance of several newly recorded seabirds including two albatrosses and seven petrels or shearwaters. Occasional waterbirds from South America drift far to the south and reach the Falklands. The Cattle Egret was recorded for the first time in 1976. Since then it has become a regular vagrant in large numbers each autumn when many immature birds disperse from South American breeding areas and arrive partly exhausted in the Falklands. Several small birds, mostly passerines, have appeared after periods of very strong west or northwesterly winds when migrating in spring or autumn. More inexplicable is the appearance of two different swifts, one found dead in 1959 and one seen flying strongly near Cape Pembroke Lighthouse in November 1986. Neither species was known to migrate southwards from their most southerly breeding regions in northwestern Argentina! It is likely that many other South American birds reach the Falklands and probable that one or two more species will have been identified by the time this book is published.

The human factor

Human activities have rarely proved beneficial to Falkland birds. From the earliest days of settlement, at Port Louis and at Saunders Island, the new arrivals were impressed by the abundance and tameness of the birds. Early reports and letters such as those from Byron (1765), Pernety (1771) and Clayton (1774) were concerned mainly with the edibility of several species, including geese, ducks, birds of prey, waders and thrushes.

Pernety described how the ships' companies of two frigates totalling 150 men, found sufficient game for a stay of more than two months in 1764, within three leagues (about 14km or 9 miles) and remained in perfect health. Amongst other birds, they ate 150 'Bustards' (Upland Geese) and found them, 'exquisite either boiled, roasted or fricasseed.' Byron said that his people lived on nothing apart from wild fowl during their stay at Port Egmont. He commented that they, 'seldom took less than 100 wild geese in a day for each ship (*Dolphin* and *Tamar*) and they by only knocking down with stones.' Clayton and his party started on albatross eggs, followed by penguin, 'Sea hen' (Skua) and gulls eggs and commented that there was no lack of refreshment till the end of November, while after December the wild geese, 'are grown fitt food and their young large enough to eat.' Many species were, however, ignored until Garnot (1826) and Darwin (Gould & Darwin 1841) listed the species observed and commented on their plumage, habits or distribution.

As sheep farming became established, the numerous Upland and Ruddy-headed Geese drew further attention from farmers. Both species probably increased as sheep grazed the native vegetation, leading to the development of coastal greens.

Geese congregated on these greens, where the grass was palatable and, inevitably, farmers were persuaded that they competed with sheep. The quality of pastures had declined by 1900 and farmers claimed that between four and seven geese ate as much grass as one sheep.

No studies were made, instead, pressure on Government caused an Ordinance to be passed in 1905 which allowed for payment of ten shillings per 100 goose beaks, for up to 25,000 beaks each from East and West Falkland in the first year. There was opposition before legislation but the Ordinance was apparently approved by a small majority (Harradine 1976). The limit was raised to 50,000 from East Falkland in 1906 and, after irregular beak payments, the Ordinance ceased effect in 1912. By that date, over 500,000 beaks had been bought by Government. Payments continued, however, until 1924 when Munro's report on sheep farming recommended the use of grain poisoned with phosphorus to kill geese. This suggestion was apparently considered seriously but was not adopted. The controversy continues, with some claiming loss of reseeded pastures to heavy grazing by geese, while others maintain that a high goose population indicates good pastures.

Another agricultural investigation by visiting specialists was carried out in 1969/70 (Davies et al 1971) and in 1974, John Harradine was employed by the Falkland Islands Government to study geese and their effects on sheep farming (Harradine 1976). His study was later integrated with the newly formed Grassland Trials Unit, which had been established to obtain basic information to improve farming systems. Harradine was followed by Ron Summers, from 1977 to 1980, who reported in 1983 that about 25,000 geese were being killed annually and that a population of several hundred thousand survived. Summers' work on the diets of geese (Summers & Grieve 1982) was thorough and amongst other findings, showed that goose droppings had similar digestability and nitrogen content to good quality grass and that sheep often ate goose droppings. The studies (Summers 1985) also showed that consumption was greatest on greens and reseeded pastures. At North Arm farm, it was found that sheep and cattle ate about 20% of the annual herbage production of pastures while geese took only about 2%. Summers concluded that goose populations did not present a serious economic threat to the sheep industry. Summers and Crocker (1983) suggested that farmers would have less trouble from geese if they sited reseeded pastures away from water and would improve their flocks if they fertilised pastures or gave food supplements to lactating ewes. The culling of geese was shown to be an ineffective control method.

Three birds of prey also attracted condemnation from sheep farmers. The Striated Caracara, Crested Caracara and the Turkey Vulture were classified as vermin in 1908, when an Ordinance for the 'Destruction of Birds of Prey' authorized the payment of four pence for each Turkey Vulture beak and two pence for each beak of Crested and Striated Caracaras. All three species were condemned for their attacks on fallen sheep and new-born lambs, though the amount of damage they do remains a matter of debate. Bounties were being paid at least to 1959 and the 1964 Wild Animal & Birds Protection Ordinance specifically stated that Crested Caracaras and Turkey Vultures could be killed by any means. The Striated Caracara, however, was given protected status in the 1920s after its numbers had declined seriously and J E Hamilton had made representations to the Government. Forty years later, this species was still being shot unlawfully at far western islands. Since then, numbers seem to have increased slightly and it is seen frequently at West Falkland settlements. One bird of prey, the Cinereous Harrier, appears to have been exterminated as a breeding species since sheep farming developed. Darwin reported that it was extremely tame, like the Striated Caracara, and Abbott (1861) noted that it preyed on rabbits. Over grazing and burning of grassland probably contributed to its decline.

There are a few records of four small passerines, observed or collected by Darwin in 1833/34 or Ross in 1842, apparently originating from the Falklands. Darwin's description of the Andean Tapaculo and its habits and habitat, strongly suggest that it was a breeding species before long grass and shrubby vegetation was eaten out by sheep. There have been no certain records since 1833/34. The Thorn-tailed Rayadito and Austral Canastero have both been collected once and attributed to the Falklands (Sclater & Sharpe 1885–98). The Yellow-bridled Finch, a bunting which is widespread in southern South America, was described in some detail by Darwin. He considered it was common in the Falklands, often at higher altitudes than the Black-throated Finch. Abbot (1861) failed to see or collect the Yellow-bridled about 25 years after Darwin and no certain records have been made since an immature was collected by Brooks in 1916. If any of these species did inhabit the Falklands, vegetation changes could have led to their extermination.

In the 1964 Ordinance several species were classed as pests. The Kelp Gull, Antarctic Skua, Thin-billed Prion and the House Sparrow could be killed at any time. The first two species are alleged to do appreciable damage to sheep but it is certain that they are useful scavengers of dead sheep, particularly those thousands culled annually. They also kill goslings and provide some natural control over populations of Upland and Ruddy-headed Geese. The Thin-billed Prion was apparently classed as vermin because its largest breeding colony was on New Island, where many thousands burrow and undermine the heathland, reputedly making it dangerous for horses and leading to soil erosion. The House Sparrow was seen as an alien that ate seeds and damaged seedlings in vegetable gardens but it occurs only at some settlements and seems unlikely to become a major pest.

At least four species of penguins have been victimised in the Falklands since the first voyagers arrived. Gentoo and Rockhopper Penguin eggs have been collected for human consumption in vast numbers and are still taken under licence, though the practice, fortunately, seems to be declining. The eggs of the Black-browed Albatross have been taken for food since the earliest days. Collecting is also controlled by licencing and few are now taken. From the early years of sealing in the late eighteenth century, and intermittently until about 1871, millions of penguins were corralled, clubbed and tried out for their oil. The crews of some small vessels were reported to have killed 70–100,000 penguins annually per vessel (Sclater 1868, Brooks 1917), each bird producing about 0.6 litres (1 pint) of oil. King Penguins, though apparently never numerous, were also killed for oil and for their plumage, leading to temporary extinction in the islands from the late nineteenth to the early twentieth century. All penguins are now officially protected as species and have been recognised as one of the great tourist attractions of the Falklands.

Several other species have been shot as game-birds in the past. Under the 1953 Wild Animals & Birds Protection Ordinance, five species of ducks and the Rufous-chested Dotterel, Common Snipe and the Long-tailed Meadowlark were considered as game species that could be shot in the open season between 1 March and 31 July. The 1964 Ordinance reduced the list to four ducks (Crested Duck, Silver Teal, Chiloe Wigeon, Speckled Teal) and the Common Snipe, reflecting the growing knowledge of Falkland birds and interest in their conservation.

It is not surprising that in a pioneer country with a resident population never exceeding 3,000, there have been few people with sufficient time to study birds. Until recently, all systematic studies of distribution or biology have been undertaken by expatriate residents or visiting biologists. This situation has changed since the Breeding Birds Survey started in 1984 and local people have begun to record the presence of all species in their home areas.

Terrestrial mammals

Only one terrestrial carnivore was native to the Falkland Islands. This animal was known from the early days of settlement as the warrah and was variously described as a wolf, dog or fox. It was absurdly tame and apparently lived on geese, penguins, other birds and eggs before livestock were introduced. Settlers and visiting sealers regarded it either as fair game or a pest and the last warrah was killed at Shallow Bay, West Falkland in 1876, only a century after colonisation. Two recent investigations of museum skins and skeletons have both suggested that the Falkland Fox (Warrah) *Dusicyon australis* was a close relative of South American foxes, wild dogs or wolves of the same genus. Gorham (1972) and Clutton-Brock (1977) felt that the warrah could have reached the Falklands on driftwood or, perhaps more likely, that a semi-domesticated form of *Dusicyon* was carried to the Falklands by early man from southern South America in the late Pleistocene or early Holocene period, about 10,000 years ago. Whatever its origin, the warrah was remarkable as the only terrestrial carnivore. Because no evidence of prehistoric man has been found in the Falklands, it is obvious that the predator-prey relationship between warrahs and birds was in balance for thousands of years before modern man arrived.

Domesticated animals were introduced by the French settlers who came into Berkeley Sound and established Port Louis (1764) and by the English who garrisoned Port Egmont, Saunders Island (1766). De Bougainville's expedition brought ten pigs, nine cattle, three horses, a few sheep and a goat, while McBride's group left pigs, goats and rabbits on Saunders Island which all thrived on the plentiful grass, especially on the tussac. The East Falkland cattle increased to about 80,000 by 1847 but, through unscrupulous killing for hides or tallow and uncertainties over land tenure, they were virtually exterminated within 40 years (Cawkell, Maling & Cawkell 1960). Pigs were released on some small islands, 'multiplied exceedingly' on Saunders (Gower 1803) but most had been killed by sealers and whalers by the mid nineteenth century. Garnot, however, found pigs occupying thickets of 'shrubby trees' around a bay north of Berkeley Sound in 1822. The goats also thrived on Saunders and were apparently numerous on New Island in 1802. By 1842, Moody could not confirm their presence anywhere, though Miller (1975) mentioned 40 at the South American Missionary Society station on Keppel Island in 1863. Horses also multiplied on East Falkland north of the Wickham Heights; Moody quoted Tyssen's estimate of about 3,000 in 1842.

These introduced pigs, goats and horses have all apparently died out or been killed by hunters. From 1764 to about 1840 there were few sheep of several breeds around the Port Louis settlement. They were well established by 1852 on East Falkland and were introduced in 1867 by the first colonists to West Falkland. By 1867 there were about 65,000 sheep in the Falklands and the population expanded rapidly to a maximum of over 800,000 in 1898.

The rabbits placed on Saunders Island in 1766 were present in 'thousands' in 1836–7 (Grey). They must have been introduced to other islands, probably by sealers or whalers, because Grey also stated that New Island abounded with rabbits while Lowcay (1838) reported them as abundant on Speedwell Island. Between 1833 and 1842, grey, piebald and black rabbits were common in the northern part of East Falkland where they favoured valleys near the coasts (Darwin 1845; McCormick 1884). By 1896, Mowat stated that there were none to contend with, as far as sheep farming was concerned though a few were reserved on some small islands for naval crews to shoot. Rabbits were still present on New Island in the 1980s and possibly survive on other small islands. Hares *Lepus europaeus* were probably introduced during the nineteenth century. The earliest published record appears to be one of 25 shot on Phillimore Island near Fitzroy in 1881 (Anon. 1882). In recent years they have been recorded on Cape Pembroke, around San Carlos, Salvador, Fitzroy and North Arm settlements. The herbivorous Guanaco *Lama guanicoe* was introduced to Staats Island (c500 hectares/1,236 acres), probably in the 1930s. They survived and form a population of several hundred which graze the grassland heavily and have apparently killed most of the tussac.

All the above introduced mammals were herbivores, liberated in an environment where no native herbivores existed. The detrimental effects of cattle and sheep on the natural vegetation are well known. It seems likely that the other animals also contributed to the decline of grasses, particularly tussac, and therefore reduced available habitat for breeding birds.

Five carnivorous or omnivorous mammals have also been introduced, which have had variable but probably more direct effects on birds. Domestic cats now occur on many inhabited islands and there are feral cats on East and West Falkland. The New Island cats were deliberately introduced to reduce the population of Thin-billed Prions. At other settlements and in Stanley, they certainly kill passerine birds. 'Grey Rats' (probably *Rattus norvegicus*, also known as Norway or Brown Rat) were described by Darwin (Waterhouse & Darwin 1839) as infesting East and West Falkland, occurring 50km (30 miles) from habitation and on some outlying islets. Their predation particularly on burrow-nesting birds of oceanic islands has often been recorded (Bourne 1981, Atkinson 1985). Cobb (1933) noted that Tussac-birds did not as a rule live on islands where rats were present. Recent field work has shown, however, that Tussac-birds can exist on an island with rats (Woods 1985). Recently, the Black or Ship Rat *R. rattus* has been identified on New Island (Thompson & Hale pers. comm.) where they co-exist with Thin-billed Prions, though passerine bird populations appear to be less dense than those on Sea Lion Island, which is free of cats, rats or mice (R Wilson pers. comm.). House Mice *Mus musculus* have been recorded from East Falkland and many off-shore islands since at least 1839 (Waterhouse & Darwin). They apparently adapted quickly to a feral existence (Bernsee 1855) and evidence that they inhabited dense tussac and fed on tussac seeds or flowers was found on West Point Island in 1983 (Woods 1985). It is probable that mice take some birds' eggs, as rats are known to do. The Patagonian Fox *Dusicyon griseus*, a close relative of the extinct Falkland Island Fox, was introduced to islands of the Hamilton Estate, probably towards the end of the nineteenth century. The Patagonian Fox now survives on Beaver and Weddell Islands where it probably kills lambs and on Staats and Split Islands, where it presumably preys on ground-nesting birds and Magellanic Penguins. Sonia Felton reported that attempts to reduce the number of foxes on Beaver Island had resulted in 57 being shot in January 1987, though there were apparently many more surviving.

History of ornithology

Interest in the birds of the Falkland Islands started in 1764, when the islands were first settled. The difficulties of travel within the Falklands and the settlers' preoccupation with establishing themselves and surviving in an alien climate, led to a shortage of contemporary written information on status and distribution of species throughout the islands.

Published ornithological records are very uneven until the 1920s. Before 1860, most records came from naturalists on expeditions that touched at the islands. In 1819 Messrs Quoy and Gaimard were wrecked in the *Uranie* in Berkeley Sound and lost all their collection of skins from previous countries visited. They made good use of their enforced stay, collected many specimens and named several new species, including the Falkland Thrush.

P Garnot, surgeon and naturalist on the corvette *La Coquille* spent a month at Port Louis in November–December 1822 during a voyage around the world between 1822 and 1825. He listed 45 species, described some in detail, barely mentioned others and misidentified a few. Charles Darwin visited in the autumns of 1833 and 1834, each time for about a month. He listed only 20 species and seemed particularly fascinated by the Striated Caracara which had also intrigued Garnot by its daring. Darwin collected some specimens as did McCormick who was naturalist with James Ross' Antarctic Expedition. This expedition on HMS *Erebus* and *Terror* spent a total of six months in Falkland waters, mainly at Port Louis in 1842. McCormick's written records are sparse while labels on specimens are not completed in detail. There is doubt about the origin of some specimens as they visited islands near Cape Horn for two months during their period in Falkland waters. The same doubts apply to some of Darwin's specimens (W Bourne pers. comm.).

After McCormick, the next ornithologist who took an interest was Captain Pack, who lived in Stanley for several years before 1860 and sent many skins back to England. Another, Captain C C Abbott, was in charge of the military detachment at Stanley between February 1858 and October 1860. He travelled as widely as possible, collected many skins and eggs and in 1861, published observations on 66 species in volume 1 of *Ibis*. P L Sclater, Secretary to the Zoological Society of London, wrote up a Catalogue of 57 species of Falkland Islands birds in 1860 with corrections in 1861, based on the collections of Pack and Abbott.

Unfortunately, during the forty-year period up to 1900, when most of the Falklands had been sold in vast areas as farms and when sheep numbers reached their greatest total, there was no resident ornithologist and apparently few specimens collected. Therefore, the impact of sheep-farming and the establishment of settlements on the number and distribution of birds can only be surmised from the sparse information available and scattered reports from 1901 onwards.

In November 1898, R Vallentin, a naturalist and marine biologist arrived and stayed for six months. He returned in 1901 and stayed in Stanley and at Hill Cove, West Falkland until 1902. His third visit was between October 1909 and March 1911 when he lived at Shallow Bay, West Falkland. His records of birds published in 1901, 1904 and later in Boyson's *The Falkland Islands* (1924), where he discussed 44 species, were uneven, giving much information on the sizes of eggs and colonies of penguins yet omitting mention of the smaller passerines.

In the second decade of the twentieth century, five ornithologists were active in the Falklands. Dr R Wace was resident for several years, mainly at Darwin and returned to England in 1917. He left a manuscript list of 105 species of Falkland birds with R Dabbene, of the Natural Sciences Museum of Argentina. This was published by Dabbene under Wace's name in 1921, incorporating several records submitted by A G Bennett. During Wace's residence two separate United States collectors spent the same period (October 1915 to February 1916) in and around the Falklands. R H Beck photographed birds and collected specimens at sea from small boats and at several islands, whilst on the Brewster-Sanford Expedition of the American Museum of Natural History (Murphy 1936) and W S Brooks visited for the J C Phillips Expedition of the Museum of Comparative Zoology at Harvard. He lived at Stanley, San Carlos and Port Stephens and found travel very difficult. In 1917 Brooks listed 42 species in variable detail. Arthur F Cobb was a farmer on Bleaker in the first quarter of this century. His book *Birds of the Falkland Islands* (1933), the first devoted to Falkland birds, described 30 species anecdotally and from farming and gastronomic points of view.

A G Bennett, at some time a magistrate at South Georgia and a customs officer in Stanley, was resident from about 1912 to the 1930s. In 1926 Bennett collated records, including those of Wace and published a list with mostly brief comments of the birds of the Falkland Islands and Dependencies in *Ibis*. He noted 106 Falkland species, a few of which are not now recognised or acceptable. Further records were published by Bennett between 1931 and 1937 in *Ibis* and in the Argentine journal *El Hornero*. Though he was mostly restricted to Stanley, Bennett collected many specimens and was largely responsible for a fine display of local birds in the Stanley Museum, which was unfortunately destroyed in the Town Hall fire of 1945.

Dr J E Hamilton was Government Naturalist, between about 1919 and the late 1940s and died in Stanley in 1957. In contrast to Bennett, who was for a time Assistant Naturalist, Hamilton was able to travel widely in the Falklands but devoted much of his time to studying seals. His ornithological interest was apparently irregular, apart from his work on skuas published in 1934. He also published several short notes on Falkland birds in *Ibis* between 1937 and 1954.

E M Cawkell lived in Stanley as Superintendent of Education from 1950 to December 1955 and was able to travel widely and collect a large quantity of notes on all Falkland species and many vagrants, but could not devote as much time to birds as he would have liked. Edwin Cawkwell incorporated notes left by Hamilton and published a joint list of 126 species in *Ibis* for 1961. In this useful paper he critically examined earlier records, included many of his own observations and some from local residents.

Dr O S Pettingill Jr, former director of the Cornell Laboratory of Ornithology and his wife were in the Falklands from October 1953 to March 1954 filming for Walt Disney Productions. Eleanor Pettingill vividly described their experiences on Kidney and New Islands in *Penguin Summer* (1962). They revisited between November 1971 and March 1972 partly under the auspices of the National Geographic Society. Sewall Pettingill published papers on the effects of weather and climate on breeding birds (1960a), passerines (1974), Gentoo, Rockhopper and Magellanic Penguins (1960b & 1964) and Kelp Geese and Steamer Ducks (1965). *Another Penguin Summer* contained many photographs and described breeding cycles of the five resident penguins (O S Pettingill 1975).

A Falkland-born sheep farmer, R B Napier, became owner of West Point Island in 1959 and continued the pasture conservation practices and natural history interests of his father, (manager 1942–59) and his great-uncle Arthur Felton, who managed the island from 1879 to 1933. Roddy Napier recorded a mixed pair of Rockhopper and Erect-crested Penguins on West Point Island between 1961 and 1966 (1968). Roddy and his wife, Lily, started large scale banding of Black-browed Albatross fledglings in 1961 under the auspices of the Bird-banding Program, United States Antarctic Research Program. Banding of up to 3,000 fledglings a year continued until about 1968 with help, in different seasons, from Peter and Rosemary Richards, Don Davidson, and Anne and Robin Woods. There were sufficient recoveries to show that West Point Island albatrosses generally stayed within South Atlantic waters. The Napiers' relatives, Cecil and Kitty Bertrand bought nearby Carcass Island in 1954 and continued the conservationist policies of the former owner, Jason Hansen. The Bertrands and the Napiers have all been keen observers of birds for many years and have supplied large numbers of records for publication. Kitty Bertrand publicised the history of tussac re-establishment and wildlife conservation on Carcass Island (1968, 1981) and the island is now well known as an example of good farming and conservation in harmony.

R W Woods (the author) lived in Stanley from late 1956 until 1963 while working for British Antarctic Meteorological Service, and collected information for a field guide, trapped, measured and ringed birds of many species and obtained much helpful information from local residents. Work carried out over several seasons on Kidney Island, East Falkland led to a paper demonstrating the importance of tussac grass to about half the Falkland breeding species (1970a). *The Birds of the Falkland Islands*, a comprehensive handbook and guide with many photographs and listing 149 species, was eventually published in 1975. In the autumn of 1981 when that book was out of print, a smaller pocket guide to the breeding birds was commissioned, using photographs by Cindy Buxton and Annie Price of Anglia Television. This book, *Falkland Islands Birds*, was published in July 1982. Through a submission to the F I Government on 5 September 1961, Roddy Napier and the author were instrumental in establishing the need for more conservation-oriented legislation for birds and the importance of making Kidney Island a nature reserve.

I J Strange came to the Falklands in late 1959 as manager of a Falkland Islands Company experimental mink farm, which was not successful. He joined Roddy Napier and the author later in 1961 in pressing for better conservation legislation and continued to develop the arguments with Government. Ian Strange has written many popular articles on Falkland wildlife, reported a Fairy Prion colony on Beauchêne Island (1968), summarised the first records of Cattle Egrets (1979) and has published results of studies at New Island of Thin-billed Prion (1980) and Rockhopper Penguin (1982).

Dr J Harradine and Dr R W Summers, biologists with the Grassland Trials Unit at Stanley, published several papers (some with other authors) between 1976 and 1985. Their field work on the diets and life cycles of Upland and Ruddy-headed Geese, carried out between 1974 and 1980, has certainly clarified the effects of these geese on pastures. It is probable that their findings need more publicity in the Falklands before farmers generally change their attitudes towards these birds and accept them as an integral and interesting part of the avifauna. This work was continued until 1987 by Dr A F G (Andy) Douse.

R S (Steve) Whitley, a veterinary officer, lived from 1976 to 1984 in Stanley and was able to travel widely. He collected many useful records, particularly of seabird colonies. Between 1979 and 1982, J Peatfield was headteacher of Stanley school. He and his wife are keen ornithologists and they made some valuable observations around Stanley. John Peatfield edited the first published list of bird records since 1975 in volume 1 of *Warrah* (1981), a journal started soon after the Falkland Islands Trust was formed.

Dr R I Lewis Smith and Dr P A Prince, biologists from the British Antarctic Survey, made the most comprehensive study to date of a single island in 15 days of December 1980 (Smith & Prince 1985). On Beauchêne Island, the most southerly and isolated of the archipelago, they counted the Black-browed Albatross, Rockhopper Penguin and Striated Caracara populations, listed all bird species they recorded and showed, through radiocarbon dating, that the tussac grasslands of Beauchêne Island had existed almost unchanged for 12,500 years. Beauchêne Island is of unique biological significance because it has an exceptionally uniform tussac ecosystem and supports one of the largest Black-browed Albatross colonies in the world (up to 170,000 pairs), a larger colony of Rockhopper Penguins (up to 300,000 pairs) and a population of the very locally distributed and rare Striated Caracara (about 250 birds). Their collections of invertebrates revealed species new to the Falklands or to science. Smith and Prince stressed the need for strict conservation measures to protect this island and its potential for biological research, particularly to test ecological hypotheses.

Conservation

Conservation activity and ornithology have developed since *The Birds of the Falkland Islands* and *Falkland Islands Birds* were published. Interest in the conservation of habitats, knowledge of the general distribution of birds and studies of individual species and families have all increased.

There are now about 30 islands, parts of islands or East Falkland peninsulas that have been declared as Sanctuaries or Nature Reserves under the Wild Animals and Birds Protection or the Nature Reserves Ordinances of 1964. About 14 more islands are wildlife reserves, maintained as such by their owners but not yet given official status under either Ordinance. Strange (1985) stated that of those islands declared as official Sanctuaries, only Beauchêne Island and the islands in the Jason group had been free of grazing animals since declaration. The original Wild

Animals and Birds Protection Ordinance specified that no grazing was to be permitted, so it appears that this condition was not enforced.

In January 1979, a meeting between Sir Peter Scott, Michael Wright of World Wildlife Fund – United States, and others at New Island led to the formation of the Falkland Islands Foundation, a charitable body and pressure group based in the United Kingdom. The aims of the Foundation are to promote the conservation of wildlife, wrecks and places of historic interest in the Falklands and their Dependencies and to aid scientific research into the fauna and flora that comprise Falkland ecosystems. A local group with similar aims, the Falkland Islands Trust, was established in Stanley in 1981. These two organisations are closely linked, with the Trust suggesting and facilitating projects that need support and the Foundation being in a position to raise the necessary funds. The conflict of mid-1982 led to great disturbance of the human population with an additional 4,000 military personnel and to H M Government's decision to support the economic development of the Falklands. These sudden pressures on the environment provided impetus for both organisations and in 1983 the Foundation began to take a more active role in conservation and in supporting scientific studies.

K T Standring, a Conservation Officer with the Royal Society for the Protection of Birds, visited the Falklands between November 1981 and January 1982. He produced comprehensive and stimulating reports and suggestions, in part discussed with Legislative Council in January 1982. Kevin Standring proposed a radical revision of Wild Mammals and Wild Birds Protection legislation and put forward a comprehensive draft Nature Reserves Ordinance (Standring 1982). If both draft revisions were accepted by F I Government, their legislation for 'living resource conservation for sustainable development' would be in line with World Conservation Strategy and conservation would be built in to all development plans from the start, instead of being added later as a response to crisis situations. As yet, these proposed changes have not been made under the new Constitution of the Falkland Islands Government.

At the xviiith World Conference of the International Council for Bird Preservation in Cambridge (August 1982), a symposium on seabird conservation was held. Data on the size and location of breeding colonies of Falkland Island seabirds were presented and later published by Croxall et al (1984). Their rough estimates of species' total breeding populations suggested that the Falkland Islands were the most important breeding site for Black-browed Albatross, Gentoo Penguin, Rockhopper Penguin and Thin-billed Prion and had important populations of Grey-backed Storm-Petrel, (Falkland) Antarctic Skua, Fairy Prion and possibly Dolphin Gull and (King) Imperial Shag.

Croxall et al concluded that although there were a good number of wildlife reserves, some species were not adequately protected and there was a dearth of recent quantitative data on Falkland seabirds. Several species were at risk of predation by cats and rats, potentially threatened by risks of oil-pollution and possibly the effects of fishery and agricultural developments. They stressed an urgent need for a comprehensive review of Falkland Islands requirements for wildlife conservation. In particular, they pointed out that the distribution of burrow-dwelling petrels was very poorly known. Surface breeding colonial species needed to be counted using high resolution aerial photography and it was essential to record the presence, or absence, of cats and rats before decisions were made about planned introduction or eradication programmes.

Suggestions for research into populations of burrow-dwelling petrels and dietary studies were also made, though they stressed that a two-year ornithological survey programme for seabirds should take priority. Croxall *et al* made several valuable proposals concerning the establishment and management of reserves, echoing Standring's arguments for a review of existing conservation legislation.

Since the conflict of 1982, there has been an increase in the number of observers, particularly of birds in Falkland waters and the 200 mile zone. Many well-authenticated records have been collected by W F Curtis, a Radio officer with the Royal Fleet Auxiliary, Dr W R P Bourne, a ship's surgeon and others on HM Ships. Bill Bourne has also spent considerable time researching collections of early museum skins and published material, to establish which species have been collected in the Falklands, with the intention of publishing a documented record. Bill Bourne and Bill Curtis have made repeated voyages since 1982 and have added several species to the Falkland list (Bourne and Curtis 1985, 1987 *in litt.*).

In late 1983, the author revisited the Falklands to carry out the first sample census of songbirds in tussac grass. Field work in 1958–63 had indicated that several species achieved higher population densities in tussac than in other habitats and 1983 results (Woods 1985) showed the hypothesis to hold for some songbirds. Other species reached higher population densities in a mosaic of dense tussac and short grazed grass without mammalian predators.

Although opportunities for travel to the Falklands have improved since 1982, visiting ornithologists are still hindered by the difficulties of travel inland and to offshore islands if time is limited. The author believed that residents in Stanley and the camp settlements know the local birds and could be sufficiently interested to record evidence systematically of all the breeding species. In 1983 a project linking local people, the Falkland Islands Trust in Stanley and the Falkland Islands Foundation in UK was discussed with Kitty Bertrand, Jess and Stuart Booth and Tom Davies, all officers of the Trust. Later negotiations with the Foundation in England led to the inauguration of the Breeding Birds Survey in the following season.

Local publicity by Tom Davies in 1984/85 produced many records based on the 10k² Grid Square system. In early 1986, R P S Wolsey, a geologist and experienced ornithologist came to Stanley as assistant general manager of the F I Development Corporation. He became editor of the F I Trust Newsletter and journal 'Warrah' and has already published many valuable records including more new species for the list. Shane Wolsey assumed local responsibility for the Breeding Birds Survey with Andy Douse, a biologist working on geese for the Agricultural Research Centre in Stanley. Local people, military personnel, civilian visitors and tourists have contributed to the survey. Three seasons' results have been encouraging and have confirmed the author's belief in this project. The first general picture of the distribution of breeding birds will be available in a few years, to be published as an Atlas of Falkland Breeding Birds. This will provide a baseline for later detailed studies.

The Shackleton Report (1976) proposed the subdivision of large farms into smaller, owner-occupied holdings. After the 1982 conflict, this recommendation was suddenly seen as an essential move to give local people a stake in the development of the Falklands. As subdivision gained momentum, the F I Foundation took the opportunity to purchase or lease several offshore islands as wildlife reserves. In Falkland Sound, Inner (35ha/86 acres) and Outer Northwest (65ha/161 acres), Cat (3ha/7 acres) and Rookery Islands (3ha/7 acres) were acquired with generous financial help from a member of the Foundation. To the west of the Falklands, nine islands off New Island and Carcass Island, previously owned by the Royal Society for Nature Conservation were formally given to the Foundation in May 1985. More recently, Split Island (220ha/543 acres) south of West Point Island was bought from Hamilton Estates. This island has not been stocked recently, has a population of introduced Patagonian Foxes and carries tussac and native 'Box'. Unfortunately Inner Northwest Island was badly damaged accidentally by fire in 1983 and worse, Outer Northwest Island was burnt out in October 1986. Although Outer Northwest Island had been colonised by rats, it held an interesting group of at least 25 bird species and it had not been grazed. These accidents show how vulnerable the remaining dense tussac is to fire, even when islands have been set aside as wildlife reserves. It is probable that tussac will regenerate on the Northwest Islands and that birds will return. A scientific study could be valuable for future conservation planning.

Concern about the effects of over-fishing on seabirds has increased since 1983, but little is known of the particular marine forms taken by Falkland seabirds. In October 1986, a two-year research project employing two biologists was started after months of fund-raising by the Foundation and support from the British Antarctic Survey. Dan Hale and Kate Thompson, working on islands off West Falkland, are studying the diets and populations of the three common penguins (Gentoo, Rockhopper and Magellanic), the Black-browed Albatross, Thin-billed Prion and the Imperial Shag. After the second season's work, some reliable data on the dietary needs of Falkland seabirds will be available.

Earlier in 1986, many dead and dying Rockhopper Penguins had been found at several sites (Douse 1986). Both chicks and adults died, apparently of starvation, while high lead concentrations were found in some birds examined at veterinary laboratories in UK. Speculation that starvation was linked to over-fishing by hundreds of foreign vessels was politically attractive, but had little factual support because the squid species eaten by these penguins appeared not to be one of those taken by fishing vessels; the simplest explanation seemed to be food shortage, possibly connected with the incursion of unusually warm currents into Falkland waters (Bourne 1987). Support from F I Government and the World Wildlife Fund allowed the Foundation to organise a short visit by two pathologists, Ian Keymer and Dave Horsley, in early 1987. They obtained blood samples to investigate the possibilities of viral infection and contamination by heavy metal residues and took specimens for later examination. Their studies have supported the hypothesis of a natural food shortage associated with temporary changes in sea temperature, leading to starvation during post-breeding moult, when penguins have high energy needs (R Wilson pers. comm.).

Promotion of tourism is a further development, which will help to publicise the attractions of the Falklands. In 1975, annual visits were being made by cruise ships, some spending only one day at Stanley while others visited good wildlife centres such as Carcass, West Point or New Island. Many groups of military personnel have also been able to spend a few days at these islands and Sea Lion Island since 1982. International tourism using the direct air route to the new airport at Mount Pleasant, started in 1986, mainly for wildlife enthusiasts who enjoyed several successful tours. Increased publicity in 1987 by a new organisation, Falkland Islands Tourism, should attract more visitors to stay for short periods at the new lodge on Sea Lion Island and in converted houses at Pebble Island and Port Howard. Guide lines for tourists have been published to control disturbance at important sites and income from tourism should make effective conservation measures more economically attractive.

Conclusion

The history of man's occupation of the Falklands is largely one of extraction and destruction of the natural resources. Millions of birds and animals have been killed for gain, or even exterminated; the vegetation has been depleted and the land impoverished. Cats, dogs, rats, mice, rabbits, hares, patagonian foxes, guanacos, cattle, sheep, pigs, horses and blowflies have been introduced within two centuries and all are affecting the natural balance.

In contrast with Antarctica, very little scientific research has been done in the Falklands. Greater interest in the economy of the islands and concern for the environment has been shown locally and in the United Kingdom since the events of 1982. A commitment to the natural sciences in these sub-Antarctic islands is long overdue and funding from Governments or charitable foundations is now essential. Many basic ecological and biological investigations are needed if environmental factors are to be taken into account when development decisions are made. With radical changes in farming practices and tourism and fishing rapidly assuming importance, increased productivity must not be won at the expense of the most attractive natural inhabitants, the birds of the Falkland Islands.

Checklist of Falkland Islands birds

This checklist includes all species known to have occurred on the Falkland Islands or within the 200 mile zone of surface water surrounding the archipelago. The order of species generally follows R Meyer de Schaunsee's *A Guide to the Birds of South America* (1971), with minor changes in nomenclature and sequence.

Status is shown by the following code letters or symbols:

† = Local race
B = Breeds in the Falkland Islands
N = Non-breeding regular visitor
V = Irregular vagrant
X = Lost breeding species: not recorded recently
M = Migrates regularly to and from the islands or adjacent waters
? = Status in doubt due to lack of information
* = Introduced species

Most species are illustrated on plates 1 to 21; page references are given to the plates where relevant and the main text entry.

			Plate no.	Text page
		Order SPHENISCIFORMES Family Spheniscidae		
1	B	King Penguin *Aptenodytes patagonicus*	1	93
2	V	Emperor Penguin *Aptenodytes forsteri*	1	94
3	B	Gentoo Penguin *Pygoscelis papua*	1	94
4	V	Adelie Penguin *Pygoscelis adeliae*	1	95
5	V	Chinstrap Penguin *Pygoscelis antarctica*	1	95
6	BM	Rockhopper Penguin *Eudyptes chrysocome*	1	96
7	BM	Macaroni Penguin *Eudyptes chrysolophus*	1	97
8	V?	Fiordland Crested Penguin *Eudyptes pachyrhynchus*	–	97
9	V	Erect-crested Penguin *Eudyptes sclateri*	1	98
10	BM	Magellanic Penguin *Spheniscus magellanicus*	1	98
		Order PODICIPEDIFORMES Family Podicipedidae		
11	B	White-tufted Grebe *Rollandia rolland*	2	99
12	V	Great Grebe *Podiceps major*	2	100
13	B	Silvery Grebe *Podiceps occipitalis*	2	101
		Order PROCELLARIIFORMES Family Diomedeidae		
14	N	Wandering Albatross *Diomedea exulans*	3	102
15	N	Royal Albatross *Diomedea epomophora*	3	103
16	BM	Black-browed Albatross *Diomedea melanophris*	3	103
17	V	Buller's Albatross *Diomedea bulleri*	–	104
18	V	Shy Albatross *Diomedea cauta*	–	105
19	V	Yellow-nosed Albatross *Diomedea chlororhynchos*	3	106
20	N	Grey-headed Albatross *Diomedea chrysostoma*	3	106
21	V	Sooty Albatross *Phoebetria fusca*	3	107
22	N	Light-mantled Sooty Albatross *Phoebetria palpebrata*	3	108
		Family Procellariidae		
23	NB?	Northern Giant Petrel *Macronectes halli*	3	109
24	BM	Southern Giant Petrel *Macronectes giganteus*	3	109
25	N	Southern/Silver-grey Fulmar *Fulmarus glacialoides*	4	110
26	V	Antarctic Petrel *Thalassoica antarctica*	5	110
27	N	Cape Petrel *Daption capense*	4	111
28	V	Snow Petrel *Pagodroma nivea*	5	111
29	N	Kerguelen Petrel *Pterodroma brevirostris*	21	112
30	V	Atlantic Petrel *Pterodroma incerta*	–	112
31	V	White-headed Petrel *Pterodroma lessonii*	5	113
32	V	Great-winged Petrel *Pterodroma macroptera*	–	113
33	V	Soft-plumaged Petrel *Pterodroma mollis*	5	114
34	N	Blue Petrel *Halobaena caerulea*	5	114
35	N	Dove/Antarctic Prion *Pachyptila desolata*	5	115
36	N	Broad-billed Prion *Pachyptila vittata*	5	115
37	BM	Thin-billed Prion *Pachyptila belcheri*	4	116
38	BM?	Fairy Prion *Pachyptila turtur*	4	117
39	V	Grey Petrel *Procellaria cinerea*	–	117
40	BM	White-chinned Petrel *Procellaria aequinoctialis*	4	118
41	V	Cory's Shearwater *Calonectris diomedea*	–	118
42	BM	Great Shearwater *Puffinus gravis*	4	119
43	BM	Sooty Shearwater *Puffinus griseus*	4	120

			Plate no.	Text page
81	B	Silver Teal *Anas versicolor*	10	150
82	B	Cinnamon Teal *Anas cyanoptera*	10	150
83	V	Red Shoveler *Anas platalea*	10	151
84	V	Rosy-billed Pochard *Netta peposaca*	10	152
85	V	Lake Duck *Oxyura vittata*	10	152
86	V	Black-headed Duck *Heteronetta atricapilla*	–	153
		Order CATHARTIFORMES Family Cathartidae		
87	B†	Turkey Vulture *Cathartes aura*	11	154
		Order ACCIPITRIFORMES Family Accipitridae		
88	V	Sharp-shinned Hawk *Accipiter striatus*	11	155
89	B	Red-backed Hawk *Buteo polyosoma*	11	155
90	X?V	Cinereous Harrier *Circus cinereus*	11	156
		Order FALCONIFORMES Family Falconidae		
91	V	Chimango Caracara *Milvago chimango*	11	157
92	B	Striated Caracara *Phalcoboenus australis*	11	158
93	B	Crested Caracara *Caracara plancus*	11	160
94	B	Peregrine Falcon *Falco peregrinus*	11	161
95	VB?	American Kestrel *Falco sparverius*	11	162
		Order GRUIFORMES Family Rallidae		
96	V	Plumbeous Rail *Rallus sanguinolentus*	–	163
97	V	Speckled Crake *Coturnicops notata*	12	163
98	V	American Purple Gallinule *Porphyrula martinica*	12	164
99	V	Red-gartered Coot *Fulica armillata*	12	164
100	V	White-winged Coot *Fulica leucoptera*	12	165
101	V	Red-fronted Coot *Fulica rufifrons*	12	165
		Order CHARADRIIFORMES Family Haematopodidae		
102	B	Blackish Oystercatcher *Haematopus ater*	13	166
103	B	Magellanic Oystercatcher *Haematopus leucopodus*	13	167
		Family Charadriidae		
104	V	Southern Lapwing *Vanellus chilensis*	14	169
105	B	Two-banded Plover *Charadrius falklandicus*	13	170
106	BM?	Rufous-chested Dotterel *Charadrius modestus*	13	171
107	V	Tawny-throated Dotterel *Eudromias ruficollis*	14	172
		Family Pluvianellidae		
108	V	Magellanic Plover *Pluvianellus socialis*	14	173
		Family Scolopacidae		
109	V	Hudsonian Godwit *Limosa haemastica*	14	174
110	N	Whimbrel *Numenius phaeopus*	14	175
111	V	Eskimo Curlew *Numenius borealis*	–	176
112	V	Upland Sandpiper *Bartramia longicauda*	14	176
113	V	Lesser Yellowlegs *Tringa flavipes*	14	177
114	V	Ruddy Turnstone *Arenaria interpres*	–	178
115	BM?	Common (Magellan) Snipe *Gallinago (gallinago) paraguaiae*	13	178
116	B?	Cordilleran Snipe *Gallinago stricklandii*	13	180
117	V	Red Knot *Calidris canutus*	–	180

			Plate no.	Text page
		Family Emberizidae		
181	V	Mourning Sierra-Finch *Phrygilus fruticeti*	–	234
182	B†	Black-throated Finch *Melanodera melanodera*	20	235
183	X?	Yellow-bridled Finch *Melanodera xanthogramma*	20	236
184	V	Rufous-collared Sparrow *Junco capensis*	20	237
		Family Icteridae		
185	B†	Long-tailed Meadowlark *Sturnella loyca*	20	239

Notes on the text

There are 21 colour plates illustrating 154 species, mostly in Checklist order. In the petrel and wader families breeding and regularly visiting species have been shown separately from vagrant species. Scales vary between plates. On Plate 17 the owls are at a smaller scale than the passerines below. On all other plates, the birds are drawn to the same scale to show relative size. Plate captions give the individual species number in the Checklist, the accepted English and scientific names and brief identification notes. On plates 3, 4, 5, 6 & 11, wing-span (ws) measurements are given to aid identification in flight.

Reference to the plate and facing text will often be sufficient for identification, but it has not been possible to illustrate every plumage stage nor every vagrant species. Page references to the main text are given for all species and for those plumage stages not illustrated.

The main text is in Checklist order. General characteristics of families precede descriptions of species in that family. World distribution and occurrence in adjacent lands or waters are given, followed by a summary of family status in the Falkland Islands.

English and scientific names are followed by Argentine and Chilean booknames, according to Olrog (1984) *Las Aves Argentinas: Una nueva guia de campo* and Mödinger & Holman (1986) *Guia de campo de las aves de Chile*. Local names are also given. Body-length ranges in inches and centimetres are from published sources and the author's data. The relative size from bill tip to tail tip is described according to the scale below.

ADJECTIVE	BODY-LENGTH	EXAMPLE
Very tiny	< 5in : < 13cm	Grass Wren
Tiny	5– 6in : 13–15cm	Black-chinned Siskin
Very small	6– 8in : 15–20cm	Two-banded Plover
Small	8–12in : 20–30cm	Falkland Thrush
Small-medium	12–16in : 30–41cm	Speckled Teal
Medium	16–20in : 41–51cm	Dolphin Gull
Medium-large	20–24in : 51–61cm	Kelp Gull
Large	24–28in : 61–71cm	Turkey Vulture
Very large	28–32in : 71–81cm	Gentoo Penguin
Immense	32–36in : 81–91cm	Giant Petrel
Gigantic	> 36in : > 91cm	Black-necked Swan

IDENTIFICATION: Prominent field characteristics are followed by plumage descriptions, including differences between males, females and immature birds where these are noticeable, and notes on behaviour.

VOICE: Typical calls are described, sometimes phonetically, though the limitations of this method are accepted. For birds that have songs or special calls associated with the breeding season, there is a description of the song, an indication of song period and types of perches used.

FOOD: Main items are given where known, with notes on some feeding methods and the results of a few dietary investigations.

HABITAT, STATUS & BREEDING: A brief indication of status and abundance in the Falkland Islands is followed by a description of the usual habitats, with seasonal changes if they occur. For migrants, approximate arrival and departure dates are given. Breeding behaviour includes data on laying season, egg colour, clutch size, nest site and materials. Unless stated otherwise, most species are thought to be single-brooded in a season.

Non-breeding species and vagrants are described under some different headings from breeding species. STATUS & RECORDS replaces VOICE, FOOD, and HABITAT, STATUS & BREEDING, while notes on calls are included under IDENTIFICATION.

DISTRIBUTION ABROAD: The number of geographical races is stated where relevant and landbirds have their distribution in southern South America outlined. Breeding areas of visiting seabirds are described with a summary of their non-breeding oceanic (pelagic) range. The breeding distribution of migrants from the Northern Hemisphere is summarised with their wintering range in South America or at sea.

Knowledge of breeding biology, diet, habitat preferences and distribution of most Falkland birds is still very limited. Opportunities for useful field work are vast. Any careful investigations examining Falkland birds in their habitats would be valuable for planning future conservation measures.

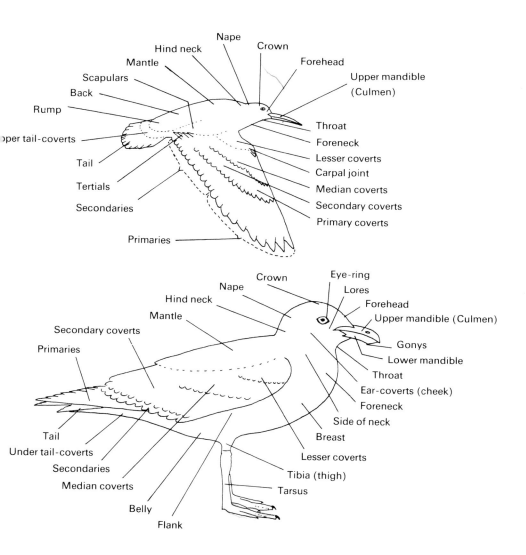

The plumage of a bird

The colour plates

1 Penguins

The heads of penguins have all the marks needed for identification. They are quite easily recognised on land but look carefully at shape and origins of yellow crests on Rockhopper (6), Macaroni (7), Fiordland Crested (8) and Erect-crested (9). At sea, identification is difficult because they rarely remain long at the surface.

1. King Penguin   p.93
Aptenodytes patagonicus
36–38in/91–96cm
A. ADULT: Largest breeding penguin; golden ear-patch on blackish-brown head.
B. IMMATURE: Smaller with shorter, darker bill and yellow ear-patch.
JUVENILE: see page 93.

2. Emperor Penguin   p.94
Aptenodytes forsteri
40–48in/101–122cm
IMMATURE: Taller and with shorter bill than (1); whitish ear-patch and whitish throat.
ADULT: see page 94.

3. Gentoo Penguin   p.94
Pygoscelis papua
30in/76cm
ADULT: Large common penguin with a white bar over crown and white flecks behind eye; orange bill with black ridge and tip.
IMMATURE: see page 94.

4. Adelie Penguin   p.95
Pygoscelis adeliae
27–31in/69–79cm
ADULT: Blue-black head and 'button-eyed'; white iris and eye-ring; bill half-feathered, reddish with black tip.
IMMATURE: see page 95.

5. Chinstrap Penguin   p.95
Pygoscelis antarctica
27–30in/68–76cm
ADULT: White face and throat, crossed by narrow black 'chinstrap'; bill black.
IMMATURE: see page 95.

6. Rockhopper Penguin   p.96
Eudyptes chrysocome
24–25in/60–64cm
ADULT: Smallest common penguin with thin yellow stripe over red eye ending in long yellow plumes, projecting behind eye; no pink at gape, compare with (7); spiky black crest, raised when excited. Underside of flipper mainly white with small black tip and outer half of leading edge white, compare with (9).
IMMATURE: see page 96.

7. Macaroni Penguin   p.97
Eudyptes chrysolophus
27–30in/69–76cm
ADULT: Slightly larger than (6) with different head pattern; golden-yellow head plumes spring from patch of same colour on forehead; bill has pink fleshy gape.
IMMATURE: see page 97.

8. Fiordland Crested Penguin   (not illustrated) see page 97.

9. Erect-crested Penguin   p.98
Eudyptes sclateri
26–28in/66–71cm
ADULT: Resembles (6) but has a golden-yellow crest starting close to the pink gape and extending upwards like a bristle-brush. Underside of flipper has a wide blackish front edge and large black tip, compare with (6).
IMMATURE: see page 98.

10. Magellanic Penguin   p.98
Spheniscus magellanicus
28in/71cm
ADULT: Common; the only burrow-nesting penguin; black chin and crown; white band from throat to eye; black, white and black breast bands, lower band extending to flanks; heavy black bill with grey band.
IMMATURE: see page 98.

C.J.F.Coombs.

2 Shags and Grebes

Shags and Grebes are grouped on this plate for convenience. Though not closely related, they show superficial similarities and two species on this plate (11) and (52) can be confused at a distance.

11. White-tufted Grebe p.99
Rollandia rolland
13–14in/33–36cm
Commoner of two resident grebes. Tame; note horizontal carriage of head and neck; compare with (52).
A. ADULT BREEDING: Black above with triangular white patch behind crimson eye; underparts chestnut.
B. ADULT NON-BREEDING: Dull brown above; red-brown neck; face, throat and rest of underparts white.
C. DOWNY YOUNG: Mottled brown above; whitish throat, foreneck and underparts.
IMMATURE: see page 100.

12. Great Grebe p.100
Podiceps major
26–30in/67–77cm
Much larger than (11) and (13), about the size of Imperial Shag (53) but has tail-less appearance; long, thin neck and massive dagger-shaped bill are distinctive. Dives frequently; in flight shows a broad white trailing edge bar.
A. ADULT BREEDING: Head black with short tufted crest; black throat and hindneck; foreneck chestnut; below mainly white; above brownish-black.
B. ADULT NON-BREEDING: Whitish cheeks; red-grey foreneck and dull grey hindneck; above dark grey-brown.
IMMATURE: see page 100.

13. Silvery Grebe p.101
Podiceps occipitalis
10–11in/25–28cm
Smaller than (11); in flight white neck and wing-bar are prominent.
A. ADULT BREEDING: Much paler than (11); grey above, white below streaked black on flanks; foreneck pure white; nape jet-black, tapering down hindneck; frill of dull gold plumes behind crimson eye.
B. ADULT NON-BREEDING: Lacks gold plumes.
IMMATURE: see page 101.

52. Rock Shag p.127
Phalacrocorax magellanicus
26in/66cm
Smaller of two resident shags; usually flies low over water.
A & B. ADULT BREEDING: Glossy black above, white below with variable black, or black and white, foreneck; red facial skin; black bill; white ear-patch and inconspicuous curved black crest on crown; pink legs.
C. SECOND YEAR IMMATURE: Dull brown head, upperparts and neck with white chin and throat; whitish belly; reddish facial skin.
ADULT NON-BREEDING: & JUVENILE: see page 127.

53. Imperial/King Shag p.128
Phalacrocorax atriceps albiventer
27–29in/69–74cm
Larger of two breeding shags; neck fully extended in flight appears all white from a distance, broad wings flap rapidly and tail looks long.
A. ADULT BREEDING: Glossy black above, white underparts continuous from below eye to belly (see text for related race); white wing-bar near shoulder; thighs and underwing black; blue eye-ring; orange caruncles above a dark bill.
B. IMMATURE: Similar pattern to non-breeding adult but dark brown above.
ADULT NON-BREEDING: see page 128.

54. Red-legged Shag p.129
Phalacrocorax gaimardi
28–30in/71–76cm
Large white patch at side of neck is characteristic at all ages.
ADULT NON-BREEDING: Similar size to (53) but dark grey, heavily chequered silvery above; bright red legs and feet; yellow bill; red facial skin.
ADULT BREEDING & IMMATURE: see page 129.

53A

53B

54

52A

52B

52C

12B

12A

11C

11B

13B

13A

11A

G.F.Coombs

14. Wandering Albatross   p.102
Diomedea exulans
42–53in/107–135cm. ws 250–350cm
Largest albatross, far bigger than (16).
Underwing white with black wingtips.
A. SUB-ADULT: White head, body and tail, often
with narrow black edge to tail; bill pale, see
(15); wings above have blackish trailing edge,
blackish and white coverts, most white is in
the centre inner half of wing.
B. POST-JUVENILE: White face, brown mask;
brown wings above; body dark brown, white
mottling increases with age. Most birds seen
are immature.
JUVENILE & ADULT: see page 102.

15. Royal Albatross   p.103
Diomedea epomophora
42–50in/107–127cm. ws 300–350cm
Similar size to (14); white head, body and tail;
juveniles resemble adults; black cutting edge
to bill separates from adult of (14) at close
range.
ADULT *D. e. epomophora*: Wings white with
black tips; difficult to separate from adult of
(14) unless the bill is seen clearly.
ADULT *D. e. sanfordi*: White head, body and tail
with black upperwing.
JUVENILE: see page 103.

16. Black-browed Albatross   p.103
Diomedea melanophris
32–37in/81–94cm. ws 213–250cm
Commonest of the smaller albatrosses
(mollymawks) in Falkland waters in summer.
A. ADULT: White head with black 'brow', white
rump and underparts; upperwing and back
blackish; tail grey; underwing white with a
broad black leading edge and narrow black
trailing edge; bill orange/pink.
B. JUVENILE: Dark bill, whitish head with dark
'eyebrow' and grey nape; underparts white,
sometimes with a grey breast band. Wings
above as adult; below dark, with variable
white centre. See juvenile (20).
IMMATURE: see page 104.

17. Buller's Albatross   (not illustrated) see
page 104.

18. Shy Albatross   (not illustrated) see page
105.

19. Yellow-nosed Albatross   p.106
Diomedea chlororhynchos
28–32in/71–81cm. ws 178–207cm
Smaller and more slender than (16) with
longer bill. Easily confused with (20) though
underwing pattern is different.
ADULT *D. c. chlororhynchos*: Head mainly grey;
bill black with a yellow ridge (not prominent);

upperparts and body as (16); white
underwing has narrow black margins.
ADULT *D. c. bassi*: Paler grey cheeks and nape,
appearing white at a distance.
JUVENILE: see page 106.

20. Grey-headed Albatross   p.106
Diomedea chrysostoma
28–33in/71–84cm. ws 203–250cm
Resembles (16) in size and proportions; see
also (19).
ADULT: Head blue-grey, dark 'eyebrow'; bill
black with bright yellow ridge and lower edge
visible at close range; underwing like (16)
though black leading edge narrower, white
centre more prominent.
IMMATURE: see page 106.

21. Sooty Albatross   p.107
Phoebetria fusca
32–35in/81–89cm. ws 198–213cm
Both this species and (22) slender; very
narrow wings, long wedge-shaped tails,
mainly brown plumage and white partial eye-
rings. Compare with (23) and (24).
ADULT: Sooty-brown, slightly lighter on body;
bill black with yellow central streak.
IMMATURE: see page 107.

22. Light-mantled Sooty Albatross   p.108
Phoebetria palpebrata
28–35in/71–89cm. ws 183–218cm
ADULT: Head, wings and tail dark grey-brown;
back and rump pale grey; underparts paler;
bill black with a pale blue central streak visible
at close range.
IMMATURE: see page 108.

23. Northern Giant Petrel   p.109
Macronectes halli
30–37in/76–94cm. ws 180–200cm
ADULT: Grey-brown above and below, darkest
on wings and tail; brown crown over whitish
face gives capped effect; bill pinkish with a
darker reddish tip; very dark leading edge to
underwing.
IMMATURE: see page 109.

24. Southern Giant Petrel   p.109
Macronectes giganteus
34–39in/86–99cm. ws 180–240cm
A. ADULT DARK PHASE: Similar to (23) but head
and neck mainly white, not capped; bill
yellowish with a greenish tip; pale leading
edge to underwing.
B. JUVENILE: Black or brownish-black; large
pale bill; difficult to separate from (23).
C. PALE PHASE: White at all ages, with few
black spots.
IMMATURE: see page 109.

14B　14A　15

16B

16A　19

20

21　22

23

24B　24C　24A

C.J.F. Coombs

4 Breeding and regularly visiting Petrels, Prions and Shearwaters

Fast-flying oceanic birds, with long narrow wings; they often occur in flocks. Identification of some species is easy but several need careful observation, which is not always possible in bad conditions or poor light. Adults and immatures are not separable at sea.

Prions are difficult to identify at sea due to their rapid, twisting flight and similarities between species. All are blue-grey above, white beneath and show a dark 'M'-shaped pattern across wings and back. Compare with (34), plate 5.

25. Southern/Silver-grey Fulmar p.110
Fulmarus glacialoides
18–20in/46–51cm. ws 107–145cm
Pale blue-grey above, white beneath; black wingtips show a variable white flash; tail looks white. Bill pale blue-pink. Stiff-winged flight with long glides.

27. Cape Petrel p.111
Daption capense
15–16in/38–41cm ws 81–94cm
Conspicuously chequered black and white above; usually two white patches on each wing, black tail with white base and speckled rump; underparts white; head, throat and back dark brown. Bill black. Stiff-winged flight with long glides.

32. Great-winged Petrel (not illustrated) see page 113.

34. Blue Petrel see Plate 5 and page 114.

35. Dove/Antarctic Prion see Plate 5 and page 115.

36. Broad-billed Prion see Plate 5 and page 115.

37. Thin-billed Prion p.116
Pachyptila belcheri
10–12in/26–30cm. ws 56–61cm
Commonest species in Falkland waters; long white eye-stripe and dark stripe below eye; underside of tail has narrow dark central stripe; tail above has narrow black tip and whitish sides. Bill and legs blue. Often seen in huge flocks, sometimes with other prion species. Compare with (35) and (36).

38. Fairy Prion p.117
Pachyptila turtur
9–11in/23–28cm. ws 48–59cm
Pale blue-grey head with a small pale eye-stripe; tail above has a broad black tip; underside of tail white.

40. White-chinned Petrel or Shoemaker p.118
Procellaria aequinoctialis
20–21in/51–53cm. ws 134–152cm
Sooty-black with a very pale bill; white chin is not easily seen at sea. Powerful slow wingbeats and long glides. Much smaller than (23) and (24). larger than (43).

42. Great Shearwater p.119
Puffinus gravis
17–20in/43–51cm. ws 99–117cm
Upperparts dark brown, including tail and cap to eye; white half-moon (variable) across the tail base; white cheeks and sides of neck, sometimes extending across hindneck as a collar; underparts white, irregularly blotched brown on belly and underwing; bill black. Compare with (41).

43. Sooty Shearwater p.120
Puffinus griseus
16–18in/40–46cm. ws 94–109cm
Sooty-brown above, paler beneath with silvery-white under wing-coverts that flash as bird turns and are visible at long range. Long, narrow wings backswept slightly; flight rapid, quick shallow beats and long glides near surface. Bill slender, black. Compare with (32).

42

40

25

43

27

37

38

C.J.F.Coombs.

5 Non-breeding Petrels, Prions and Shearwaters

A mixed group of medium and small petrels and shearwaters that visit Falkland waters, mostly from Antarctic and sub-Antarctic breeding grounds; adults and immatures are not separable at sea.

26. Antarctic Petrel p.110
Thalassoica antarctica
16–18in/40–46cm. ws 92–104cm
Conspicuously patterned; dark brown head, back and forewings, broad white trailing half of wing; lower rump and tail white with broad black tip; all underparts white. Stiff-winged flight, often high above sea.

28. Snow Petrel p.111
Pagodroma nivea
12–15in/30–38cm. ws 76–91cm
Small white petrel with a short black bill and a black eye; tail looks square. Flight batlike with shallow beats and erratic direction; rarely follows ships.

29. Kerguelen Petrel see Plate 21 and page 112.

30. Atlantic Petrel (not illustrated) see page 112.

31. White-headed Petrel p.113
Pterodroma lessonii
16–18in/40–46cm. ws 92–109cm
Distinctive; wings blackish above, back lighter; white head and white or grey rump and tail; underwing grey, contrasts with white body; dark eye patch and black bill noticeable when close. Flight fast and strong, ignores ships.

33. Soft-plumaged Petrel p.114
Pterodroma mollis
13–15in/33–38cm. ws 83–95cm
Slate-grey crown, back, tail and underwing; wings grey-brown above, with darker coverts forming 'M' shape; underparts white, variable grey sides, sometimes a partial breast band; face and throat white, dark patch through and below eye; bill short, black. Flight fast and erratic; occasionally follows ships.

34. Blue Petrel p.114
Halobaena caerulea
11–12in/28–30cm. ws 58–69cm
At a distance resembles prions; separated at close range by white-tipped tail; other differences are a blackish cap, grey and white mottled forehead, grey sides of neck. Flight less erratic than prions, tending to glide low over sea; will approach ships closely but does not follow.

35. Dove/Antarctic Prion p.115
Pachyptila desolata
11–12in/28–30cm. ws 58–66cm
Slightly larger than other prions; dark grey nape extends as a partial collar to sides of neck; short white eye-stripe, dark mark through eye; narrow black tail tip. Bill broad, blackish. Flight less erratic than (37), plate 4.

36. Broad-billed Prion p.115
Pachyptila vittata
10–12in/25–30cm. ws 58–66cm
Closely resembles (35), but bill very broad, blue; usually lacks partial collar; tail has narrower black tip than (38); shows dark central line beneath tail like (37). See Plate 4.

39. Grey Petrel (not illustrated) see page 117.

41. Cory's Shearwater (not illustrated) see page 118.

44. Manx Shearwater (not illustrated) see page 121.

45. Little Shearwater (not illustrated) see page 121.

C.J.F. Coombs.

Storm-Petrels and Diving Petrels are very small oceanic birds; they differ markedly in shape, flying actions and feeding habits.

Diving Petrels are stout, short-necked and small-winged. Bills of both species are short and black, the legs and feet bright blue. Flight is rapid, with whirring wingbeats as they emerge from the sea and fly quickly below the surface again. Specific identification is often difficult.

46. Wilson's Storm-Petrel   p.122
Oceanites oceanicus
6–7in/15–18cm. ws 38–42cm
Sooty-black body, wings, head and tail, with broad white rump extending to flanks; variable grey streak across secondary coverts. Long black legs; yellow webs not easily seen. Flight similar to (49); often follows ships.

47. White-faced Storm-Petrel   (not illustrated) see page 123.

48. Black-bellied Storm-Petrel   p.123
Fregetta tropica
7½–8in/19–20cm. ws 45–48cm
More heavily built than (46) and similar above with black upperparts and white rump; head, breast and undertail black, belly and sides of body white with narrow central black line from breast to undertail; underwing dark with conspicuous white triangle on coverts. Flight differs from (46) when feeding; feet hang down, the body swings like a pendulum and the bird drops breast first to water, springing off with the feet. Rarely follows ships. Black central breast streak is often difficult to see; beware of confusion with the White-bellied Storm-Petrel *Fregetta grallaria*, not recorded near Falklands.

49. Grey-backed Storm-Petrel   p.124
Garrodia nereis
6–7½in/15–19cm. ws 33–39cm
Black head, breast and wings above; back and tail grey with a broad black tip, rump pale grey; belly and under wing-coverts white, with a black margin. Bill and long legs black. Flutters and glides like a swallow, often pattering on the surface; sometimes follows ships.

50. Common Diving Petrel   p.125
Pelecanoides (urinatrix) berard
7½–9in/19–23cm. ws 33–38cm
Cheeks and sides of neck mottled grey, often forming an incomplete breast band, under wing-coverts grey, otherwise black above and white below; similar to (51).

51. Magellan Diving Petrel   p.126
Pelecanoides magellani
7½–9in/19–23cm. ws 38cm
Blackish above and white below; white from throat extends up towards nape as a half collar; sharp contrast between grey cheeks and white throat; broad white stripe either side of back; underwing whiter than on (50).

C. F. Coombs.

7   Herons and Egrets

Long-legged wading birds with dagger-shaped bills, herons and egrets have broad, slow-flapping wings, fold their necks back to give a typical thick-chested appearance and their feet project beyond the tail.

55. Cocoi Heron   p.130
Ardea cocoi
38–50in/97–127cm
ADULT: Twice the size of the resident species (60); long, thin white neck streaked black down centre; black face and cap; black sides from shoulder to flanks and black patches on belly; grey back and wing-coverts; black flight feathers and tail; very heavy yellow bill and very long legs.
IMMATURE: see page 130.

56. Great White Egret   p.130
Egretta alba
33–40in/85–102cm
ADULT NON-BREEDING: Very large, all white heron with sharply kinked very long neck; bill yellow; legs and feet black. Compare with (57) and (59). Black line from gape to eye is seen at close range.
ADULT BREEDING & IMMATURE: see page 130.

57. Snowy Egret   p.131
Egretta thula
22–26in/56–66cm
ADULT NON-BREEDING: Medium size, all white egret; bill black, slender with a yellow base; legs black, feet yellow. More graceful than (59) and much smaller than (56).
ADULT BREEDING: see page 131.

58. Green-backed Heron   p.131
Butorides striatus
15–19in/38–48cm
A. ADULT: Thickset, small and dark; glossy green above with scaly buff sides and grey below; heavy-looking head with a black cap, white mark below eye; bill black with a yellow base; legs dull yellow.
B. IMMATURE: Browner above with white spotted wing-coverts; buffish below heavily streaked dark brown.

59. Cattle Egret   p.132
Bubulcus ibis
19–21in/48–53cm
IMMATURE: Stocky, small white egret, with rounded head; variable buff patches on head and breast; a short yellow bill, dark greenish legs and faster wingbeats distinguish it from (57). Associates with grazing animals on pasture.
ADULT BREEDING: see page 132.

60. Black-crowned Night Heron   p.132
Nycticorax nycticorax
21–23in/53–58cm
Heavy build, with flight silhouette and pattern unlike any other resident species; wings broad, rounded and slow flapping.
A. ADULT: Black back, grey wings, pale grey neck and below; white or cream forehead, cap black with long white plumes; iris bright red; bill blackish; legs variable, slaty and yellow or pink.
B. FIRST YEAR IMMATURE: Dark brown above, heavily flecked and spotted buff; underparts buff streaked dark brown; iris orange; legs yellow green.
SECOND & THIRD YEAR IMMATURES: see page 132.

55

57

56

59

60B

58B

58A

60A

C. F. Coombs.

8 Swans, Ibis, Stork, Spoonbill and Flamingo

All species in these four families fly with the neck outstretched; bill size, wing shape and flight silhouette provide good identification points.

61. Maguari Stork p.133
Ciconia maguari
38–43in/97–110cm
ADULT: White body, upper and under wing-coverts; black flight feathers and short forked tail; heavy reddish dagger-shaped bill; very long white neck and long reddish legs project in flight, which is powerful with slow wingbeats.
IMMATURE: see page 133.

62. Buff-necked Ibis p.134
Theristicus caudatus
26–29in/66–73cm
ADULT: Goose-size with a long orange neck and head, slender downcurved black bill and black face; broad, rounded wings; back and inner half of wings grey with a broad white band across centre and black flight feathers; tail short, blackish; red legs and feet extend to tip of tail. Often uses loud harsh calls in flight.
IMMATURE: see page 134.

63. Roseate Spoonbill p.134
Ajaia ajaja
27–32in/69–81cm
ADULT: Long spoon-shaped greenish bill, long white neck, pink and white body, long pink wings with red shoulder patch make it easily identifiable. In flight the dark red legs project beyond the yellowish tail. Face is bare, greenish with a black border. Feeds by sweeping bill from side to side.
IMMATURE: see page 134.

64. Chilean Flamingo p.135
Phoenicopterus chilensis
39–44in/100–112cm
ADULT: Flight silhouette distinctive; extremely long thin white neck with heavy curved bill and very long legs outstretched; wing-coverts red with contrasting black flight feathers. Flies with rapid wingbeats and few glides.
IMMATURE: see page 135.

65. Coscoroba Swan p.136
Coscoroba coscoroba
36–45in/90–114cm
ADULT: Smaller than (66) with all white plumage except for small black tips on rather long wings; bill bright red, duck-like. Flight call is a loud musical triple trumpeting. Beware confusion with Feral Domestic Goose (71), [plate 21 and page 141] which has a thicker neck, stouter orange bill and honking calls in flight.
IMMATURE: see page 136.

66. Black-necked Swan p.136
Cygnus melancoryphus
39–49in/99–124cm
ADULT: Distinctive large and shy freshwater bird; plumage white except for a black neck with white eye-streak; bill blue-grey with red basal knob, larger on male. Flies with regular slow wingbeats, pink feet hidden by tail.
IMMATURE: see page 137.

62

61

64

63

66

66

65

C.J.F.Coombs.

All of the Sheldgeese except the male Kelp Goose (70) have a similar wing pattern to the Ruddy-headed Goose (68).

67. Ashy-headed Goose   p.137
Chloephaga poliocephala
22–24in/55–61cm
ADULT: Male and female alike; separated from (68) by grey head and neck, chestnut breast and mantle, black/white barred flanks and white belly.
IMMATURE: see page 137.

68. Ruddy-headed Goose   p.138
Chloephaga rubidiceps
20–22in/51–56cm
ADULT: Male is slightly larger than the female; both are smaller than female (69). Sharp demarcation between chestnut upper neck and finely barred black/grey lower neck; eye-ring white; barred flanks merge into chestnut belly and undertail; bill black, legs orange, often spotted black, compare with (69). In flight shows black rump and tail, metallic green secondary converts.
IMMATURE: see page 138.

69. Upland Goose   p.139
Chloephaga picta
28–30in/71–76cm
A. MALE: Appears mainly white with black legs at a distance, see male (70); head, neck mantle and underparts white, heavily barred black on mantle and flanks; rump white, tail black with variable white fringe; bill black.
B. FEMALE: Larger than (68); rusty-brown head and neck merge into finely barred brown/black breast; flanks heavily barred black/white; rump and tail black, see female (70); bill black, legs and feet dark yellow.
IMMATURE MALE & FEMALE: see page 139.

70. Kelp Goose   p.140
Chloephaga hybrida
26–29in/66–74cm
A. FEMALE: Black, white and brown, well camouflaged; head dark brown, lighter cap and white eye-ring; underparts barred black/white; white tail, rump and undertail, see female (69); bill pink, legs yellow.
B. MALE: White and conspicuous; bill black with pink culmen, legs yellow. Compare with (125), [plate 15 and page 185].
IMMATURE MALE AND FEMALE: see page 140.

71. Feral Domestic Goose: see Plate 21 and page 141.

72. Crested Duck   p.143
Lophonetta specularioides
20–24in/51–61cm
ADULT: Male and female similar; long-bodied, with whitish neck and cheeks; dark cap surrounds red eye; ragged crest not conspicuous; mottled brown/buff mantle and underparts; elongated tail and undertail black. Bill mainly black. In flight, dark brown above, pale below, with black rump and tail; white trailing edge bordered glossy black in front.
IMMATURE: see page 143.

73. Falkland Flightless Steamer Duck   p.144
Tachyeres brachydactyla
24–30in/61–76cm
Bulky, scaly grey, with rounded head and a massive bill; large broken white bar on back; white belly; short, spiky tail; wingtips reach to top of rump; cannot achieve free flight, see (74).
A. MALE: Head white, grey cheeks; bill bright orange. In territorial disputes, 'steams' over surface creating much spray.
B. FEMALE: Smaller than male; dark brown head, white eye-ring and curved streak; bill greenish-yellow.
IMMATURE: see page 144.

74. Flying Steamer Duck   p.145
Tachyeres patachonicus
23–28in/58–71cm
Often confused with (73), but more slender and wingtips reach to tail base; in flight unmistakable, showing large white secondary patch and white belly. More shy than (73); 'steams' with less spray.
MALE: Grey head, white behind eyes, throat red-brown; bill smaller than (73), orange-yellow, bluish around nostrils.
FEMALE & IMMATURE: see page 145.

68

68

68

67

70B

69B

69A

70A

72

72

73A

73B

74

C. J. F. Coombs.

All birds illustrated are adults. Except where shown, males and females are similar.

75. Mallard   (not illustrated) see page 146.

76. Spectacled Duck   (not illustrated) see page 146.

77. Speckled/Yellow-billed Teal   p.147
Anas flavirostris
15–16in/38–41cm
Smallest duck, grey-brown with a dark brown head, black streak through eye, yellow bill with black ridge. Looks down-at-the-front on water. In flight, brown with a darker head; black/green speculum bordered narrowly buff in front and white behind.

78. Chiloe Wigeon   p.148
Anas sibilatrix
19–21in/48–53cm
Head glossy black, forehead and variable 'ear' patch white, bill blue-grey; breast barred black/white, underparts white, orange at the sides; back black streaked with white. In flight, dark with large white forewing crescent, white rump and black tail.
IMMATURE: see page 148.

79. White-cheeked Pintail   (not illustrated) see page 148.

80. Yellow-billed Pintail   p.149
Anas georgica
19–21in/48–53cm
Larger and paler than (77); long, slender pale brown neck and round head with a darker crown; dark brown streaked buff above; breast warm buff spotted brown; dark yellow bill with black ridge and blue-grey tip. In flight, separated from (77) by pale head, long neck and whitish belly patch; brown wings with greyish shoulder, black speculum with buff edges.
JUVENILE: see page 149.

81. Silver Teal   p.150
Anas versicolor
17–18in/43–45cm
Conspicuous head pattern of wide brown cap to nape and cream cheeks; flanks barred black/white; bill blue with orange base. In flight, brown wings with grey-brown shoulder, glossy blue/green speculum bordered white; pale grey rump and tail; underwing mainly white.

82. Cinnamon Teal   p.150
Anas cyanoptera
16–19in/41–48cm
A. MALE BREEDING: Chestnut head, neck and below; black undertail; long black bill.
B. FEMALE & ECLIPSE MALE: Dark brown above flecked lighter; head, neck and underparts buff mottled dark brown. Black bill, yellow legs and dark undertail separate it from (80), larger size and black bill from (77); see also (86).
C. In flight, black primaries, white line between pale blue forewing and glossy green/black speculum.

83. Red Shoveler   p.151
Anas platalea
18–21in/46–53cm
A. MALE BREEDING: Huge, spoonlike black bill; head grey-buff speckled black, underparts red-brown spotted black, white at side of tail and black undertail; back and rump black streaked whitish.
B. FEMALE & ECLIPSE MALE: Brown streaked buff above, buff mottled and spotted dark brown below; legs dull yellow, bill brown.
C. In flight, male similar to (82); paler head, looks longer-necked with larger bill; forewing blue with white bar above glossy speculum; white sides to tail.
FEMALE FLYING: see page 151.

84. Rosy-billed Pochard   p.152
Netta peposaca
19–22in/48–55cm
A. MALE: Purple-black head, neck and breast; black back; flanks grey, undertail white. Iris red, bill and large basal knob rose-red.
B. FEMALE: Red-brown above; dull brown below, whitish throat and belly; white undertail. Bill blue-grey with small knob.
C. In flight, sexes are similar; blackish with white speculum, tipped black.

85. Lake Duck   p.152
Oxyura vittata
15–16in/38–40cm
Dumpy, short-necked, long fan-shaped tail often held vertically.
MALE BREEDING: Head black, back and underparts chestnut, belly mottled white/brown. Bill blue, legs grey. In flight, male shows black head, chestnut back, blackish wings and tail.
MALE IN WINTER & FEMALE: see page 152.

86. Black-headed Duck   (not illustrated) see page 153.

77

78

80

81

82C

82B

82A

83C

83B

84C

84B

84A

83A

85

C.J.F.Coombs

11 Birds of prey

87. Turkey Vulture p.154
Cathartes aura
26–28in/66–71cm. WS 157–170cm
Flight leisurely and rocking, wings held in a shallow 'V'-shape.
ADULT: Black plumage; wings long, undersides of flight feathers grey; naked red head.
IMMATURE: see page 154.

88. Sharp-shinned Hawk p.155
Accipiter striatus
10–14in/25–36cm. WS 51–71cm
Slender; rounded wings and long, white-tipped tail; low level twisting flight.
IMMATURE: Dark brown above flecked buff; underparts white heavily streaked buff/brown. Tail dark brown with four or five broad black bars and a narrow white tip.
ADULT: see page 155.

89. Red-backed Hawk p.155
Buteo polyosoma
18–22in/46–56cm. WS 110–130cm
Glides with wings flat. Two main colour phases and others known. ADULTS have a white tail with a black subterminal band; yellow legs, bluish and yellow bill.
A. LIGHT FEMALE: Chestnut mantle, grey head and white underparts.
B. DARK FEMALE: Chestnut mantle, underparts red-brown.
C. LIGHT MALE: Slate-grey back and wings above, white underparts.
D. JUVENILE: Tail grey with fine black bars; heavily mottled and flecked brown, chestnut and buff; whitish patch on nape.
DARK MALE & IMMATURES: see page 156.

90. Cinereous Harrier p.156
Circus cinereus
16–20in/41–51cm. WS 100–120cm
Long narrow wings, slender body, long tail; flaps and glides at low level.
A. MALE: Pearl-grey above with white rump; tail centre grey, white sides barred black, narrow black subterminal band; underparts barred red-brown on white; legs, iris and cere yellow.
B. FEMALE: Dark brown above, flecked buff on head and shoulders; rump white, tail grey with four broad dark bands; breast brown.
IMMATURE: see page 156.

91. Chimango Caracara p.157
Milvago chimango
15–17in/38–43cm
MALE: Smaller than (92) or (93); brown above, whitish heavily mottled brown and buff below. In flight; blackish wingtips and large whitish patch on primaries, white rump, whitish tail with black subterminal band. Legs blue-grey.
FEMALE & IMMATURE: see page 158.

92. Striated Caracara p.158
Phalcoboenus australis
23–25in/58–63cm. WS not known
Darker than (93), with a smaller pale patch on wings; tail white-tipped or brown.
ADULT: Female larger; black with collar of white streaks extending to breast; belly and leg feathers bright rufous. In flight; small buff patch at base of primaries, tail black with broad white tip, wings below dark with buff central patches. Bill blue-grey, cere and facial skin orange, legs yellow.
IMMATURES: see page 158.

93. Crested Caracara p.160
Caracara plancus
21–25in/50–63cm. WS c130cm
Looks flat-headed, black cap contrasts with pale cheeks, see (92).
A. ADULT: Dark brown flecked buff above; face, foreneck and undertail sandy-buff, neck and breast buff barred brown, belly and tibia dark brown. Bill yellowish, cere orange/pink, legs yellow. In flight; long parallel-sided wings, large whitish patch on primaries, tail whitish with broad black tip. Flies with deep flaps and glides, wings held almost flat.
B. IMMATURE: Underparts darker, heavily streaked brown; above streaked buff. Face pinkish, legs dull yellow.

94. Peregrine Falcon p.161
Falco peregrinus
15–19in/38–48cm. WS 90–105cm
Rapid agile flight; quick beats and glides on swept back, sharp-pointed wings; tapered tail.
ADULT: Female larger and darker; dark grey above; black 'helmet' contrasts with pale throat; underside whitish heavily barred dark brown. Cere, eye-ring and legs yellow, bill slate-blue.
IMMATURE: see page 161.

95. American Kestrel p.162
Falco sparverius
9–11in/23–28cm. WS 50–60cm
Flight buoyant on sharp-pointed wings, often hovers. Variegated grey and chestnut head with double black bar on white cheeks; back chestnut; underparts buff/white spotted black.
A. FEMALE: Inner wing and tail chestnut barred black, primaries blackish.
B. MALE: Inner wing blue-grey flecked black; black subterminal bar and white edge to tail.
IMMATURE: see page 162.

87

89C

89A

89B

89D

90B

90A

91

91

92

93B

95A

94

93A

88

95B

C.J.F. Coombs.

A varied family that includes swamp-dwelling crakes, rails and gallinules, which usually remain hidden in dense vegetation, and coots that frequent open pools with waterside plants. Usually silent outside the breeding season. All three Coots have velvet-black heads and necks, red eyes, slate-black bodies and a small patch of white beneath the tail. Shape and colour of the frontal shields above the bill are the best field marks. The Coots shown are adults; immatures are paler below and have duller frontal shields. Legs trail in a weak-looking flight.

96. Plumbeous Rail   (not illustrated) see page 163.

97. Speckled Crake   p.163
Coturnicops notata
5½in/13–14cm
ADULT: Minute; rotund and short-tailed; dark brown above spotted with white; flanks barred white and brown; head heavily spotted white. A secretive and little known species.

98. American Purple Gallinule   p.164
Porphyrula martinica
10–14in/26–36cm
FIRST YEAR IMMATURE: Greenish-brown above, buff-brown head, neck and flanks. Conspicuous white undertail noticeable in flight when long trailing greenish legs, long neck and rapidly beating rounded wings are distinctive.
ADULT: see page 164.

99. Red-gartered Coot   p.164
Fulica armillata
16–21in/41–53cm
Largest of the three species; frontal shield oval, yellow or red with a yellow border; bill yellow with red patches at base. Red 'garter' visible above the ankle joint when walking and sometimes when swimming. In flight shows faint white leading edge to black wings.
IMMATURE: see page 164.

100. White-winged Coot   p.165
Fulica leucoptera
14–17in/35–43cm
Smallest of the coots recorded; large, round-topped, bright yellow or orange frontal shield above a lemon-yellow to ivory bill. Wings have barely visible white lines along leading and trailing edges of secondaries.

101. Red-fronted Coot   p.165
Fulica rufifrons
15–19in/38–48cm
Between (100) and (99) in size; frontal shield all red, long, narrow and pointed at the top. In flight shows all black wings.

C.J.F.Coombs.

13 Oystercatchers, Plovers, Sandpipers and Snipes

102. Blackish Oystercatcher   p.166
Haematopus ater
19–20in/48–50cm
ADULT: Sooty-black head, neck and underparts; dark brown back, wings and tail; red bill shorter than (103) and deeper; iris yellow, eye-ring red, legs pink.
IMMATURE: see page 166.

103. Magellanic Oystercatcher   p.167
Haematopus leucopodus
17–18in/43–46cm
ADULT: Shiny black head, breast and back; white belly; long red bill, orange iris and yellow eye-ring, pink legs. In flight black wings have a large white triangle on inner trailing half; white inner half of tail, black outer half.
IMMATURE: see page 167.

105. Two-banded Plover   p.170
Charadrius falklandicus
7–7½in/18–19cm
A. MALE BREEDING: Grey-brown above, white face and below; chestnut nape and hindneck; black over crown, through eye to side of narrow, sometimes incomplete neck band; broader black breast band. In flight, dark tail with white sides and narrow white bar across primaries, see (118) and (119).
B. FEMALE BREEDING: As male but duller chestnut and black bands.
C. JUVENILE: Speckled buff head, back and breast band.
NON-BREEDING ADULT: see page 170.

106. Rufous-chested Dotterel   p.171
Charadrius modestus
8–9in/20–23cm
A. ADULT BREEDING: Sexes similar, female less bright; prominent white stripe across forehead and over eye; blue-grey face; bright chestnut breast with black band, rest of underparts mostly white. Flight rapid, showing white sides to dark tail and white streaks on outer primaries; larger than (105).
B. ADULT NON-BREEDING: Buff head stripe; brown neck and breast.
JUVENILE: see page 171.

115. Common (Magellan) Snipe   p.178
Gallinago (gallinago) paraguaiae
10–11in/25–28cm
ADULT: Blackish above heavily spangled and streaked chestnut and buff, showing broad buff lines along back; head brown with a buff stripe over eye; underparts whitish, heavily marked brown except on belly. In flight long bill, short brown tail, broad pointed and angled wings are distinctive; often flies erratically and pitches very quickly; tame and usually runs from intruders.

116. Cordilleran Snipe   p.180
Gallinago stricklandii
12–14in/30–35cm
ADULT: Larger with longer bill than (115); red-brown above, barred and streaked black; underparts warm buff mottled and barred brown. In flight, very long bill and broad, rounded wings are prominent, see (115).

118. Sanderling   p.181
Calidris alba
8–8½in/20–21cm
A. ADULT NON-BREEDING: Very active on sand beaches; pale grey above; white face and underparts, black 'shoulder' patch sometimes visible.
B. ADULT FLYING: Long, broad white bar across blackish wings; white sides to black tail; call-note similar to (105).
IMMATURE: see page 181.

119. White-rumped Sandpiper   p.182
Calidris fuscicollis
6–7in/15–18cm
A. ADULT NON-BREEDING: Inconspicuously coloured, grey-brown above streaked darker; white below streaked brown on breast; bill black, slender and slightly downcurved. In flight, has white patch above dark tail, narrow white wingbar and a typical squeaky call, see (105), (118) and (120).
B. ADULT PRE-BREEDING: From March acquires buff edges above and clearer streaking on white flanks.

103

102

105A   105B   105C

106A   106B

119A

119B

118B

118A

116   115

C. J. F. Coombs.

104. Southern Lapwing   p.169
Vanellus chilensis
13–14in/33–36cm
Sexes similar; black forehead, foreneck and
breast band with a white line in front of the
red eye; belly white; dull grey above; long
crimson legs; dark red bill with a black tip.
Wary; often calls loudly.
In flight: black primaries, grey and white
inner wing, white rump and tail with a broad
black subterminal bar; slow beats of broad
rounded wings.

107. Tawny-throated Dotterel   p.172
Eudromias ruficollis
10–11in/25–28cm
Sexes similar; tall and slim; thin bill as long
as the head, see (106) [plate 13]; grey crown
and nape, black bar from bill to large dark eye,
cream eye-stripe and face; neck orange, breast
dark grey, belly buff with a central black spot;
mantle grey-brown, wings blackish heavily
streaked buff and chestnut.
FLIGHT PATTERN: see page 172.

108. Magellanic Plover   p.173
Pluvianellus socialis
8–8½in/20–21cm
Grey head and above, white below with
brown-grey breast band, rump and tail black
with broad white sides. Short black bill, iris
red.
IMMATURE: see page 173.

109. Hudsonian Godwit   p.174
Limosa haemastica
14½–15½in/37–39cm
NON-BREEDING: Tall and slim; slightly
upcurved dark bill twice as long as head; very
long dark legs; upperparts grey-brown edged
buff; breast brownish-grey, belly white;
narrow whitish stripe from bill over eye.
ADULT & FLIGHT PATTERN: see page 174.

110. Whimbrel   p.175
Numenius phaeopus
16–18in/40–46cm
IMMATURE: Tall; very long downcurved
blackish bill; long blue-grey legs; dark brown
flecked buff and spotted with white above;
underparts buff lightly streaked brown from
face to breast; head brown with buff central
crown stripe; broad buff eye-stripe. Rippling
call is diagnostic.
ADULT & FLIGHT PATTERN: see page 175.

111. Eskimo Curlew   (not illustrated) see
page 176.

112. Upland Sandpiper   p.176
Bartramia longicauda
11–12in/28–30cm
Resembles (110) in colour but smaller; small
rounded head with large dark eye on pale
face; neck thin, buff finely spotted brown, belly
whitish; long dull yellow legs, slender yellow
bill.
FLIGHT PATTERN: see page 177.

113. Lesser Yellowlegs   p.177
Tringa flavipes
9–10in/23–25cm
NON-BREEDING: Long yellow legs; thin dark
bill, as long as the head; pale stripe over the
eye; grey-brown above flecked whitish; white
below streaked brown, see (122) [plate 21].
FLIGHT PATTERN: see page 177.

114. Ruddy Turnstone   (not illustrated) see
page 178.

117. Red Knot   (not illustrated) see page
180.

120. Baird's Sandpiper   p.182
Calidris bairdii
5½–7in/14–18cm
NON-BREEDING: Similar to (119) but more buff
with a duller eye-stripe and very slender tip to
the dark bill.
FLIGHT PATTERN: see page 182. Compare with
(119) [plate 13].

123. White-bellied Seedsnipe   p.184
Attagis malouinus
10½–11½in/26.5–29cm
A. ADULT: Stocky and plump with short, thick
brown bill; head and neck buff, spotted
brown; breast buff with dark crescents
extending to flanks; belly white; dark brown
above heavily scalloped chestnut and buff.
B. JUVENILE: More scaly above and whiter
below.
FLIGHT PATTERN: see page 184.

124. Least Seedsnipe   p.185
Thinocorus rumicivorus
6–7in/15–18cm
A. MALE: Dark brown above mottled buff and
white with a white belly; grey sides of neck,
white throat edged black, extending to narrow
black breast band; short curved brownish bill;
short yellow legs.
B. FEMALE FLYING: Very narrow, sharp-pointed
dark wings with faint pale bar; dark tail with
white sides and broad white tip to outer
feathers.

104

107

108

120

113

124A

124B

112

110

123B

123A

109

C.J.F.Coombs.

15. Sheathbill, Gulls, Terns and Skua

125. Snowy Sheathbill p.185
Chionis alba
15–16in/38–41cm.
A. ADULT: White, pigeon-like; bill yellowish with black tip and ridge and a horny sheath around the base; pink wattled skin below and around eye.
B. IMMATURE: As adult, without bill sheath and wattles.

126. South Polar Skua (not illustrated) see page 186.

127. Antarctic Skua p.187
Catharacta antarctica
20–23in/53–58cm
ADULT: Dark brown, heavy build with a stout hooked black bill and black legs; plumage varies, some are lighter with a yellowish hindneck and a dark cap, see (126) and (128). In flight, large white flash on primaries; see juvenile (134).

128. Chilean Skua (not illustrated) see page 188.

129. Long-tailed Skua (not illustrated) see page 189.

130. Arctic Skua (not illustrated) see page 189.

131. Dolphin Gull p.190
Larus scoresbii
16–18in/40–46cm
A. ADULT BREEDING: Pale grey head and below; white tail; slate-black back and wings with white edge to secondaries; stout bill, eye-ring and legs deep red.
B. ADULT AUTUMN: As adult breeding, with dark grey hood.
C. FIRST WINTER: Sooty head, mottled grey/brown breast; white tail has black subterminal bar; bill dull pink with a broad black tip; legs dark brown.
D. SECOND WINTER: Sooty-grey head, mostly pale grey below; tail white; bill pink with broad black subterminal bar; legs brown tinged red.
OTHER PLUMAGES & FLIGHT PATTERN: see page 191.

132. Grey Gull p.192
Larus modestus
18in/46cm
A. ADULT BREEDING: Whitish head, dull grey underparts and back; wings black with white edged secondaries; grey tail with black band and white tip; legs black; slim blackish bill, see first year (131).
B. ADULT NON-BREEDING: Head brown.
JUVENILE & IMMATURE PLUMAGES: see page 192.

133. Band-tailed Gull (not illustrated) see page 192.

134. Kelp Gull p.193
Larus dominicanus
22–24in/56–60cm
A. ADULT BREEDING: White head, neck, underparts and tail; sooty-black mantle, back and wings above with white tips; bill orange-yellow with a red patch, eye-ring red; legs vary; green/grey-yellow or orange-yellow.
B. ADULT NON-BREEDING: Brown streaked nape and head.
C. JUVENILE/FIRST WINTER: Dark brown mottled buff; tail blackish, barred brown; bill black, legs pink-brown.
D. SECOND WINTER: Variable white on head, rump and below, some slate on mantle; bill mostly cream; legs grey-brown.
OTHER PLUMAGES & FLIGHT PATTERN: see page 193.

135. Franklin's Gull (not illustrated) see page 195.

136. Brown-hooded Gull p.196
Larus maculipennis
14–15in/36–38cm
A. ADULT BREEDING: Pearl grey back and wings; chocolate brown head and white underparts often suffused rose pink; slender dark red bill, crimson legs.
B. NON-BREEDING: Head white, dark ear-coverts and crown; see (135).
JUVENILE & IMMATURE PLUMAGE & FLIGHT PATTERN: see page 196.

137. Common Tern p.198
Sterna hirundo
12–14in/31–35cm
ADULT NON-BREEDING: Smaller than (140); white forehead, black crown and nape; bill blackish. In flight, variable dark wedge on outer primaries; forked tail lacks streamers. Compare with (138) and (139).

138. Arctic Tern see Plate 21 and page 198.

139. Antarctic Tern see Plate 21 and page 199.

140. South American Tern p.200
Sterna hirundinacea
16–17in/40–43cm
ADULT BREEDING: Appears white with a black cap; very slender, long thin pointed wings and a deeply forked tail; bill blood-red, fairly heavy; legs red. Compare with (138) and (139).
NON-BREEDING & IMMATURE: see page 200.

125B

125A

131B

131A

131C

134C

131D

134D

134A

136B

134B

136A

132A

132B

140

127

137

C.J.F.Coombs.

16 Doves, Parakeet and other vagrants

141. Chilean Pigeon p.201
Columba araucana
14–15in/35–38cm
Much larger than Eared Dove (142); purple back, head and underparts with a narrow whitish collar on nape; wings blackish with grey coverts; tail grey with a black subterminal band; bill black, legs red.

142. Eared Dove p.201
Zenaida auriculata
10–11in/25–28cm
MALE: Small, olive-brown above with black spots on scapulars; grey crown, pinkish underparts. Rises rapidly from ground showing long, graduated fanned tail, grey-brown with broad white edge and black subterminal band.
FEMALE & IMMATURE: see page 201.

143. Burrowing Parrot (not illustrated) see page 202.

144. Austral Parakeet p.202
Enicognathus ferrugineus
13–14in/33–36cm
Very long red-brown pointed tail; dull green crown and back; yellow-green face and below; dull red forehead, lores and centre of belly; wings dark green above, yellow and grey below, see (143).

145. Dark-billed Cuckoo p.203
Coccyzus melacoryphus
10–11in/25–28cm
Pale grey-brown above with very long, distinctively marked tail, brown in the centre, black sides with large white tips; head dark grey with white cheeks, underparts buff; wings long and rounded, uniform grey-brown; bill and legs black.

151. White-collared Swift (not illustrated) see page 208.

152. Ashy-tailed Swift p.208
Chaetura andrei
5–6in/12–15cm
Tiny, fast flying, blackish with extremely long and narrow curved wings; tail short and square with projecting feather shafts; rump and throat paler brown. Compare with (151) which is much larger.

153. Green-backed Firecrown p.209
Sephanoides sephanoides
4–4½in/10–11cm
MALE: Very slender bill, longer than the head; bronzy green above with blackish flight feathers; whitish below speckled bronze on breast; crown glittering red.
FEMALE: see page 209.

176. Patagonian Mockingbird p.228
Mimus patagonicus
8½–9½in/21–24cm
Smaller than a Thrush; long black tail edged white; brown-grey above, red-brown rump; head and below brown-grey, white eyebrow, throat and belly; strong, slightly curved black bill; black legs. In flight, black wings show two broad white bars.

141

142

144

176

145

152   153

C.F.Coombs.

NB Owls 146–150 are at a smaller scale than 154–157.

146. Barn Owl p.204
Tyto alba
14–16in/35–41cm
Very pale above and below, appearing white in twilight; heart-shaped white facial disc with dark eyes. Flight wavering; slow deep flaps of long wings.

147. Great Horned Owl (not illustrated) see page 205

148. Burrowing Owl p.205
Athene cunicularia
8–10in/20–25cm
Small brown owl heavily spotted and mottled white above; facial disc brown with white forehead, 'eyebrows' and throat; whitish below barred brown; long whitish legs; yellow eyes.
IMMATURE: See page 205

149. Rufous-legged Owl p.206
Strix rufipes
14–15in/35–38cm
Darker than (150); blackish head, red-brown facial disc bordered black, white 'eyebrows' lores and throat; brown eyes; brown, heavily barred white, buff and black above and below.

150. Short-eared Owl p.206
Asio flammeus
14–15in/35–38cm
Rich buff, mottled and barred dark brown above, streaked dark brown on neck and breast with paler flanks and belly; rounded buff facial disc with white lores and 'eyebrows'; bright yellow eyes set off by black feathers; legs feathered buff.
  Flight distinctive; long, broad and round-ended wings show dark mark on underside at carpal joint; body tapers from bulky head to short tail; wing beats deep and slow; usually flies at low level.

154. Thorn-tailed Rayadito p.210
Aphrastura spinicauda
4–5½in/10–14cm
Tiny, noisy and active, distinctively patterned; head black with a long buff eye-stripe to nape; back brown; rump and centre of long tail orange-brown, outer feathers black, all with a projecting shaft; underparts white tinged grey on flanks; wings blackish with double buff bar. Short, thin black bill, legs greenish. Climbs vertically, frequently bobbing; tail trails in flight.

155. Tussac-bird p.210
Cinclodes antarcticus
7¼–8¼in/18–21cm
Small, dark brown, tame, restless and inquisitive; stout-based, slightly curved black bill and black legs; throat variably flecked buff; wing-coverts edged red-brown. In flight shows a faint red-brown wing bar.

156. Austral Canastero p.212
Thripophaga anthoides
6½in/16cm
Secretive; dull olive-grey heavily streaked black above with red-brown wing-coverts; long tail, blackish tipped, chestnut on sides; head streaked black, throat yellowish, breast and belly pale grey streaked black on breast. Bill short, greyish, legs dull grey.

157. Andean Tapaculo p.212
Scytalopus magellanicus
4–4½in/10–11cm
Tiny, dark slaty-grey, secretive bird resembling a House Wren (175, plate 19) in shape; wings and belly tinged red-brown; bill black, legs yellow-brown. General colour varies; some almost black, others have grey on crown.
JUVENILE: see page 212.

146

148

149

150

150

155

157

154

156

C.J.F. Coombs.

158. Black-billed Shrike-tyrant   p.213
Agriornis montana
9–10in/23–25cm
Dark brown above with white edges to flight
feathers; tail brown in centre with broad
white outer edge; head brown with buff lores,
streaked black and grey throat; belly pale
chestnut, flanks and undertail white. Bill
heavy, black with a hooked tip, legs black.

159. Fire-eyed Diucon   p.214
Pyrope pyrope
8–8½in/19–21cm
Darker above and larger than (161); sooty
grey from crown to back with light edges to
flight feathers; rump pale grey, tail grey in
centre with broad white sides; eye
conspicuously bright red; throat white, upper
breast pale grey, darker below; buff patch on
flanks; white belly and undertail. Bill and legs
black.

160. White-browed Ground-tyrant   p.215
Muscisaxicola albilora
7in/17–18cm
Resembles (161) but mantle, forehead, crown
and nape red-brown, brightest on nape; long
narrow white 'eyebrow'; wings grey-brown,
edged whitish; tail black with white sides;
underparts whitish tinged grey. Bill and legs
black, iris brown.

161. Dark-faced Ground-tyrant   p.215
Muscisaxicola macloviana
6½in/16cm
Slim, upright stance, often flicks and fans tail;
pale grey-brown nape and back; wings brown
with light edges; crown dark brown, lores and
around the eye black, pointed black bill; grey-
white below; lower rump and tail black with
a prominent white outer edge; long black legs.

162. Rufous-backed Negrito   p.216
Lessonia rufa
4½–5in/11–12cm
A. MALE: Very tiny and unmistakable; black
head, wings and underparts, chestnut back.
B. FEMALE: Grey-brown head, pale rufous
back, wings black edged rufous, tail black;
underparts pale grey-brown with chestnut on
the belly.

163. Fork-tailed Flycatcher   p.217
Tyrannus savana
Body: 5–6in/13–15cm. Tail:
8–11in/20–28cm
MALE: Body size as (161) but black, deeply
forked tail twice as long as the body; black
head to below eye, white throat and
underparts; back grey; wings blackish. Bill
and legs black. Tail streams like ribbons in
flight.
FEMALE & JUVENILE   see page 217.

164. Eastern Kingbird   (not illustrated) see
page 217

165. Great Kiskadee   p.217
Pitangus sulphuratus
8–10in/20–25cm
About thrush size, handsomely marked; head
has black and white bands, a partly hidden
yellow crown and a white throat; breast and
belly bright yellow; back, wings and tail dark
brown, tinged rufous on coverts. Stout black
bill; legs black.

166. White-crested Elaenia   p.218
Elaenia albiceps
5½–6in/14–15cm
Tiny and inconspicuous; olive-green above,
head darker with a thin white crest on the
crown; yellowish eye-ring; blackish wings
have two jagged white bars on the coverts;
tail darker than back; pale olive-grey below
becoming creamy on the belly. Bill short, dark
brown with a pinkish base; legs brown.

158   159   161

160

166   163

165   162B

162A

C. J. F. Coombs.

19 Swallows, Plantcutter, Wrens and Thrush

167. Rufous-tailed Plantcutter p.219
Phytotoma rara
7½–8in/19–20cm
A. MALE: Bright chestnut head and underparts; orange iris and black sides of head; back olive-brown heavily streaked black; wings black with white bars; tail chestnut and brown with black edges. Strong conical bill and legs are yellow-brown.
B. FEMALE: Much paler; back and underparts buff, heavily streaked brown; wingbars buff; tail, bill and legs as the male.

168. Chilean Swallow p.220
Tachycineta leucopyga
4½–5¼in/11–13cm
Blue-black above; square white rump, slightly forked tail; head blue-black to the gape, with a very narrow white streak above lores (not easily seen); [compare with White-rumped Swallow, page 220]; underparts white. Triangular wingspread of flight silhouette is characteristic, see (171); flight often erratic in direction, with few wingbeats and long glides.

169. Southern Martin p.221
Progne modesta
8–8¾in/20–22cm
A. ADULT MALE: Large and very dark; flight similar to (171); blue-black above and below; tail forked without streamers.
FEMALE: Blackish above, grey-brown below with a paler throat.
B. IMMATURE: Resembles female, tail is less forked.

170. Rough-winged Swallow see Plate 21 and page 222

171. Barn Swallow p.222
Hirundo rustica
6–7in/15–18cm
A. ADULT: Larger than (168); longer wings and deeply forked tail with streamers, see also (172). Blue-black above and on sides of breast; forehead and throat chestnut, underparts buff; tail blackish with white patches on inner webs near the tip. Flight rapid, graceful and more direct than (168).
B. JUVENILE: Brownish above, paler below, no tail streamers

172. Cliff Swallow (not illustrated) see page 223

174. Grass Wren/Short-billed Marsh Wren p.225
Cistothorus platensis
4½–5in/11–12cm
ADULT: Smaller than (175), recognised by heavy black streaks on buff back and head; small buff eye-stripe; bill shorter, light brown; tail barred black on red-brown; underparts creamy, paler on throat.
JUVENILE: see page 225.

175. House Wren p.226
Troglodytes aedon
4¾–5¼in/12–13cm
A. ADULT: Uniform red-brown back and grey-brown head without an eye-stripe separate it from (174); chestnut wings and tail closely barred brown; bill blackish, slightly curved, longer than (174); whitish below, shaded buff.
B. ABERRANT ADULT: Has irregular white or grey patches on head, wings, flanks or back.
JUVENILE: see page 226.

177. Wood Thrush (not illustrated) see page 228

178. Falkland Thrush p.229
Turdus falcklandii
10–10½in/25–26cm
A. MALE: Plump, long-legged and noisy; olive-brown back and wing-coverts, blackish wings, grey rump and black tail; black crown, nape and around eye; grey ear-coverts; throat white with large brown streaks, rest of underparts rich buff. Stout, pointed orange bill, yellow eye-ring and legs.
B. JUVENILE: Olive-brown flecked buff above; underparts buff, heavily spotted with black; breast appears patchy as speckled feathers are moulted from January. Bill and legs brownish.
C. FEMALE: As male and often indistinguishable; usually has red-brown crown and nape, buff throat with narrow dark streaks. Plumage of both sexes fades rapidly through spring.

168

167B

167A

171B

171A

169B

175B

169A

175A

174

178C

178B

178A

C.J.F.Coombs.

173. Falkland Pipit   p.223
Anthus correndera
6–6½in/15–16cm
Inconspicuous; buff heavily streaked dark brown from crown to back; paler below, streaked dark brown, particularly on sides; wings brown, broadly edged buff; tail brown with clear white outer edges, see (182); yellowish bill broad-based, tapering sharply; pink legs. Flight jerky or undulating; has characteristic song-flight.

179. House Sparrow   p.231
Passer domesticus
6–6½in/15–16.5cm
A. MALE BREEDING: Plump and perky, separated from (184) by chestnut sides of head, grey crown, black lores, white cheeks and black 'bib'; streaked brown above with small white wingbar; pale grey underparts. Bill black; legs brownish.
B. FEMALE: Dull brown above, streaked darker; pale grey-brown below; faint buff eye-stripe; no white in tail.
JUVENILE & NON-BREEDING MALE: see page 231.

180. Black-chinned Siskin   p.232
Carduelis barbatus
4¾–5in/12–13cm
A. FEMALE: Smaller than (182); olive-yellow streaked brown on back with greyish cheeks and a curving yellow face stripe; breast yellow, belly white; short conical bill brownish, legs black. In flight shows yellow rump and double yellow wing-bar, slightly forked blackish tail with yellow basal sides.
B. MALE: Black crown and throat, brighter yellow side of neck and breast; yellow on wings and base of tail brighter; back streaked blackish.

181. Mourning Sierra-finch   (not illustrated)
see page 234

182. Black-throated Finch   p.235
Melanodera melanodera
5½–6in/14–15cm
A. MALE: Blue-grey crown, mantle and sides of breast; lores and throat black prominently bordered white; breast yellow centred, fading to white under tail; back and rump grey-green; tail blackish with bright yellow sides noticeable in flight, see (173); wings blackish bordered yellow, but no wingbar, see (180). Short, conical, blue-grey bill. Amount of yellow and olive-green varies.
B. FEMALE: Drab, streaked brown and buff above; buff below variably tinged yellow and heavily streaked brown on sides; wings edged white or yellow; tail fringed yellow, less than on male, see (173). Bill horn-coloured.

183. Yellow-bridled Finch   p.236
Melanodera xanthogramma
6–6¾in/15–17cm
GREY PHASE MALE: Similar to male of (182) though larger; yellow border to black lores and throat; usually more yellow on breast and belly. Southern race has broad yellow edges to the tail; northern has white edges.
GREEN PHASE MALE & FEMALE: see page 236.

184. Rufous-collared Sparrow   p.237
Junco capensis
5½–6½in/14–16cm
MALE: Slender, fairly long-tailed, buffish, heavily streaked brown above and resembling (179). Separated by chestnut collar across the hindneck, white throat and grey head, with or without black stripes through the eye and on the crown; brown forked tail has faint white edges.
FEMALE: Similar.
JUVENILE: see page 238.

185. Long-tailed Meadowlark   p.239
Sturnella loyca
9½–10in/24–25cm
A. MALE: Unmistakable; brilliant red throat and breast; broad, curving white eye-stripe; conical sharp-pointed whitish bill; back heavily mottled black and buff; tail barred brown and black.
B. FEMALE: Paler red breast, thinner eye-stripe and darker bill.
JUVENILE: see page 239.

173

185B

185A

183

182B

182A

180A

180B

184

179B

179A

C.J.F.Coombs.

29. Kerguelen Petrel   p.112
Pterodroma brevirostris
13–14in/33–36cm
Slate-grey, showing a silvery underwing in
good light; large rounded head, short black
bill, long wings with narrow white leading
edge. Compare with (32) page 113.

71. Feral Domestic Goose   p.141
Anser anser
c30–32in/c74–81cm
Thick neck, heavy orange-pink bill and
paunch separate it from Coscoroba Swan (65),
[plate 8 and page 136]. When seen swimming
at a distance, the thick neck and horizontal
carriage of head are distinctive. Plumage of
MALE: varies from all white to variegated,
white with grey-brown streaking on neck,
back and flanks. FEMALE: varies more; head
and neck may be all white, white streaked
brown on neck or all dark grey-brown; breast,
belly and undertail white with a brown flank
patch; back grey-brown with narrow white
bars; wings vary from white and brown to all
brown; tail white with narrow central dark
band.

121. Pectoral Sandpiper   p.183
Calidris melanotos
7½–9in/19–23cm
ADULT NON-BREEDING: Larger than (119),
[plate 13 and page 182]; the greyish breast
heavily streaked with dark brown contrasts
sharply with the white belly; back and wing-
coverts brown with a scaly pattern of buff
edges; legs yellowish.
FLIGHT PATTERN & CALLS & IMMATURE PLUMAGE:
see page 183.

122. Wilson's Phalarope   p.183
Phalaropus tricolor
8½–9½in/22–24cm
ADULT NON-BREEDING: Resembles (113), [plate
14 and page 177] but is paler above and
below; the very long, needle-like black bill is
the best distinguishing feature; feeding
behaviour also differs from (113) and it swims
readily.

138. Arctic Tern   p.198
Sterna paradisaea
13–15in/33–38cm
FIRST WINTER IMMATURE: Smaller than (140),
[plate 15]; from below, most primaries appear
translucent, see (137), [plate 15 and page
198.] and gaps caused by moulting may show
in flight feathers; wings darker grey above
than on (137) with blackish bar along inner
leading edge; underwing white, showing clear
narrow black trailing edge; forehead white,
crown and nape black; bill blackish. Difficult
to separate from immature (137).
NON-BREEDING ADULT: see page 199.

139. Antarctic Tern   p.199
Sterna vittata
15–16in/38–41cm
ADULT BREEDING: Slightly smaller than (140),
see plate 15 and page 200; generally darker
grey above and below; underwing white with
narrow black edge only on trailing edge of
primaries. Closely resembles (138) but most
birds are in breeding plumage when (138) has
its non-breeding pattern.
ADULT NON-BREEDING & IMMATURE: see page
199.

170. Rough-winged Swallow   p.222
Stelgidopteryx ruficollis
4½–5¼in/11–13cm
Small swallow, earth-brown above with a
paler rump, darker brown wings and slightly
forked tail; underparts lighter, brownish,
without a dark breast band, yellowish on
belly. Flight erratic and fluttering. See page
222 for comparison with Bank Swallow
Riparia riparia.

29

139

138

122

71

170

121

C. f. f. Coombs.

Falkland Islands birds

Penguins *Spheniscidae*

Penguins are very specialised birds. Their wings have become modified into efficient paddles which are ideally suited to swimming under water. When at the surface their heads show all the specific identification marks. Sixteen species occur in the Southern Hemisphere, mostly between 45°S and 60°S. The New Zealand area and the Falkland Islands hold more species than are found in other parts of their range.

Nine (possibly ten) species have been seen in the Falklands and five of these breed regularly. Four of the breeding species have a circumpolar distribution on Antarctic and sub-Antarctic islands, while the Magellanic Penguin is restricted to South America. The remaining four (or five) species are infrequent vagrants from Antarctic or New Zealand waters.

Gentoo Penguin

1. King Penguin *Aptenodytes patagonicus* Plate 1

A. & C. Pingüino rey

Gigantic. 36–38in/91–96cm

IDENTIFICATION: The largest and most handsome penguin breeding in the Falklands, it can only be confused with the very rare Emperor Penguin (2). *Adults* have a long, slender black bill with a bright orange-red patch on the lower mandible. Head blackish-brown with large golden-yellow ear patches extending as a narrow band to meet a golden patch on the breast, fading into the white underparts. Back blue-grey, separated from white front by a narrow black line; feet black. *Immature* birds are smaller with pale yellow head patches and mostly dark bills. Chicks are covered in a thick, woolly brown down. Noticeably more tame than other penguins; it usually occurs in association with Gentoo penguins.

VOICE: The adults' usual call is a loud musical trumpeting uttered with the bill pointed skywards. First year birds have a soft triple whistling call.

FOOD: Small fish and squid.

HABITAT, STATUS & BREEDING: Prefers flat ground near the shore, where it breeds, usually in the company of Gentoo Penguins. Early records from the eighteenth century suggest it was never plentiful but by 1870 it was possibly nearly exterminated. Breeding was first proved again in 1933; by the 1940s small numbers were breeding in the area where they were last recorded in 1867. There are at least five colonies now, the largest holding about 100 pairs. The complete breeding cycle takes 12–13 months, which means that a pair can only rear two chicks in three years. A single large egg is laid and then incubated beneath a fold of the lower abdomen, resting on the feet. Most eggs are laid during November, though some may not lay till February. Incubation takes about eight weeks and the chick is fed for 11–12 months. King Penguins may be seen throughout the year near their colonies.

DISTRIBUTION ABROAD: Circumpolar, on sub-Antarctic and low Antarctic islands. Formerly abundant at the South Shetlands and may possibly breed on islands off Tierra del Fuego. Vagrants have occurred north to Gough Island, South Africa and southern Australia.

2. Emperor Penguin   *Aptenodytes forsteri*   Plate 1
A. & C. Pingüino emperador
Gigantic. 40–48in/101–122cm
IDENTIFICATION: Resembles King Penguin (1), but is much larger; has a larger pale yellow or whitish patch on the side of the neck, fading into the pale yellow foreneck and white underparts. Head, throat and nape black, back blue-grey with black border extending from the side of the neck to the flanks. Bill shorter than that of King, slightly downcurved, black with narrow purplish streak on lower mandible. Feet black. *Immature* has whitish throat and ear patches.

STATUS & RECORDS: Vagrant from Antarctica, recorded three times in the Falklands: an adult stayed on Pebble Island for five days in late April 1936 and 'probable immature' was seen in or near Foul Bay, East Falkland in early April 1954. Both birds were photographed (Hamilton 1954). W Curtis saw an immature bird off Lively Island on 14 January 1987 (Wolsey 1987a).

DISTRIBUTION ABROAD: Circumpolar in Antarctic waters; breeds on sea-ice close to Antarctic shores in June, laying a single egg. The chicks hatch in about eight weeks and are able to swim after about six months. Emperor Penguins usually stay in cold Antarctic waters throughout their lives though a few birds occur further north; has been recorded at the South Orkneys, South Shetlands and Tierra del Fuego.

3. Gentoo Penguin   *Pygoscelis papua*   Plate 1
A. Pingüino de pico rojo
C. Pingüino papua
Very large. 30in/76cm
IDENTIFICATION: The largest common Falkland penguin, easily recognised by a white bar over the crown and the long orange and black bill. The head is black, frequently with a scattering of white feathers behind the bar. Back and flippers blue-black, becoming brown when worn; underparts white. Legs and feet orange. *Immature* resembles adult, but has shorter, less bright bill. Very inquisitive; will approach close to an observer if one remains still, but rushes away if suddenly disturbed. Typically walks to colonies in a leisurely manner, by traditional and circuitous routes. These may be up to 5km (3 miles) inland though usually with a view of the sea.

VOICE: Has a variety of calls. The most frequent is a loud trumpeting uttered with the head thrown up. A higher pitched *wha-r-r-r* is used in courtship or when disturbed on the nest. A short *caw* is often used when coming ashore or at sea when resting at the surface.

FOOD: Takes mainly fish and some crustaceans (Croxall *et al* 1984). At South Georgia, Croxall & Prince (1980) found that adults feeding well-grown chicks took a considerable quantity of fish and large krill *Euphausia superba*.

HABITAT, STATUS & BREEDING: Resident throughout the year; widespread and very numerous, breeding in colonies up to thousands on flat ground usually near the coasts of East and West Falkland and on offshore islands. Nests may be bulky piles of diddle-dee torn from nearby plants, constructed of small stones or hard, rounded lumps of mud. Two large round white eggs are laid between late September and mid-October.

DISTRIBUTION ABROAD: Circumpolar in sub-Antarctic zones; the larger race *Pygoscelis p. papua* breeds on many sub-Antarctic island groups apart from the Falklands; the smaller race *P. p. ellsworthi* breeds on the Antarctic Peninsula south to about 65°S and adjacent islands; Gentoo Penguins have been reported in the South Atlantic to about 43°S.

4. Adelie Penguin *Pygoscelis adeliae*   Plate 1
A. & C. Pingüino de Adelia
Large to very large. 27–31in/69–79cm

IDENTIFICATION: Recognised by its blue-black head face and throat ending in a 'V' where it joins the white underparts; has white iris and eyelids, which give it a characteristic button-eyed appearance; upperparts blue-black; tail long, black; bill, feathered black at the base, mainly brick-red with black tip; feet flesh pink. *Immature* has black eyelids for at least one year, a whitish throat, black head extending well below the eye and a dark bill. At breeding colonies is inquisitive and bold.

STATUS & RECORDS: Vagrant from Antarctica to Falklands: one photographed by A Carey at the head of Berkeley Sound, East Falkland early December 1961 (Woods 1975).

DISTRIBUTION ABROAD: Circumpolar on the Antarctic continent and adjacent islands, including the Antarctic Peninsula and South Shetlands. Breeds in very large colonies on flat areas, sometimes well above beaches. Birds travel up to 300km (186 miles) over ice to reach colonies early in the breeding season. Migrates northward in winter to about 60°S and winters on free pack-ice; rarely occurs on coasts of New Zealand and at South Georgia.

5. Chinstrap Penguin *Pygoscelis antarctica*   Plate 1
A. Pingüino de barbijo
C. Pingüino antártico
Large to very large. 27–30in/68–76cm

IDENTIFICATION: Black crown, white cheeks and a narrow black line extending across the throat from ear to ear make this penguin easily recognised. Bill black, not feathered at the base; feet pale pink. *Immature* similar but has a smaller bill and some dark markings on the cheeks. Notoriously the most aggressive of the *Pygoscelis* penguins on its breeding colonies.

STATUS & RECORDS: Vagrant visitor, probably from colonies in the Scotia Arc; single birds of unknown age have been recorded seven times: in Stanley harbour, June 1915 (Bennett 1926); at Port Stephens, January 1916 (Brooks 1917); at Bleaker Island, March 1959 (Woods 1975); at Long Island, Berkeley Sound, December 1980 (Peatfield 1981); in Stanley harbour, September 1983 and at Pebble Island sand beach by S Whitley, January 1984 (Wolsey 1986c); and at Carcass Island on 14 March 1987 where one was found dead by H Muller (Wolsey 1987b).

DISTRIBUTION ABROAD: Antarctic waters, mainly in southern South Atlantic though it is apparently spreading to coasts and Antarctic islands in the southern Indian Ocean. Breeds in very large, close-packed colonies on slopes above shores. In winter may wander in ice-free waters well away from colonies, but movements scarcely known.

6. Rockhopper Penguin *Eudyptes chrysocome* Plate 1
A. & C. Pingüino de penacho amarillo
Local name: Rocky
Large. 24–25in/60–64cm

IDENTIFICATION: One of the two crested penguins breeding in the Falklands and by far the most common, the Rockhopper is separated from the Macaroni (7) by its straight bright yellow eyebrow ending in long yellowish plumes projecting sideways behind the small red eye. The forehead is black (see 7) and there is a spiky frill on the crown which is raised when excited. Head, throat and upperparts blueblack becoming brown when worn; underparts white; underside of flipper white with small black tip and the outer half of the leading edge is white; compare with Erect-crested (9). Bill stout, orange-red, without the pink fleshy margin at the gape found on the Macaroni. Legs and feet are pink. Males are generally larger than females. *Immature* birds have paler yellow eyebrows and lack the plumes. A very noisy and quarrelsome bird, aptly named 'Rockhopper' from its habit of bounding up quite steep slopes with both feet together. Traditional routes up cliffs from the sea have grooves worn in the rocks by thousands of climbing Rockhoppers.

VOICE: Adults call at any time of day or night using a harsh, grating and very loud bark, repeated rhythmically. Cobb (1933) accurately describes the sound from a large colony; '. . . as if thousands of wheelbarrows, all badly in need of greasing, are being pushed at full speed.' The chick has a plaintive *peeeep* call.

FOOD: Croxall *et al* (1985) sampled the diet at Beauchêne Island and found that it consisted of roughly equal proportions by weight of squid *Teuthowenia* sp. and crustaceans *Euphausia lucens, E. vallentini* and *Thysanoessa gregaria* and only 2% small fish.

HABITAT, STATUS & BREEDING: Very numerous around the outer coasts and offshore islands. Returns in early October from its winter pelagic wanderings to breed in close-packed colonies on cliff-tops and steep cliff-sides, often in association with Black-browed Albatrosses and Imperial Shags. One of the largest colonies is on Beauchêne Island; in 1980, about 300,000 nests were calculated by Smith & Prince (1985), using sample counts and estimates of area covered. Two pearshaped, whitish, limy eggs are laid between the last days of October and midNovember, in a shallow depression on the soil. The first egg is usually much smaller and the resulting chick is rarely reared to fledging. Immature and non-breeding birds moult from mid-January, breeding adults a little later; most have completed moult by late March and the colonies are deserted by the end of April.

DISTRIBUTION ABROAD: Circumpolar in the sub-Antarctic zone. Three races recognised; *E. c. chrysocome* breeds in the Falklands and islands off Tierra del Fuego; *E. c. moseleyi* breeds at Tristan da Cunha, Gough, St Paul and Amsterdam Islands; *E. c. filholi* breeds at other southern Indian Ocean and southern Pacific Ocean islands south of New Zealand. At least two pairs were found breeding amongst Macaroni Penguin colonies on South Georgia (Prince & Payne 1979). The extent of winter pelagic movements is unknown but it has reached 35°S off Argentina.

7. Macaroni Penguin   *Eudyptes chrysolophus*   Plate 1
A. Pingüino anaranjado
C. Pingüino macaroni
Large to very large. 27–30in/69–76cm

IDENTIFICATION: Resembles the Rockhopper (6) but is slightly larger and has golden-yellow head plumes springing from a patch of the same colour on the forehead which droop back and out over the eyes. Head and throat are blue-black; upperparts blue-black and underparts white. Has a heavier orange-red bill than a Rockhopper with a noticeable pink gape. Sexes alike, though the male is larger. *Immature* birds resemble adults but have sparse head plumes.

VOICE: Loud trumpeting, harsher and deeper than that of the Gentoo is used in displays; also has chattering and deep throbbing calls. At sea has a harsh, nasal barking call.

FOOD: At South Georgia, adults brought mostly krill *Euphausia superba* to their chicks (Croxall & Prince 1980). In Falkland waters it is probable that local species of krill are taken.

HABITAT, STATUS & BREEDING: Rare breeding bird; probably the rarest penguin, found in very small numbers (maximum 20 pairs) at several Rockhopper colonies where mixed pairs have been recorded by A Douse (Wolsey 1986c). Lays two white eggs, probably later than the Rockhopper, in mid-November. Migratory, but information on arrival and departure dates is lacking.

DISTRIBUTION ABROAD: Circumpolar at the cooler sub-Antarctic islands and on the Antarctic Peninsula; it breeds mainly at islands in the southern South Atlantic and Indian Oceans and is the most abundant penguin at South Georgia. Pelagic movements in winter are little known; it probably stays within the zone between 45°S and 65°S. A closely related race, the Royal Penguin *Eudyptes chrysolophus schlegeli* breeds only at Macquarie Island, south of New Zealand; it has a white or grey face and throat and tends to be larger than the Macaroni.

8. Fiordland Crested Penguin   *Eudyptes pachyrhynchus*   Not illustrated
A. & C. Not recorded
Large to very large. 28in/71cm

IDENTIFICATION: Similar in size to the Macaroni (7); recognised by a broad yellow line running from the base of the bill over the eye, with plumes hanging loose at the side of the nape. Bill brownish-red, lacking the pink fleshy margin shown by the Macaroni. Several small parallel white lines usually show on the cheeks.

STATUS & RECORDS: One doubtful record; an undated specimen from 'King George's Bay' presented to the British Museum by the Admiralty in the nineteenth century (W Bourne pers. comm.).

DISTRIBUTION ABROAD: Breeds in July/August in caves or hollows beneath tree roots in coastal forests on southern coasts of South Island, New Zealand. Pelagic movements unknown though it occurs at sea south of Australia.

9. Erect-crested Penguin *Eudyptes sclateri* Plate 1
A. & C. Not recorded
Large to very large. 26–28in/66–71cm
IDENTIFICATION: Intermediate in size between Rockhopper (6) and Macaroni (7), this vagrant species is recognised by its golden-yellow crest running from the base of the upper mandible, over the eye and projecting upwards like a bristle-brush above and behind the eye. The head is all blue-black apart from the crest; underparts are all white; underside of flipper has a wide, blackish leading edge and a large black tip; compare with Rockhopper (6). The heavy bill is red-brown with a pink fleshy line along the junction between bill and feathers; there is also a pink fleshy gape, as in the Macaroni. *Immature* birds have white and grey mottled throats and a sparse crest.

STATUS & RECORDS: One record in the Falklands; an adult was seen at West Point Island from 1961 to 1966, where it was paired with a Rockhopper and nested twice, both attempts apparently being unsuccessful (Napier 1968).

DISTRIBUTION ABROAD: Breeds on sub-Antarctic islands south of New Zealand. Pelagic movements in winter not well known; has occurred on eastern coasts of New Zealand and off southern Australia.

10. Magellanic Penguin *Spheniscus magellanicus* Plate 1
A. & C. Pingüino de Magallanes
Local name: Jackass Penguin
Large to very large. 28in/71cm
IDENTIFICATION: Easily recognised in the Falklands by the conspicuous black and white bands on the face and neck. Head black with a broad white band from either side of the crown, looping behind the cheeks and meeting on the throat. Upperparts dark slate-grey; underparts white with an inverted horseshoe of black from upper breast to flanks; often shows scattered black feathers on breast. Bill heavy, black with a grey band; bare, pink skin between eye and bill; eye-ring also pink. Legs and feet blackish, flecked with white. *Immature* bird has greyish throat and foreneck and lacks the striking head pattern. Much more shy than other Falkland penguins; usually retreats into the sea or down its burrow if disturbed. Nesting birds defend their burrows vigorously, turning their heads deliberately from side to side; they are respected because the stout, hooked bill can inflict a nasty wound on an unwary hand.

VOICE: The local name of Jackass is derived from its loud, mournful, braying call, frequently uttered at the entrance to the burrow. This 'song', resembling the braying of a donkey, is a repetition of short honking notes alternating with sudden intakes of breath, reaching a crescendo with a long-drawn howl that rises and then falls in pitch as it dies away. The sound of many Jackasses braying forms a common background to the dawn chorus in the Falklands. Large chicks in the burrow utter a monotonous repeated *pee-pee-pee-pee*.

FOOD: There is no quantitative information for the Falklands. Croxall *et al* (1984) noted a Chilean study which found that 90% of food by weight was fish, the remainder being crustaceans of *Munida* sp..

HABITAT, STATUS & BREEDING: Generally a summer resident returning in early September and leaving about mid-April, though a few are seen during the winter, this species is numerous around all coasts. It breeds in large and small colonies, less densely packed than those of other penguins because it burrows into soft soil or peat on slopes near the shores. Can be seen at many places around both main islands and on most offshore islands. Most, if not all colonies are on ground that formerly carried dense tussac grass. Still breeds under this vegetation in the very soft waterlogged peat formed where mature tussac survives. The burrows slope down, are up to 2m (6 feet) deep and have a nest-chamber slightly higher than the adjacent tunnel floor; rain water therefore tends to collect away from the eggs. The two white eggs, which rapidly become stained by the damp soil or peat, are laid between mid-October and mid-November on a nest of diddle-dee or tussac grass.

DISTRIBUTION ABROAD: Breeds on the Pacific coast of South America from 37°S in Chile to the Magellanic islands and on the Atlantic coast to about 41°S in Argentina; also at Juan Fernandez (34°S) off the coast of Chile. Ranges north in winter to about 30°S off Chile and to southern Brazil, occasionally reaching Rio de Janeiro (23°S). Vagrants have occurred at South Georgia and reached New Zealand.

Grebes *Podicipedidae*

Grebes are small to large diving birds that rarely fly. Under water they are propelled by their feet which are set far back on the body, and have separate lobes on each toe. On the surface they appear tail-less and round-bodied with a long, thin neck and dagger-shaped bill. Podicipedidae is the only family in the order Podicipediformes. Twenty-two species in eight genera occur almost throughout the world, though most are found in temperate regions. Fifteen species are known from the Americas, six of which occur in Argentina. Three species with a wide distribution in southern South America have been recorded in the Falkland Islands. Two are resident and the third is a much larger vagrant.

White-tufted Grebe

11. White-tufted Grebe *Rollandia rolland*   Plate 2
A. Macá común
C. Zambullidor pimpollo
Local names: Brown, Black, Golden Grebe
Small–medium. 13–14in/33–36cm

IDENTIFICATION: *Adult breeding*: recognised by a prominent triangular white patch streaked with black on each side of the peaked and crested black head and shiny black upperparts. Upper neck black; chestnut underparts with black streaked flanks are rarely seen in the field. Bill pointed, black; iris glowing crimson. In flight shows a broad white bar along trailing edge of the secondaries, white under wing-coverts, extended neck and hump-backed shape. *Adult non-breeding*: upperparts dull brown except for white chin, throat and lower ear-coverts; neck red-brown; rest of underparts white. *Immature* resembles non-breeding adult but has two irregular black lines across cheeks. Can be confused with Rock Shag (52) at a distance; separated by horizontal carriage of its shorter head and bill. Rarely flies but dives when alarmed; is tame and inquisitive of a stationary observer.

VOICE: Both sexes use jarring or creaking notes during the breeding season. Young birds have similar but higher-pitched calls. Usually silent in winter.

FOOD: Fish up to 15cm (6 in), crustaceans and aquatic plants. All food obtained by diving, using only the lobed feet for propulsion; average dive lasts about 15 seconds, maximum about 20 seconds.

HABITAT, STATUS & BREEDING: Breeding resident race *R. r. rolland* is confined to the Falklands and is larger than mainland South American races. It is found on freshwater ponds with emergent vegetation, streams and rivers when breeding. Occurs in creeks and close inshore on coastal waters in winter. Widespread throughout the Falklands and fairly common, it breeds between mid-October and January, laying one to three white eggs, that rapidly become stained, in a floating nest of waterweeds and grass placed under the overhang of a stream bank or in rushes.

DISTRIBUTION ABROAD: The smallest race *R. r. chilensis* occurs in South American lowlands from 10°S in Peru through Argentina to Tierra del Fuego. An intermediate-sized race *R. r. morresoni* breeds in the Andes of central Peru at Lake Junín.

12. Great Grebe   *Podiceps major*   Plate 2
A. Macá grande
c. Zambullidor huala
Large to very large. 26–30in/67–77cm
IDENTIFICATION: Similar in size to the Imperial Shag (53), this species has a very long thin neck and a massive dagger-shaped black bill. *Adult breeding*: head black with short tufted crest on the nape, grey cheeks, black throat and hindneck with green gloss; foreneck chestnut; underparts white shaded with chestnut on flanks; back brownish-black. *Adult non-breeding*: cheeks and sides of the head whitish, foreneck reddish-grey, hindneck dull grey, back grey-brown with light grey freckling. In flight shows dark wings above with broad white bar across trailing edge of secondaries; under wing-coverts white.

STATUS & RECORDS: Vagrant from South America, recorded at least six times: one dead at San Carlos, spring 1941 (Cawkell & Hamilton 1961); one in Carcass Island harbour for several days in February 1966 (C & K Bertrand in Woods 1975);

one spent nearly two months in West Point Island harbour from 16 January 1967 (R Napier in Woods 1975); one near Horse Point, Stanley Common 24–27 October 1981 (J & A Peatfield); two close to shore at Goose Green on 11 February 1983 after a period of strong winds (P Lackey pers. comm.); a pair seen at Mare Harbour by K Layman in late January 1987 (Wolsey 1987a).

DISTRIBUTION ABROAD: Found on freshwater lakes in South America, though not in the andean region, from about 30°S in Chile and 25°S in southeastern Brazil, through Paraguay, Uruguay and Argentina to Tierra del Fuego. Also occurs in coastal Peru between 5°S and 10°S. Possibly the commonest grebe in the Magellanic region. Though reluctant to fly when disturbed, it migrates into coastal waters in winter and has been recorded far offshore. One seen (R Woods) on the sea, 19 April 1963, about 40km (25 miles) off Cape San Antonio, Argentina (37°S 56°15′W).

13. Silvery Grebe   *Podiceps occipitalis*   Plate 2
A. Macá plateado
c. Zambullidor blanquillo
Local name: White Grebe
Small. 10–11in/25–28cm

IDENTIFICATION: Separated from the White-tufted Grebe (11) by its generally grey plumage and shining white foreneck. Nape jet-black extending halfway down hindneck as a narrow line. Back and wings dark grey; underparts mainly white streaked black on flanks. Bill black, iris crimson. *Adult breeding* has large frill of dull gold plumes from eyebrow to ear-coverts. *Adult non-breeding* has no plumes. *Immature* similar to winter adult but has white hindneck tinged brown. Dives frequently, averaging about 20 seconds below water. Rarely seen flying; white neck and white wingbar are prominent.

VOICE: Has short clucking, twittering and squeaky notes.

FOOD: Obtains insects and their larvae, fish and their eggs, small crustaceans and plant food by diving.

HABITAT, STATUS & BREEDING: Locally common resident, breeding on freshwater ponds, often with White-tufted Grebe but not as numerous. Occurs in coastal kelp patches in autumn and winter. Little information on breeding in Falklands; probably lays two blue-white eggs in a floating weed nest in December, possibly earlier. A pair with a small downy chick were seen at Bertha's Beach pond on 20 January 1963 (R Woods) and six pairs with young seen by A Douse (pers. comm.) on Green Pond (1.25km/¾ mile long), Pebble Island in January 1982.

DISTRIBUTION ABROAD: Two races: *P. o. occipitalis* occurs in the Falklands and in South America from Tierra del Fuego to about 25°S in Chile and Argentina. It is migratory in the south, arriving in Tierra del Fuego late September and leaving by May. *P. o. juninensis* has white plumes and white hindneck; it occurs in andean regions of northern Chile, northwestern Argentina, Bolivia, Ecuador and Peru.

Albatrosses *Diomedeidae*

Albatrosses are very large to gigantic seabirds with exceptionally long, narrow wings on which they glide superbly, using air currents over the sea or land for lift. In calm weather they tend to settle on the sea. All have heavy, hooked bills for catching squid and fish; some species also take refuse from ships. Their heads are large and rounded and their tails are either short, broad and square as in the three species of Great Albatrosses and nine species of Mollymawks or long and wedge-shaped as in the two species of Sooty Albatrosses. Ten of the 14 known species breed on islands in the Southern Hemisphere, three in the North Pacific and one on the Galapagos Islands.

Nine species have been recorded in Falkland waters; one breeds in the Falklands and eight at other sub-Antarctic and Antarctic islands. Some species occur regularly on migration while others have been seen occasionally.

14. Wandering Albatross *Diomedea exulans*   Plate 3
A. & C. Albatros errante
Local name: Albatross
Gigantic. 42–53in/107–135cm

IDENTIFICATION: This species and the Royal Albatross (15) are easily separated from the common Black-browed (16) by size alone. Specific identification is more difficult, particularly in some plumage stages. The Wandering Albatross matures slowly, not breeding until nine to ten years old. *Juvenile*: all brown body above and below, including crown and nape which form a dark mask around its white face; underwing white with black wingtips at all ages (see Royal Albatross). This is probably the commonest stage seen at sea. *Immature (2nd stage)*: white beneath with a brown breast band. As birds mature, the back gradually becomes more white, starting in the centre of the inner wing. Over several years white extends forward and backward until upperwings are largely white with black wingtips and black trailing edge. *Males* and *females* are similar, but the female retains more dark colouring on head and body and is generally smaller. *Old males* are white above with black wingtips and trailing edge and even these mature birds usually show some black on the outer edges of the tail (see Royal Albatross). Separation of fully adult males of *chionoptera* race from some Royal Albatrosses is difficult. At close range, the pale bill without any black is a useful feature. Regularly follows ships and takes refuse thrown overboard.

STATUS & RECORDS: Non-breeding visitor to Falkland waters. Occurs throughout the year in small numbers offshore; comes closer to the Falklands in strong easterly winds (Bourne & Curtis 1985).

DISTRIBUTION ABROAD: Two races; *D. e. exulans* breeds at Inaccessible and Gough Islands and *D. e. chionoptera* breeds at South Georgia in the South Atlantic. Both races breed at other islands in the southern Pacific and Indian Oceans, *exulans* at more temperate locations and *chionoptera* at colder islands. Ranges widely through the southern oceans from about 60°S to 22°S, and reaches 10°–15°S in the Humboldt Current off western South America. Pairs usually breed successfully in alternate years because incubation and fledging take about 11 months. The nestling remains on the nest and is fed by the adults throughout the winter.

15. Royal Albatross   *Diomedea epomophora*   Plate 3
A. & C. Albatross real
Local name: Albatross
Gigantic. 42–50in/107–127cm
IDENTIFICATION: The Royal Albatross is similar in size to the Wandering Albatross (14). Two races of the Royal may be seen in Falkland waters; these are separable at sea. *Juvenile* of *D. e. epomophora* has mainly white head and body apart from dark markings on lower back; upperwings mostly black with white at base of leading edge; tail white with narrow black tip, not outer edges. In later *immature* stages, upperwing whitens from leading edge backwards (see Wandering Albatross) and tail all white. *Adult*: head, body and tail all white; wings mostly white with black tips; difficult to separate from adult male Wandering, though at close range black cutting edge visible on pink bill. *Juvenile* of *D. e. sanfordi* shows some brown mottling on crown, dark streaks on lower back and narrow black tail tip. *Adult*: all white head, body and tail; wings above all dark, sharply separated from white back; underwing white with black wingtips and trailing edge; underside of forewing has thickened black leading edge by outer (carpal) joint.

STATUS & RECORDS: Non-breeding visitor to Falkland waters. More frequently seen than Wandering Albatross over the continental shelf, near fishing fleets and off headlands around the Falklands, particularly with westerly winds (Bourne & Curtis 1987). Until 1987, few documented records distinguished the two races, but W Curtis (in Wolsey 1987b) found a high proportion of the southern race *epomophora* in autumn and winter. Of the hundreds reported in February and March 1987 by Curtis, most of the 87 seen off Cape Pembroke in late February were of the northern race *sanfordi*, while about half of 81 seen off Fox Bay on 28–29 March were of each race. A juvenile of the race *epomophora* banded at Campbell Island in September 1980 was found dead near Volunteer Point, East Falkland on 11 March 1981 (Peatfield 1981). Another Campbell Island banded bird was found on Great Island, Falkland Sound in April 1985 (A Douse pers. comm.). W Curtis saw two *sanfordi* 21km (13 miles) east of Mengeary Point on 29 November 1982.

DISTRIBUTION ABROAD: Two races: *D. e. sanfordi* breeds at Chatham Islands and on Taiaroa Head near Dunedin, New Zealand. *D. e. epomophora* breeds on Auckland and Campbell Islands, south of New Zealand. Earlier suspicion of breeding in Tierra del Fuego (Murphy 1936) has not been substantiated. Range not fully known; occurs off both coasts of South America, to about 10°S off Peru and to about 23°S off Brazil, after dispersal from breeding grounds.

16. Black-browed Albatross   *Diomedea melanophris*   Plate 3
A. Albatros chico
C. Albatros de ceja negra
Local name: Mollymawk
Immense to gigantic. 32–37in/81–94cm
IDENTIFICATION: The commonest albatross in Falkland waters, this species resembles the Kelp Gull (134) in colour but has far longer wings, a thick-necked appearance and a 'scowling expression' due to the black streak over and through the eye. *Adult*: pure white head, underparts and rump; upperwing and back black-

ish; tail grey; bill heavy, hooked, orange or pink-yellow, sometimes with a reddish tip; iris brown; underwing has a broad black leading edge, widest on inner half of wing, white centre and narrow black trailing edge. *Juvenile*: has dark bill, often showing a black tip; head mainly white with a dark eyebrow; nape grey extending sometimes to join a variable grey breast band; wings above similar to adults, below mainly dark with variable, usually much reduced central white streak. Older *immatures* have paler nape and dull yellow bill with black tip; underwing pattern similar to adult. Juveniles are difficult to separate from juvenile Grey-headed (20); bill colour is probably the best feature to differentiate the species.

Black-browed Albatrosses often follow ships and will settle to take offal or refuse.

VOICE: Usually silent at sea; breeding adults use loud braying notes during courtship and when meeting at the nest. Nestlings produce hollow clopping noises with their bills when humans approach.

FOOD: Prince (1982) estimated from a few samples obtained at Beauchêne Island in December 1980 that the diet consisted almost equally of fish, lobster-krill *Munida* sp. and squid *Loligo* sp.

HABITAT, STATUS & BREEDING: Falkland breeding birds are present between September and April. They nest in large colonies on steep slopes or open rocky plateaux of several islands off West Falkland, particularly Grand Jason Island, Steeple Jason Island and West Point Island. At Beauchêne Island, south of East Falkland, there is a huge colony which held 140,000 to 170,000 pairs in 1980 (Prince 1982).

The nest, a solid pillar up to 50cm (20in) high of mud and guano with some tussac grass and seaweed incorporated, is re-used annually. A single whitish egg variably marked with red-brown is laid in early October; fledged young birds leave the nest between mid-March and early April. This species may be seen throughout the year in Falkland waters though it is more numerous during the breeding season.

DISTRIBUTION ABROAD: Circumpolar in sub-Antarctic waters; the race *D. m. melanophris* also breeds at 51°S off the coast of Chile (Clark 1985), at Diego Ramirez (56° 32′S), Ildefonso to the west of Cape Horn, Staten Island off Tierra del Fuego and several other sub-Antarctic islands including South Georgia, Heard, Kerguelen and Antipodes Islands. The race *D. m. impavida* can be distinguished at sea by its pale yellow iris and darker underwing. It has not been identified in Falkland waters and breeds only at Campbell Island, south of New Zealand. The species generally ranges between 65°S and 20°S in the southern oceans, but reaches 10°S off Peru in the Humboldt Current and at least 16°S off the coast of Angola. Results from the banding of several thousand fledglings at West Point Island indicate that dispersal occurs northwards and that Falkland-bred mollymawks tend to stay in the South Atlantic (Tickell 1967).

17. Buller's Albatross *Diomedea bulleri* Not illustrated
A. Not recorded
c. Albatros de Buller
Very large. 30–32in/76–81cm
IDENTIFICATION: Slightly smaller than Black-browed (16) and Grey-headed (20),

this species is recognised at all ages by the underwing pattern. Black leading edge is moderately wide (narrower than on Black-browed) and black trailing edge is very narrow, the whole underwing pattern similar to that of Yellow-nosed (19). *Adult* has mainly grey head, darker in front of the eye, with clear white forehead; bill black with broad yellow top ridge and narrow yellow lower edge, though it appears all black at long distances; underparts all white; back and wings above dark brown with white rump and blackish tail. *Juvenile* has similar head pattern but bill brownish with a darker tip. *Immature* has dull horn coloured ridge to bill, a greyer head and patchy dark markings on neck. Can be confused with Shy Albatross (18), but that species is larger, the bill appears pale at a distance and the underwing pattern is different.

STATUS & RECORDS: Vagrant, recorded once; three birds, an adult and two immatures seen off the southern end of Falkland Sound on 28 March 1987 by W Curtis.

DISTRIBUTION ABROAD: Two races are described of this uncommon albatross, both breeding on islands off New Zealand. *D. b bulleri* apparently disperses only to Australasian waters. *D. b. platei* breeds earlier at Chatham Islands and apparently migrates across the Pacific to the western coast of South America, where it has been recorded between about 55°S and 10°S.

18. Shy Albatross *Diomedea cauta*   Not illustrated
A. Albatros piliblanco
c. Albatros de frente blanca
Gigantic. 36–39in/91–99cm
IDENTIFICATION: Larger than the Black-browed Albatross (16), this species can be recognised in all plumage stages by its largely white underwing with a narrow black border and a characteristic black mark where the wings join the body. Back grey-brown and wings above darker brown at all ages. *Adult*: mainly white head with grey cheeks and a dark eyebrow; bill pale, greenish-grey with a yellow tip. *Juvenile*: grey head, neck and mantle; bill dark blue-grey with black tip. *Older immature*: variable head and neck colour as the grey crown and hindneck gradually become white.

STATUS & RECORDS: First recorded in Falkland waters in 1984, with four sightings between June and August (Bourne & Curtis 1985). W Curtis saw one at 51°55′S 56°54′W on 10 April 1986 and three in the southern end of Falkland Sound, 28–29 March 1987. This species is known to follow fishing boats for offal.

DISTRIBUTION ABROAD: Three races, separable at sea, are recognised. This race, the Shy Albatross *D. c. cauta*, breeds at islands near Tasmania and at Auckland Islands south of New Zealand. It is common off South Africa in winter; until 1984 it had not been recorded in the western South Atlantic. The race *D. c. salvini* (Salvin's Albatross) breeds at the Snares and Bounty Islands. It has a paler yellowish bill with a dark tip on the lower mandible; the forehead is white and the rest of the head is brown-grey blending into the grey mantle. Salvin's Albatross is frequent off the western coast of South America to about 5°S and has been recorded off Buenos Aires Province, Argentina; it could occur off the Falklands. The Chatham

Island Albatross *D. c. eremita* resembles *salvini* but lacks the white cap and has a yellow bill with a dark tip to the lower mandible. It remains in waters near its breeding grounds at the Chatham Islands east of New Zealand throughout the year; see Harrison (1983) for further details.

19. Yellow-nosed Albatross   *Diomedea chlororhynchos*   Plate 3
A. Albatros clororrinco
c. Not recorded
Very large. 28–32in/71–81cm
IDENTIFICATION: Smaller, with a more slender neck, longer tail and thinner, longer bill than the Black-browed (16). *Adult* of the South Atlantic race *D. c. chlororhynchos* has a mainly grey head, a black bill with yellow ridge (not easily seen) and white underwings with narrow black margins; upperwings and mantle appear black. Easily confused with adult Grey-headed (20); underwing pattern and general build different. *Adult* of the southern Indian Ocean race *D. c. bassi* has pale grey cheeks and nape but appears white-headed from a distance. *Juvenile* has completely white head and a black bill; underwing pattern similar to adult but may have wider black leading edge. Apparently more shy than Black-browed and rarely follows ships.

STATUS & RECORDS: R H Beck reported this species near the Falklands in September 1915 (Murphy 1936), though he may have confused it with the Grey-headed. The first substantiated record was of one seen 24km (15 miles) east of the Falklands on 30 September 1983 (Bourne & Curtis 1985).

DISTRIBUTION ABROAD: The race *D. c. chlororhynchos* breeds at Tristan da Cunha and Gough islands; *D. c. bassi* breeds at St Paul, Prince Edward and the Crozet Islands. Ranges between about 20°S and 50°S in the South Atlantic and southern Indian Oceans and occurs off New Zealand but has not been recorded in the southern Pacific.

20. Grey-headed Albatross   *Diomedea chrysostoma*   Plate 3
A. & C. Albatros cabeza gris
Very large to immense. 28–33in/71–84cm
IDENTIFICATION: Resembles the Black-browed (16) in shape and flight, though slightly smaller. *Adult*: blue-grey head with a dark 'eyebrow'; bill black with bright yellow ridge and lower edge, though this yellow is only visible at close range; underwing pattern similar to Black-browed but black leading edge narrower and white area more prominent. Can be confused with South Atlantic race of Yellow-nosed (19); differences in body proportions are best distinguishing features. *Juvenile*: difficult to separate from juvenile Black-browed; bill black rather than dark grey. *Older immatures*: gradually gain more yellow on ridge of bill, whereas bill of immature Black-browed lightens along the sides first and retains a dark tip on its pale bill to near-adult stage. Grey-headed occasionally follows ships but less often than Black-browed.

STATUS & RECORDS: Non-breeding visitor to Falkland waters. Earlier reports that it bred are unsubstantiated, though one adult occupied a nest-site alone on West

Point Island between 1952 and 1956, amongst Black-browed Albatrosses and another was present in 1969 (C Gallimore pers. comm.). Large numbers reported following fishing boats south and east of the Falklands in winter but scarce inshore (Bourne & Curtis 1985). In February and March 1987, W Curtis reported a total of 46 birds (Wolsey 1987b).

DISTRIBUTION ABROAD: Circumpolar in Antarctic and sub-Antarctic waters between about 65°S and 35°S and occurs to about 15°S in the Humboldt Current off western South America. Breeds at Diego Ramirez and Ildefonso Islands west of Cape Horn, South Georgia, Prince Edward, Kerguelen and Campbell Islands, often in association with Black-browed but not at the more temperate islands occupied by that species. Unlike the Black-browed, pairs that breed successfully in one year, may not breed in the following year because the fledging period is longer.

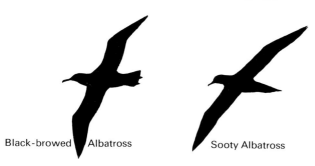

Black-browed Albatross   Sooty Albatross

21. Sooty Albatross   *Phoebetria fusca*   Plate 3
A. & C. Albatros oscuro
Immense. 32–35in/81–89cm

IDENTIFICATION: Easily separated from the 'Mollymawks' and 'Great Albatrosses' by its smaller size, generally dark brown colour and long, pointed, wedge-shaped tail. Can be confused with Giant Petrels (23 & 24) at a distance but the slender build, narrow wings and long tail give it a quite different appearance. *Adult*: sooty-brown, darker on head and wings, slightly lighter on body; has a white half-circle round the rear of the eye; light streaks visible on wingtips; bill black with yellow or orange central stripe, visible at close range. *Immature*: dark brown with variable whitish nape and light edges to back feathers but lower back and rump dark brown. *Juvenile*: head paler than adult; some pale streaks on upper back but has dark brown lower back; no light marks on wingtips; bill blackish with light stripe on side. Adults with worn plumage in autumn and immatures cannot always be distinguished from Light-mantled Sooty Albatross (22). Often follows ships; flight appears very graceful.

STATUS & RECORDS: Non-breeding visitor to Falkland waters; no certain early records. One adult spent three days in December 1953 at an old Imperial Shag nest on Kidney Island, East Falkland (Pettingill 1962). One 'Sooty Albatross' seen close to Kidney Island on 1 November 1962 (Woods 1975). A single bird seen southwest of the Falklands on 11 March 1985 (Bourne & Curtis 1985).

DISTRIBUTION ABROAD: Breeds at the more temperate islands in the South Atlantic and southern Indian Ocean, including Gough, Tristan da Cunha, St Paul, Prince Edward and Amsterdam. Also occurs with the Light-mantled at Kerguelen, Prince Edward and Crozet Islands. Pelagic range between about 60°S and 30°S from the South Atlantic east to Australasian waters, rarely into the eastern Pacific.

22. Light-mantled Sooty Albatross *Phoebetria palpebrata*   Plate 3
A. Albatros oscuro
c. Albatros oscuro de manto claro
Very large to immense. 28–35in/71–89cm
IDENTIFICATION: *Adult*: head dark grey-brown; underparts pale grey-brown; upperparts including rump pale ash-grey; wingtips and tail dark brown with whitish shaft streaks; bill black with indistinct pale blue or lilac central stripe; iris dark with incomplete white half-circle behind eye. *Immature*: shows pale tips on mantle and breast; black bill has pale grey or yellowish stripe. *Juvenile*: similar to adult but without light marks on wingtips; bill black with yellowish stripe. Flight and behaviour at sea as Sooty Albatross (21); immature birds may not be separable from that species.

STATUS & RECORDS: Non-breeding visitor to Falkland waters but few documented records. Murphy (1936) notes that Beck saw it near the Falklands in 1915–16. One seen with two Wandering Albatrosses in Port William near Stanley during an easterly gale on 18 December 1980 (Peatfield 1981). Several seen close inshore during spring 1982 (A Douse pers. comm.).

DISTRIBUTION ABROAD: Circumpolar, breeding at most colder sub-Antarctic islands and some more temperate ones where Sooty Albatross also breeds. The nearest breeding station to the Falklands is at South Georgia. Ranges on migration between northern limit of pack-ice and about 30°S; off the west coast of South America reaches about 20°S in the Humboldt Current zone.

Petrels & Shearwaters *Procellariidae*
Petrels and Shearwaters form the largest group of oceanic birds, most of which only return to land for a few months to breed. Their wings are long and narrow and they typically alternate between flapping and gliding with the wings held stiffly. About 55 species in 12 genera have been described from all oceans of the world. Twenty-three species have been recorded in Falkland waters. Six or seven species breed, most of them nesting in burrows. Six species occur as regular visitors and ten species are apparently vagrants rarely occurring in Falkland waters. Two of this latter group breed in the Northern Hemisphere and winter in southern oceans. Large flocks of one or more breeding species can be seen offshore in the evenings when adults gather on the water before returning to their nests.

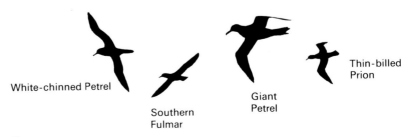

White-chinned Petrel

Southern Fulmar

Giant Petrel

Thin-billed Prion

23. Northern Giant Petrel   *Macronectes halli*   Plate 3
A. Petrel gigante picocorto
C. Petrel gigante subantártico
Local name: Stinker
Very large to gigantic. 30–37in/76–94cm
IDENTIFICATION: The two closely related species of Giant Petrel are similar in size to the Black-browed Albatross (16) but are less graceful in flight; they appear stiff-winged and clumsy, partly because they have long necks and very heavy bills with prominent external nostril tubes reaching halfway to the tip. *Juvenile* Northern Giant Petrels are completely black when first fledged but soon fade to brownish-black. *Older immatures* become whitish on the face and, with increasing age, the plumage lightens generally until the *adult* stage is reached; upperparts dark grey-brown, darkest on wings and tail; crown grey-brown giving a capped effect above the whitish face (see 24); underparts lighter grey-brown; leading edge of the inner wing, seen from below, is very dark; bill pinkish-yellow with a darker reddish tip. Immature birds are difficult to separate from the Southern species; bill colour may be sufficiently different but has not been closely studied. Flies usually with several short flaps between glides; regularly follows ships and squabbles for refuse thrown overboard.

STATUS & RECORDS: Giant Petrels are seen regularly throughout the year in Falkland waters. It was not recognised that there were two species until 1966 (Bourne & Warham) and since then, few observers have examined Falkland birds closely. The first documented record was of one off Mengeary Point, Port William on 14 November 1980 (Peatfield 1981) and others have been seen offshore (Bourne & Curtis 1985). Breeding (unconfirmed) has been reported at Beauchêne Island where several were seen close inshore in February 1987 (A Douse pers. comm.). Research is needed in the Falklands as both species could be breeding (Devillers & Terschuren 1980). At sub-Antarctic islands where both breed, *M. halli* lays about six weeks earlier and tends to nest in loose colonies or alone.

DISTRIBUTION ABROAD: Circumpolar in southern oceans, ranging far from colonies and reaching coasts of Australia and South Africa. Breeds at the more northerly sub-Antarctic islands of Gough, Marion, Crozet, Kerguelen, Campbell, Chatham, Stewart, Antipodes and Auckland. It also breeds at South Georgia in substantial numbers.

24. Southern Giant Petrel   *Macronectes giganteus*   Plate 3
A. Petrel gigante
C. Petrel gigante antártico
Local name: Stinker
Immense to gigantic. 34–39in/86–99cm
IDENTIFICATION: Size, shape and behaviour are similar to Northern Giant Petrel (23) but the bill colour, pale yellowish with a greenish tip is distinctive at all ages. The Southern species has two distinct colour phases; the *pale phase* is almost completely white with a few dark spots on the plumage from the juvenile stage while birds of the more common *dark phase* are similar to the Northern species. *Juveniles* are black when first fledged and soon become brownish-black. *Immatures* resemble

adult Northern species but are as dark below as above, with pale faces and lack the obvious capped appearance of the Northern. *Adults* have mainly white heads and whitish necks which contrast with the grey-brown body and wings. In flight shows a pale leading edge to the underwing.

VOICE: Usually silent at sea though birds competing for offal use a low guttural rattling call.

FOOD: Both species act as scavengers of carrion such as penguin, seal or whale carcasses and will follow ships for refuse. They also kill disabled seabirds and take young penguins and eggs.

HABITAT, STATUS & BREEDING: Birds of the dark phase breed in colonies of up to a few hundred pairs on several offshore islands and are common in Falkland waters throughout the year, habitually entering harbours during daylight. Nests socially on low flat ground near shores and lays a single large white egg in late October. Pale phase birds are occasionally seen offshore.

DISTRIBUTION ABROAD: Nests at colder sub-Antarctic islands than (23) and on the Antarctic Peninsula, though it also breeds at Isla Noir 54°26′S and Diego Ramirez 57°S (Clark 1985) and in Chubut, Argentina (Humphrey & Livezey 1983). Both occur at South Georgia, Kerguelen, Crozet, Marion and Macquarie Islands. Juvenile birds disperse rapidly and widely, many reaching coasts of Australia in about five weeks. Occurs between about 78°S in the Ross Sea and 30°S in southern oceans; some occur further north in cold-current zones and stragglers occasionally reach the Northern Hemisphere.

25. Southern/Silver-grey Fulmar   *Fulmarus glacialoides*   Plate 4
A. & C. Petrel plateado
Medium. 18–20in/46–51cm
IDENTIFICATION: A fairly large, light-coloured petrel resembling a gull with pale grey upperparts and white underparts but flying quite differently with stiff, bowed wings and long glides. *Adults* and *immatures* are similar; head white with pale grey crown; underparts mainly white; back and inner wing blue-grey, outer wing black with a very variable whitish patch near the tips and narrow black trailing edge to the secondaries; tail pale grey, appearing white from a distance; bill pink and pale blue with black tip; legs and feet light blue.

STATUS & RECORDS: Regular non-breeding visitor from Antarctic breeding grounds to Falkland waters throughout the year, more numerous in winter; in early summer, parties on migration southward occur close inshore.

DISTRIBUTION ABROAD: Breeds at South Sandwich, South Orkney and South Shetland Islands and on the coasts of the Antarctic continent and Antarctic Peninsula. Pelagic distribution is circumpolar between the continent and about 43°S, though reaches about 10°S in the Humboldt Current west of South America.

26. Antarctic Petrel   *Thalassoica antarctica*   Plate 5
A. & C. Petrel antártico
Medium. 16–18in/40–46cm

IDENTIFICATION: An easily recognised, fairly large petrel with typical stiff-winged gliding flight, the Antarctic Petrel has a chocolate-brown head, back and forewings with a broad white trailing edge, white lower rump and tail with a broad black tip and white underparts, including underwing. Bill brown in *adults*, black in *juveniles*. Often flies high above the sea.

STATUS & RECORDS: Vagrant from Antarctica: first probable record, a single bird flushed near the shore of Port Harriet, south of Stanley, 28 February 1957. An immature bird in fresh plumage was found dead near Eliza Cove, south of Stanley on 23 September 1959 (Woods 1975). W Curtis saw one 29km (18 miles) east of Cape Pembroke on 12 June 1984 and five near fishing vessels between Sea Lion Island and Beauchêne Island on 8 July 1984 (Wolsey 1986c).

DISTRIBUTION ABROAD: Breeds on the coast of the Antarctic continent and adjacent islands, in very large colonies. Pelagic distribution in winter usually in Antarctic waters with pack-ice but occasionally occurs further north to about 33°S. Has also occurred in waters around Cape Horn and the channels of Tierra del Fuego.

27. Cape Petrel   *Daption capense*   Plate 4
A. Petrel común or Damero del cabo
c. Petrel moteado
Small-medium. 15–16in/38–41cm

IDENTIFICATION: An unmistakable medium-sized petrel, conspicuously chequered black and white above. *Adults* and *immatures* alike: head black; throat, neck and back dark brown; upperwings black with two large white patches on inner primaries and on secondary coverts; tail black with white base and speckled brown and white rump; underparts white; bill and legs black. Follows ships and often occurs in flocks. Flight is like that of Southern Fulmar (25), though it also towers high in the air in strong winds.

STATUS & RECORDS: Regular non-breeding visitor to Falkland waters. Common offshore and inshore from early April to November, and occasionally to January.

DISTRIBUTION ABROAD: Circumpolar in Antarctic and cold sub-Antarctic regions; the race *D. c. capense* breeds on the Antarctic continent and at many islands including South Georgia, South Orkneys and South Shetlands. A slightly smaller race *D. c. australe*, not easily separated, breeds at islands south of New Zealand. Ranges north to about 25°S in winter, reaching the Equator in cold-current regions.

28. Snow Petrel   *Pagodroma nivea*   Plate 5
A. Petrel blanco
c. Petrel de las nieves
Small-medium. 12–15in/30–38cm

IDENTIFICATION: The only small white petrel, it has a short black bill and a conspicuous black eye. The wings are long and the tail appears square. Flies with characteristic shallow, bat-like wingbeats, frequently changing direction. Rarely follows ships. Groups rest on icebergs.

STATUS & RECORDS: Vagrant from Antarctic waters, said to be an occasional winter visitor by Wace (1921) and Bennett (1926). There have been only two recent records inshore: one seen in a storm off Eliza Cove, south of Stanley, 24 July 1979 and two long dead specimens found on Cape Pembroke in about September 1979 (Peatfield 1981). Offshore, W Curtis saw one 19km (12 miles) east of Cape Pembroke on 12 June 1984 and five about 40km (25 miles) southeast of Lively Island, after prolonged southeasterly gales, on 8 July 1984 (Wolsey 1986c). B Bewsher saw one 16km (10 miles) north of Falkland Sound on 13 October 1985 (Bourne & Curtis 1987).

DISTRIBUTION ABROAD: Circumpolar; *P. n. nivea* breeds on the Antarctic continent and at South Georgia, South Shetlands and South Orkneys in the Atlantic sector. Disperses from breeding grounds to adjacent seas with pack-ice and rarely occurs north of 55°S. *P. n. confusa*, a slightly smaller race which may be a separate species, occurs on the Adélie coast of Antarctica.

29. Kerguelen Petrel   *Pterodroma brevirostris*   Plate 21
A. Fardela apizarrada
C. Fardela de Kerguelen
Small-medium. 13–14in/33–36cm
IDENTIFICATION: Plumage is all slate-grey, apart from a narrow white leading edge to the wing and white edges to the under wing-coverts. Shows silvery reflections from the underwing in strong light. The short black bill, large rounded head and long wings are distinctive in flight, which is typically very fast and erratic; it also glides in strong winds, high above the sea. It is solitary at sea and rarely follows ships.

STATUS & RECORDS: Non-breeding visitor to Falkland waters; first recorded on 2 October 1980 when a single bird was seen flying parallel and close to the shore of Stanley harbour (Peatfield 1981). There have been many subsequent records at sea, particularly in the winter of 1984. Seen off Cape Pembroke, 10km (6 miles) northeast of Pebble Island and 29 were counted in half an hour when approaching Port William in September 1983. One seen in Smiley Channel and one 13km (8 miles) west of Eddystone Rock on 8 August 1984 (Bourne & Curtis 1987). Two seen east of Cape Pembroke on 23 March 1987 (Wolsey 1987b).

DISTRIBUTION ABROAD: Breeds at Tristan da Cunha, Gough, Kerguelen and the Crozet Islands. Pelagic distribution in southern oceans is little known but it appears to range between the northern edge of pack ice and about 30°S.

30. Atlantic Petrel   *Pterodroma incerta*   Not illustrated
A. Petrel pardo y blanco
C. Not recorded
Medium. 17–18in/43–46cm
IDENTIFICATION: Larger than the Kerguelen Petrel (29), the Atlantic Petrel is dark brown above with a brown head and upper breast and all brown underwing and tail; the white breast and belly contrast sharply with the otherwise dark plumage. When the plumage becomes worn, the brown feathers lighten and the hindneck may appear white. The long wings are curved and the tail is long and wedge-shaped; flight is fast and swooping. It often follows ships.

STATUS & RECORDS: Vagrant recorded several times since 1982; first recorded on 3 June 1982 when 20 seen 65km (40 miles) east of Cape Pembroke. Since then, larger numbers have been reported further out to sea throughout the year (Bourne & Curtis 1987). One was seen flying north past Cape Pembroke on 6 December 1986 (Wolsey 1987a).

DISTRIBUTION ABROAD: Breeds at Tristan da Cunha group and Gough Island in the South Atlantic. Occurs commonly between about 23°S and 52°S in the South Atlantic, more rarely to 2°S and 64°S and in the western Indian Ocean.

31. White-headed Petrel   *Pterodroma lessonii*   Plate 5
A. Fardela gargantiblanca
c. Fardela de frente blanca
Medium. 16–18in/40–46cm

IDENTIFICATION: One of the more distinctive petrels of the southern oceans, appears blackish above with a lighter grey back, a white head and a grey or whitish rump and tail. The dark grey underwing contrasts with the white body and undertail. A dark patch around the eye and the black bill are noticeable at close range. Legs and feet are pink with dark toes and outer parts of the webs. Flight is fast and strong, particularly in very high winds; it does not usually follow ships.

STATUS & RECORDS: Vagrant to offshore Falkland waters from southern Pacific and southern Indian Ocean breeding grounds, recorded three or four times. Three reported flying near the north coast of East Falkland on 23 August 1925 (Bennett 1926); W Curtis saw one 13km (8 miles) west of Beaver Island on 10 July 1984 and one 24km (15 miles) east of Bluff Cove on 27 February 1986 (Bourne & Curtis 1987).

DISTRIBUTION ABROAD: Probably has a circumpolar distribution between the Antarctic continent and 30°S, though the pelagic range from the different breeding colonies is not well known. Breeds at Kerguelen, Crozet, Auckland, Antipodes and Macquarie Islands; possibly breeds at Campbell and Prince Edward Islands. There are few records from the South Atlantic, but it has been reported as numerous in the western Straits of Magellan.

32. Great-winged Petrel   *Pterodroma macroptera*   Not illustrated
A. Fardela aligrande
c. Fardela de alas grandes
Small-medium. 15–16in/38–41cm

IDENTIFICATION: Plumage dark brown except for a greyish patch below the bill. In good light shows variable silvery flashes below wings. Bill short, black; legs and feet black. Flight is fast, soaring and swooping like other petrels of this genus. Has very long wings and a slightly wedge-shaped tail; shape recalls that of a swift (*Apus* species). Compare with Sooty Shearwater (43).

STATUS & RECORDS: Pelagic vagrant at the southern limit of its range; it has been identified twice at sea at the edge of the continental shelf. Three seen about 320km (200 miles) northeast of Cape Pembroke on 19 August 1982 and six on 24 August 1982 by W Curtis (Bourne & Curtis 1985).

DISTRIBUTION ABROAD: Two races occur in southern Indian and South Atlantic Oceans between 25°S and 50°S. *P. m. macroptera* breeds at Tristan da Cunha, Gough, Marion, Crozet and Kerguelen Islands. *P. m. gouldi* breeds on islands off South Australia and northern New Zealand. This Pacific race has a greyer face than *P. m. macroptera*. Has been observed near Cape Horn but circumpolar distribution is not well known.

33. Soft-plumaged Petrel *Pterodroma mollis*   Plate 5
A. Fardela coronigris
c. Not recorded
Small-medium. 13–15in/33–38cm
IDENTIFICATION: Slate-grey on crown, back and tail; wings grey-brown above with some darker coverts forming a variable 'M' mark across the back; underside of wings slate-grey, body white variably marked with grey at sides and sometimes with a variably complete grey breast band; throat and face white with a dark mark through and below the eye; bill short, black; legs and feet pink with black toes. Flight fast and erratic but not as wild as the Kerguelen Petrel (29). Sometimes follows ships.

STATUS & RECORDS: Non-breeding visitor to Falkland waters, first recorded in 1945 when one was found dead at Teal Inlet in late March (Hamilton 1945b); recorded several times within 130km (80 miles) north of the Falklands between 1956 and 1963 (Tickell & Woods 1972). Four were seen off Mengeary Point on 31 December 1982 and since then small numbers have been seen regularly to the east of the Falklands between December and April. A few have been identified in waters 13–16km (8–10 miles) south of the Falklands (Bourne & Curtis 1987).

DISTRIBUTION ABROAD: Four races recognised; *P. m. feae* and *P. m. madeira* breed in the North Atlantic at Cape Verde and Madeira Islands in small numbers. *P. m. mollis* breeds at Tristan da Cunha and Gough Islands in the South Atlantic. *P. m. dubia* breeds at Marion, Crozet and Antipodes Islands. Movements not well known; occurs between about 25°S and 60°S in South Atlantic and southern Indian Oceans, infrequently in southwest Pacific Ocean.

34. Blue Petrel *Halobaena caerulea*   Plate 5
A. & C. Petrel azulado
Small. 11–12in/28–30cm
IDENTIFICATION: A small blue-grey and white petrel, superficially resembling a prion but having a blackish cap, grey and white mottled forehead, grey patch at the side of the neck and a white-tipped tail which is only visible at close range. Upperwing and back blue-grey with a dark open 'M' mark; underparts mainly white. Flies less erratically than prions, tending to glide low over the sea with fewer wingbeats; may approach ships but does not follow.

STATUS & RECORDS: Non-breeding visitor to Falkland waters; there was formerly much confusion between this species and the Thin-billed Prion (37), (Bennett 1926 and 1931a). Hamilton (1951) discounted it as a breeding species, having handled many specimens of the Thin-billed Prion and Carins (1974a) concluded that it was a visiting species, though it could breed. It is widespread in offshore waters east of the Falklands, apparently more numerous in winter, and occasionally comes inshore during severe weather. Up to 40 in a day have been seen within 32km (20 miles) of Cape Pembroke in June and September between 1983 and 1985 (Bourne & Curtis 1987).

DISTRIBUTION ABROAD: Breeds at Diego Ramirez islands and many were found in burrows on Cape Horn Island 56°32'S in April 1984 (Clark 1985). Also breeds at South Georgia, Marion, Crozet, Kerguelen and Macquarie Islands. Ranges between northern limit of pack-ice and about 40°S in all southern oceans and reaches about 20°S off Peru.

Prions   *Genus Pachyptila*
Controversy has continued for many years over the number of species and island races of prions. Bill shape and size have been used as field characters, but these are of little use when viewing at sea. Harrison (1983) divides them into two basic groups: Broad-billed and Thin-billed with distinct head patterns and narrow black tail tips and Fairy Prions with less head pattern and broader black upper tail tips. All are blue-grey above, with darker primaries linked by dark tips to some coverts and across the back to form an open 'M' mark. They are not easy to separate due to their rapid flight but can be distinguished with care and experience. Rarely follow ships.

35. Dove/Antarctic Prion   *Pachyptila desolata*   Plate 5
A. Petrel-ballena picoancho
c. Petrel-paloma antártico
Small. 11–12in/28–30cm
IDENTIFICATION: The Dove Prion is slightly larger than the other prions. Distinguishing marks are the dark blue-grey nape extending to the sides of the neck as a partial collar, a short white eye-stripe and a black mark through the eye; bill broad, blackish. The blue-grey tail has a narrow black tip. Flight is less erratic than the Thin-billed Prion (37).

STATUS & RECORDS: Uncertain, probably a non-breeding visitor; one specimen was found near Stanley 11 January 1961 (Woods 1975). Two were seen off Elephant Cays, Falkland Sound on 15 November 1983 and others were recorded in small numbers offshore in summer and possibly in larger numbers during winter (Bourne & Curtis 1987).

DISTRIBUTION ABROAD: Circumpolar; breeds at South Georgia, South Orkney, South Shetland, South Sandwich, Kerguelen, Heard, Macquarie and Auckland Islands and on the Antarctic continent at Cape Denison. Ranges between the Antarctic continent and about 20°S.

36. Broad-billed Prion   *Pachyptila vittata*   Plate 5
A. Petrel-ballena picoancho
c. Not recorded
Small. 10–12in/25–30cm

IDENTIFICATION: Very similar to the Dove Prion (35) but has a blue bill and usually lacks the partial collar. Can be distinguished from Fairy Prion (38) by its narrower black tail tip and a dark central line beneath the tail, a marking also found on the Thin-billed Prion (37).

STATUS & RECORDS: Non-breeding visitor to Falkland waters, occurring throughout the year in small numbers. Three specimens obtained on land: one struck Cape Pembroke Lighthouse in August 1912 (Bennett 1926); one found dead on West Falkland in July 1940 (Cawkell & Hamilton 1961); one found dead at Eliza Cove near Stanley by D Davidson on 3 September 1963 (Woods 1975).

DISTRIBUTION ABROAD: Circumpolar; breeds at Tristan da Cunha and Gough Islands in the South Atlantic, at islands off New Zealand and some southwestern coastal sites on South Island, New Zealand. Ranges further north than the Dove Prion, between about 55°S and 10°S in the Indian Ocean.

37. Thin-billed Prion *Pachyptila belcheri*   Plate 4
A. Petrel-ballena pico delgado
c. Petrel-paloma de pico delgado
Local name: Firebird
Small. 10–12in/26–30cm

IDENTIFICATION: The commonest prion in Falkland waters, it has a long white eye-stripe and a dark stripe below the eye; bill and legs are blue; tail blue-grey with a narrow black tip and whitish sides; has a narrow dark central stripe on the underside of the tail. Flight is fast and twisting; often seen in huge flocks that seem to appear and disappear as they turn, showing alternately their white undersides and grey upperparts.

VOICE: Silent at sea; in the breeding season has several guttural cooing or churring notes and trills, sometimes rhythmic, which are used in the nest burrow. Thousands calling at night resembled the heavy roar of surf (Cawkell & Hamilton 1961).

FOOD: Takes small marine invertebrates from the sea surface. Samples from the New Island colony contained amphipods ('shrimps'), Euphausian krill and very small squid (Prince in Strange 1980).

HABITAT, STATUS & BREEDING: Breeds in very large numbers at New Island, Grand Jason Island and Steeple Jason Island and at several other islands off the west coast of West Falkland. Reputed to breed at Macbride Head, East Falkland but not confirmed. Nests in burrows up to 2m (6 feet) long, excavated in soft peat or sandy soil. Adults return to colonies in early September and a single egg is laid between late October and early November. Most chicks fledge by late February and the population leaves by mid-March (Strange 1980). Breeding birds feed over the continental shelf east and south of the Falklands during daylight. It is thought to migrate northwards during winter but some remain in Falkland waters with other prion species (Bourne & Curtis 1987).

DISTRIBUTION ABROAD: Breeds in small numbers at Kerguelen and Crozet Islands in the southern Indian Ocean and a very large colony was found on Isla Noir off southern Chile (54°28′S) in the 1983/84 season (Clark 1985). Probably has a circumpolar distribution between about 60°S and 23°S though rarely recorded in South African waters.

38. Fairy Prion   *Pachyptila turtur*   Plate 4
A. Petrel-ballena picocorto
c. Petrel-paloma chico
Small. 9–11in/23–28cm

IDENTIFICATION: Separated from other prions by the broad black tip to its blue-grey tail; undertail all white; head pale blue-grey with a small, indistinct pale eye-stripe. Flight similar to Thin-billed Prion (37); often feeds in large flocks, fluttering and picking from the sea surface.

VOICE: Staccato or rhythmic guttural cooing notes, shorter and slightly higher-pitched than those of Thin-billed Prion, are used by adults in burrows.

FOOD: Takes small marine invertebrates, including squid and crustaceans.

HABITAT, STATUS & BREEDING: One early record; a bird found dead near Stanley 11 March 1917 (Bennett 1926). First found breeding in the Falklands in January 1967 (Strange 1968) on Beauchêne Island, 80km (50 miles) south of East Falkland. In 1980 Smith and Prince (1985) found them to be quite widespread over the island and they estimated the population to be several thousand pairs. Nests in burrows or cavities beneath rock slabs were examined and birds were incubating single eggs in mid-December; small chicks were found in early January 1967. Observed at sea off the Falklands throughout the year; this local population may be relatively sedentary.

DISTRIBUTION ABROAD: Breeds at Marion and Prince Edward Islands in the southern Indian Ocean, also at islands off New Zealand and Australia. Pelagic range is not well known, but it is probably circumpolar from about 58°S to at least 25°S.

39. Grey/Brown Petrel   *Procellaria cinerea*   Not illustrated
A. Petrel gris
c. Fardela gris
Medium. 18–20in/46–51cm

IDENTIFICATION: Larger than the Atlantic Petrel (30), this species is grey-brown on the head, back, wings and tail; underwing uniform grey and undertail grey-brown; throat and underside of body white. Bill fairly heavy, greenish with a yellow tip and black ridge; legs and feet pinkish with blackish toes. Flight similar to the White-chinned Petrel (40) though it has rapid duck-like wingbeats and glides long distances. Frequently dives from the air and swims underwater, using its wings. It often follows ships, particularly trawlers.

STATUS & RECORDS: Non-breeding visitor to offshore Falkland waters, at least between February and June. Wace (1921) stated that it occurred over the seas near the Falklands. The first substantiated record was on 25 April 1960, when one was seen at 49°S 58°W, 260km (160 miles) to the north (Tickell & Woods 1972); up to 40 seen around 52°S 52°W (420km, 260 miles) to the east by W

Curtis in June 1982; one seen at 50°42′S 58°43′W, 56km (35 miles) north of Cape Dolphin on 21 March 1985 by W Bourne. Up to nine were seen within 16km (10 miles) of Port William in February, March and June 1986 and two were 24km (15 miles) east of Bluff Cove on 27 February 1986 (Bourne & Curtis 1987).

DISTRIBUTION ABROAD: Circumpolar between about 60°S and 25°S; reaching further north in cold currents west of South America and Africa. Breeds at Tristan da Cunha group, Gough, Marion, Crozet, Kerguelen, Campbell and Antipodes Islands and nests during the southern winter season.

40. White-chinned Petrel or Shoemaker   *Procellaria aequinoctialis*   Plate 4
A. Petrel negro
c. Fardela negra grande
Local names: Cobbler, Nighthawk
Medium-large. 20–21in/51–53cm
IDENTIFICATION: A large sooty-black petrel with a very pale, greenish bill, much bigger than the Sooty Shearwater (43) and much smaller, with a shorter neck than the Giant Petrels (23 & 24). The legs and feet are black. Most individuals of the Falkland breeding race have a white chin, but this is variable and rarely visible at sea. Flight is powerful with deliberate, slow wingbeats and frequent long glides. Often dives from the air and will scavenge around ships and follow trawlers.

VOICE: Silent at sea but very noisy at its breeding grounds. Returning and departing adults use an ear-piercing, screaming trill, *chiky-chiky-chiky-* . . .; other low grunting calls are also used. As many as six adults have been watched on the ground outside their burrows, trilling together in the early breeding season.

FOOD: Squid, crustaceans and fish, taken by diving or from the surface.

HABITAT, STATUS & BREEDING: A summer resident, known to breed only at Kidney Island off East Falkland (a few hundred pairs) and at New Island off West Falkland (colony size unknown). Present all year in Falkland waters but smaller numbers in winter. Returns to the breeding colony on Kidney Island in late September; lays a single egg in late October or November in a burrow about 2m (6 feet) long in soft tussac-peat below dense tussac grass. The last juvenile birds leave their burrows by the end of April.

DISTRIBUTION ABROAD: Circumpolar between about 55°S and 25°S; two races known. *P. a. aequinoctialis* breeds at the Falklands, South Georgia, Prince Edward, Crozet, Kerguelen and islands south and east of New Zealand. *P. a. conspicillata*, distinguished by a variable amount of white on the sides of the face, breeds at Inaccessible Island, Tristan da Cunha.

41. Cory's Shearwater   *Calonectris diomedea*   Not illustrated
A. Pardela cenicienta
c. Not recorded
Medium to medium-large. 18–22in/46–56cm
IDENTIFICATION: A large, long-winged shearwater, grey-brown above and all white beneath, except the underwing tips, which are dark brown. Head grey-brown

above, darker in front of the eye, fading gradually into the white throat but not having a capped appearance (see Great Shearwater, 42). Primaries and tail slightly darker, occasionally showing a narrow white crescent across the base of the tail. Bill large, hooked, yellowish with a dark tip. Flight appears leisurely, with wings held downcurved when gliding; wingbeats are deep and slow. It will follow ships and fishing boats.

STATUS & RECORDS: Vagrant at southern edge of pelagic range in South Atlantic. One record of a single bird seen 8km (5 miles) off Volunteer Point, East Falkland on 5 March 1986 by W Curtis.

DISTRIBUTION ABROAD: Three races are recognised; *C. d. diomedea* breeds at several Mediterranean islands, *C. d. borealis* breeds at Azores, Maderia, Canaries and Berlengas Islands and *C. d. edwardsii*, which is smaller, with a dark bill and darker upperparts, breeds at Cape Verde Islands. Dispersal occurs westward in the North Atlantic to 50°N and the coast of North America and south to seas around South Africa. Also small numbers off the east coast of South America to about 35°S.

42. Great Shearwater *Puffinus gravis* Plate 4
A. Petrel pardo or Pardela capitorada
c. Fardela capitorada
Medium. 17–20in/43–51cm

IDENTIFICATION: Similar in size to Cory's Shearwater (41), but with a noticeable dark brown cap, white cheeks and sides of the neck, extending around the hind-neck, sometimes as a complete collar. Wings above, back and tail are dark brown, with a conspicuous white half-moon across the base of the tail. Underparts mainly white, with an irregular brown patch on the belly and brown markings at sides of the breast and on under wing-coverts. Bill slender, hooked, black; legs pink. During moult of wing-coverts (July to early September) shows white bands across upper surface of wings. Flight appears strong, with quicker wingbeats than Cory's and the wings held more straight. Dives from the air and follows fishing boats.

VOICE: Has loud howling and rhythmic calls at its breeding grounds, similar to those of the Sooty Shearwater. Will call at sea, when squabbling over food.

FOOD: Squid, fish, crustaceans and offal from fishing boats.

HABITAT, STATUS & BREEDING: Summer resident, breeding in very small numbers at Kidney Island. Numerous in Falkland waters and east towards South Georgia between mid-November and early May. Breeding was first suspected at Kidney Island in 1954 and proved on 28 December 1961 when a pair with a chipped egg were found (Woods 1970b) Adults were present in the same area on 18 September 1983, when at least two were seen in a raft of about 1500 Sooty Shear-waters gathering offshore and one was seen entering a burrow in tussac peat on 19 September. W Curtis visited Kidney Island on 28 February 1987 and esti-mated that no more than 15 pairs were nesting there. Possibly breeds at other offshore tussac islands, judging by its abundance during the summer; for instance, W Bourne counted 588 in one hour about 115km (70 miles) northeast of East Falkland on 13 February 1986 (Bourne & Curtis 1987). More than 100 were seen passing Cape Pembroke on 1 March 1987 by S Wolsey.

DISTRIBUTION ABROAD: Breeds in very large numbers at Inaccessible and Nightingale Islands of Tristan da Cunha group and at Gough Island. Post-breeding dispersal is to the northwest then north, past the eastern coast of South America into the North Atlantic to about 66°N, returning down the eastern side to breeding grounds from September. It also occurs inshore as far south as the Magellan Straits (Clark 1985).

43. Sooty Shearwater *Puffinus griseus* Plate 4
A. Pardela oscura
c. Fardela negra
Local name: Shyer Bird
Medium. 16–18in/40–46cm

IDENTIFICATION: Smaller than the White-chinned Petrel (40), it is similarly dark sooty-brown above, slightly paler below with whitish under wing-coverts that flash as it turns and are visible from a long distance. Wings long, narrow and slightly backswept, body bulky; the head looks small and the black bill is fairly long and slender. Flight is rapid with several quick, shallow wingbeats between long glides, usually close to the sea (see Great-winged Petrel 32). Plunge-dives with wings open. Occurs in large flocks, particularly where food is plentiful or near breeding colonies, where groups (rafts) gather on the sea before coming into their burrows at and after dusk.

VOICE: Rarely calls at sea; at breeding colonies uses an eerie howling call reminiscent of a cat, *wheeoo-har, wheeoo-har, wheeoo-har* repeated rhythmically and sometimes sustained for half a minute, rising and falling in pitch towards the end. This call can be heard from adults hurtling over the colony and from birds underground.

FOOD: Mainly squid, crustaceans and small fish; also takes fish offal.

HABITAT, STATUS & BREEDING: Summer resident, first recorded in February 1919 near Stanley by Bennett (Wace 1921). It breeds at Kidney Island (probably several thousand pairs) and at Sea Lion Island (possibly 500 pairs) and may breed on islands off West Falkland. Numerous over the continental shelf from August and present in Falkland waters throughout the year except in midwinter (Bourne & Curtis 1987). Returns to Kidney Island in mid-September to excavate or renovate burrows in soft tussac peat, usually 1.3m (4 feet) or more deep, with a raised mat of tussac as a nest. The single white egg is probably laid in November, though data on the egg-laying period are not available. Adults probably leave late March and juveniles from early April to early May. An unprecedented gathering, estimated from visual and radar observations by W Curtis to be about 80,000, was observed in the southern end of Falkland Sound on 28–29 March 1987 (Wolsey 1987b).

DISTRIBUTION ABROAD: Breeds at islands off Tierra del Fuego and in large numbers on Isla Guafo (43°S) and Cape Horn Island (Clark 1985). Large populations breed at islands south and east of New Zealand. Migrates into the North Atlantic and North Pacific, reaching coasts of Canada and Alaska. Some remain in southern oceans through the winter; many were seen in Falkland waters during the winter of 1984.

44. Manx Shearwater   *Puffinus puffinus*   Not illustrated
A. Pardela pichoneta
C. Fardela atlántica
Small-medium. 12–15in/30–38cm
IDENTIFICATION: A medium-sized shearwater, noticeably smaller than the Great Shearwater (42), with all black upperparts extending from crown to include lores and ear-coverts; underparts all white from chin to under tail-coverts with small white extension behind ear-coverts. Bill slender, black; legs pinkish. Underside of wing white with black border, broader at wingtips. Flies with fast, shallow wing-beats alternating with gliding and banking to one side and the other, showing black back then white underside, with typical stiff-winged appearance. Although it will attend fishing boats, does not normally follow ships.

STATUS & RECORDS: Vagrant, recorded twice; four seen flying north off Choiseul Sound on the morning of 17 February 1987 by W Curtis and one found dead on the southern coast of Keppel Island on 18 March 1987 (Wolsey 1987b).

DISTRIBUTION ABROAD: The typical race *P. p. puffinus* breeds in the North Atlantic, mainly on the European side and migrates rapidly into the South Atlantic in August and September, returning northwards in February and March. Previous records show that some birds reached about 50°S; the winter range may be extending further southward. Two other races, which are distinguishable at sea, breed in the Mediterranean and winter in that area or off the western coast of Europe.

45. Little Shearwater   *Puffinus assimilis*   Not illustrated
A. Pardela chica
C. Fardela chica
Small. 10–12in/25–30cm
IDENTIFICATION: A small black and white shearwater, with flight reminiscent of a Diving Petrel (50); rapid whirring wingbeats alternate with short low glides, usually close to the sea surface. In the race *P. a. elegans*, plumage is dark brown to slaty grey above with dark sides to the head; underparts are white, including the cheeks below the eye and the under tail-coverts. The underwing is white, with a narrow dark fringe and dark brown tips. Bill short, dark grey or black; legs and feet mainly blue. Usually seen singly, though it occurs with other larger shearwaters and often follows ships.

STATUS & RECORDS: Uncertain, probably a vagrant at southern edge of the pelagic range; one record of a single bird seen by W Bourne 140km (85 miles) northeast of Cape Bougainville on 4 April 1986 (Bourne & Curtis 1987).

DISTRIBUTION ABROAD: Probably circumpolar in southern oceans between about 30°S and 50°S, though extent of dispersal from colonies is not known. Several races have been described from different island groups in the North and South Atlantic, South Pacific and southern Indian Ocean. The race *P. a. elegans* breeds at Tristan da Cunha and Gough Islands and has been recorded off the coasts of Argentina and South Africa.

Storm-Petrels *Hydrobatidae*
*Storm-petrels are tiny, long-winged oceanic birds, no
bigger than a swallow, yet they spend most of their lives
at sea. About 20 species in eight genera are known. They
occur in all oceans of the world, many of them migrating
long distances from cold-water breeding grounds to
tropical waters in winter. At sea they flutter and patter
over the surface, picking minute organisms from the water.
Three species breeding at Antarctic and sub-Antarctic
islands have been recorded in the Falkland Islands or
adjacent waters. There are two breeding species and the
third is a vagrant. A fourth species breeding further north
has possibly been recorded.*

Grey-backed
Storm-Petrel

46. Wilson's Storm-Petrel *Oceanites oceanicus*   Plate 6
A. Paíño común
c. Golondrina de mar
Very small. 6–7in/15–18cm
IDENTIFICATION: Mainly sooty-black plumage with broad white rump extending
to the flanks separates this species from the Grey-backed (49). Upperwing has
a variable grey streak across the secondary coverts. The tail is square; the long
black legs project beyond the tip when extended, sometimes showing yellow webs
on the feet. In flight recalls a swallow, fluttering and gliding low over the water.
When feeding, often patters on the surface or hangs with wings motionless and
feet in the water. Occurs in large flocks and often follows ships.

VOICE: Has a loud, two or three-note, grating call used in flight or from the nest
at breeding colonies. When feeding at sea it uses a very quiet squeaking call.

FOOD: Takes small shrimps, squid and offal from fishing vessels.

HABITAT, STATUS & BREEDING: Summer resident, not fully investigated in the Falklands. It probably breeds in large numbers at Beauchêne Island and Grand Jason
Island, possibly at Kidney Island, Carcass Island and other offshore islands. Nests
in deep crevices amongst rocks or burrows in soft soil; lays one white egg with
reddish-brown spots around the broad end, probably between November and
January. Dispersal from colonies is probably in March-April. It occurs in large
numbers between November and April along the edge of the continental shelf
south of the islands and off the entrances to some of the sounds, especially Falkland
Sound (Bourne & Curtis 1987). Most birds have migrated by May but a few occur
in winter.

DISTRIBUTION ABROAD: The smaller race *O. o. oceanicus* breeds at the Falklands and
at islands off Tierra del Fuego, at South Georgia and Kerguelen Island. A larger
race *O. o. exasperatus* breeds at the South Shetland Islands, at many other Antarctic
islands and sites on the coast of Antarctica. Migration is transequatorial; it is
abundant between April and August in the North Atlantic (to about 53°N) and
Indian Oceans but less common in the North Pacific.

47. White-faced Storm-Petrel   *Pelagodroma marina*   Not illustrated
A. Paíño común
C. Not recorded
Very small to small. 8–8½in/20–21cm
IDENTIFICATION: A distinctive storm-petrel with characteristic sideways dancing flight when feeding from the sea surface, it is larger than Grey-backed (49) and Wilson's (46). Recognised by the marked face pattern of white lores joining a broad white stripe over the eye, dark grey around eye extending to ear-coverts, and all white underparts from chin to vent. Crown dark grey fading to grey-brown on back and upper wing-coverts, separated from blackish flight feathers by a pronounced dark curve from carpal joint to trailing edge. Rump pale grey, tail blackish almost square. Bill black; very long black legs with yellow webbed feet not easily seen at sea, projecting, when retracted, well beyond the tail. In feeding flight, it appears to bounce off the surface as it drops the legs and splashes the body onto the water. When not feeding, flight is erratic with jerky wingbeats, somewhat resembling a prion.

STATUS & RECORDS: Uncertain, possibly recorded once as a vagrant south of its normal non-breeding range. One was reported as caught by a Peregrine Falcon using a naval ship as a convenient feeding station, 32km (20 miles) south of Falkland Sound on 26 March 1986 (Ross 1986), though there is some doubt concerning the identification (Bourne & Curtis 1987).

DISTRIBUTION ABROAD: Six races described, one breeding on subtropical Cape Verde Islands, the nominate *P. m. marina* at Gough and Tristan da Cunha and others on coasts and islands of Australia and New Zealand. North Atlantic breeders disperse south at least to the Equator, while Tristan da Cunha and Gough birds spread to about 45°S off the coast of Argentina.

48. Black-bellied Storm-Petrel   *Fregetta tropica*   Plate 6
A. Paíño ventrinegro
C. Golondrina de mar de vientre negro
Very small. 7½–8in/19–20cm
IDENTIFICATION: Slightly larger and more heavily built than the Wilson's Storm-Petrel (46); upper wing, back and tail black; rump and upper tail-coverts white; head, breast and under tail-coverts black; rest of underparts white except for a variable black line extending down from the breast to the underside of the tail; underwing shows a conspicuous white triangular patch on the coverts, contrasting with the blackish undersides of the flight feathers. Can be confused with Wilson's but has typical flight behaviour at sea; wings are usually held horizontal, the feet hang down and the body swings from side to side. It feeds by dropping breast first to the water and springing off, using its legs. Rarely follows ships but may be seen ahead; it is usually solitary at sea.

STATUS & RECORDS: Probably a non-breeding visitor to Falkland waters, though Wace (1921) mentions an egg supposed to be of this species that was collected by the Challenger expedition last century and then listed in a British Museum catalogue. Bennett (1926) had heard that it bred in the Falklands but Cawkell and Hamilton (1961) had no evidence of its occurrence. Some recent records are available; Smith and Prince (1985) observed a few near Beauchêne Island in December 1980; W Curtis saw two off Mengeary Point on 31 December 1982 and also recorded it 22km and 60km (14 and 37 miles) north of the Falklands on 2 July 1984; W Bourne saw one 48km (30 miles) north of Cape Dolphin on 19 November 1983. One seen just off the East Falkland coast in February 1985 (A Douse pers. comm.). As the November, December and February records are in the breeding season, the possibility that it breeds in the Falklands remains.

DISTRIBUTION ABROAD: Breeds at South Georgia (uncommon), South Orkney, South Shetland, Crozet, Kerguelen, Auckland, Antipodes and possibly at other colder sub-Antarctic islands. May breed at Gough Island but there is possible confusion with the closely related species, the White-bellied Storm-Petrel *Fregetta grallaria*, which breeds in the Tristan da Cunha group of islands. Some of this species were reported 320km (200 miles) north of the Falklands in December 1982 by W Curtis and in 1983 by S da Prato (Bourne & Curtis 1987). Identification of this species is difficult due to close resemblance to the Black-bellied, particularly to the white-breasted form, which also breeds at Tristan da Cunha. Pelagic distribution of the Black-bellied is circumpolar between about 58°S and the tropics, occasionally crossing the Equator.

49. Grey-backed Storm-Petrel *Garrodia nereis* Plate 6
A. Paíño gris
c. Golondrina de mar subantártica
Very small. $6-7\frac{1}{2}/15-19$cm
IDENTIFICATION: Grey back, silver-grey rump and shortish, square grey tail with a broad black tip, immediately separate this species from Wilson's (46). Head and breast blackish, remainder of underparts white; wings above, black with grey coverts sometimes marked with white. Underwing mainly white with black margins; bill and long legs black. Flight similar to Wilson's; sometimes follows ships.

VOICE: Silent at sea; during courtship uses a quiet, wheezy croaking note repeated rhythmically slightly quicker than once a second when in the nest cavity. No calls recorded in flight at the Falklands but Falla *et al* (1966) reported high-pitched twittering calls when flying over breeding colonies at islands southeast of New Zealand.

FOOD: Probably takes small crustaceans and squid, though not studied.

HABITAT, STATUS & BREEDING: Summer resident, apparently only occurring between September and late May. It is widespread over the continental shelf in summer, often feeding over drifting kelp (Bourne & Curtis 1987). Known to breed at Kidney Island, where numbers may be high; probably breeds at other islands with dense tussac grass, including Carcass Island where a courting pair were found in October 1983 and East Sea Lion Island where corpses were seen in November 1983. Distribution not known through lack of investigation. Nocturnal when breeding; most return two to three hours after sunset. Short-eared Owls catch many adults on Kidney Island; remains are often found in pellets or on plucking sites. Probably vulnerable to predation from introduced cats and rats. Nests are enlarged cavities between dead tussac stems in the skirt of leaves above the basal pedestal or at ground level. One white egg with minute reddish dots is laid between mid-October and late December. Fledglings probably leave between early February and mid-April.

DISTRIBUTION ABROAD: Circumpolar, breeding at South Georgia, Gough, Crozet, Kerguelen, Chatham, Auckland and Antipodes islands. Pelagic range not well known; it appears to stay fairly close to breeding colonies.

Diving Petrels *Pelecanoididae*

Diving Petrels are stout, short-necked and small-winged seabirds, scarcely larger than Storm-Petrels. They typically whirr over the sea surface and dive suddenly into the water. A little known family which has not been fully investigated, it contains four or five species found in southern oceans. They show a strong resemblance to the Northern Hemisphere Little Auk or Dovekie Alle alle *and thus provide an excellent example of evolutionary convergence. Two species have been recorded. One certainly breeds in the Falkland Islands and at several other sub-Antarctic islands. The second species may breed locally but has not been found nesting. A third species, the Georgian Diving Petrel* Pelecanoides georgicus *may occur in Falkland waters (Bourne & Curtis 1987). Diving Petrels are difficult birds to observe at their breeding grounds as they return after dark.*

Common
Diving Petrel

50. Common Diving Petrel *Pelecanoides (urinatrix) berard*   Plate 6
A. Potoyunco malvinero
C. Yunco de los canales
Local names: Diver, Firebird
Very small to small. $7\frac{1}{2}$–9in/19–23cm

IDENTIFICATION: Upperparts black or dark brown, glossy on back and inner wing; head black on crown, nape and around eye, mottled grey on cheeks; underparts white with variable grey mottling on sides of neck, often forming an incomplete breast band; underwing has grey coverts, black flight feathers. Bill short, black, with upward pointing nostrils; legs and feet bright blue. Compare with Magellan Diving Petrel (51). Note that specific identification is often very difficult; only fleeting views are possible as the birds suddenly emerge with whirring wings from the sea and fly quickly into the water again.

VOICE: A rhythmically repeated, double cooing or mewing note, *whooee-whip* is used by birds in the air or on the ground at nesting colonies.

FOOD: Crustaceans and possibly small fish.

HABITAT, STATUS & BREEDING: Summer breeding resident, present in large numbers at some offshore tussac islands, including Beauchêne Island, Kidney Island,

Cochon Island and Flat Jason Island. May nest at many other islands where tussac peat is suitable for excavating the 1m long burrow. Probably lays the single egg in October, but information on the breeding season is scanty. It is present in Falkland waters through the year, particularly over the edge of the continental shelf. Up to 150 were seen in an hour in the southern approaches to Falkland Sound on 27 May 1984 (Bourne & Curtis 1987).

DISTRIBUTION ABROAD: Many island races have been described from southern oceans between about 35°S and 55°S. It is possible that some should be recognised as full species. At South Georgia and other sub-Antarctic islands this species occurs with *P. georgicus*. The Common and Magellan Diving Petrels both breed on Fuegian coasts.

51. Magellan Diving Petrel   *Pelecanoides magellani*   Plate 6
A. Potoyunco magallánico
c. Yunco de Magallanes
Very small to small. 7½–9/19–23cm
IDENTIFICATION: General coloration similar to Common Diving Petrel (50) but has sharper demarcation between grey cheeks and the white throat; white extends as a half collar towards the nape; scapular feathers tipped with white, forming a broad stripe either side of the back. White fringes also show on back and rump in fresh plumage (August); by autumn (March) they are worn and often absent. Underwing whiter than in Common species.

STATUS & RECORDS: Uncertain, possibly a non-breeding visitor, though it may breed. There are two specimens in the British Museum, dated 1888 and 29 March 1930. The latter struck Cape Pembroke Lighthouse and was collected by Hamilton (Bourne in Woods 1975). Essenhigh reported 50 diving petrels in Byron Sound on 20 March 1984; W Bourne considered this record to be out of character for the Common Diving Petrel (Bourne & Curtis 1987). Clark reported seeing Magellan Diving Petrels in channels near Beaver Island in June/July 1984, but there are no other recent records.

DISTRIBUTION ABROAD: Breeds at islands of southern Chile, Tierra del Fuego and Patagonia. Is found in Fuegian waters throughout the year though it has been recorded to about 40°S off the coast of Argentina in winter.

Shags or Cormorants   *Phalacrocoracidae*
Shags (Cormorants) are large seabirds with slender sinuous necks and long, hooked bills. Their wings are broad and flight is direct and steady with rapid wingbeats. They swim with the body low in the water and the head typically uptilted; they dive frequently.

About 30 species have been described from up to five genera; relationships of several forms are still undecided. Shags occur in most parts of the world; six species are found in South America and three have been recorded in

Imperial Shag

the Falklands. The two Falkland breeding species also breed in southern South America; one of them, the Imperial Shag, is found at several other sub-Antarctic islands. The third species is a rare vagrant from the South American coast.

Carins (1974b) suggested that the Olivaceous/Bigua Cormorant *P. olivaceus* should be included on the Falkland list as a possible vagrant, on the basis of an incomplete and probably second-hand description by Garnot (1826). There have been no later sightings to support the suggestion. This species is easily confused with the juvenile Rock Shag.

The Brown Booby *Sula leucogaster* was also listed by Garnot under an old synonym, *Pelecanus fiber* and was later mentioned as a vagrant by Wace (1921), Bennett (1926), Cawkell & Hamilton (1961) and Woods (1975). It is a tropical species, not recorded further south than about 30°S. Carins (1974b) concluded that Garnot's description could be applied equally to immature Rock Shags. This seems a reasonable conclusion and therefore the Brown Booby has been omitted from the list of Falkland birds in this book.

52. Rock Shag *Phalacrocorax magellanicus*   Plate 2
A. Viguá cuello negro
C. Cormorán de las rocas
Local name: Black Shag
Large. 26in/66cm

IDENTIFICATION: Smaller than the Imperial Shag (53), generally glossy black above and on the neck, with white underparts, pink legs, black bill and red facial skin around the eye. *Adult breeding*: a white ear-patch that grows larger from October; crown has curved black crest (not illustrated) from late June to late December; variable white patches develop on throat, neck and forehead, foreneck sometimes all white. *Adult non-breeding*: lacks white ear-patches and usually has all-black neck though white patches remain on some birds; upperparts dark brown. *Juvenile*: dull brown above and below with white belly and black legs. *Immature*: similar but underparts gradually become all brown by July, except for white throat. This plumage retained for about a year, when white gradually reappears on belly and breast. Appears to be a weak flyer, almost invariably dropping close to surface of water before gaining speed. Usually flies low over water with neck extended straight and rounded wings beating rapidly.

Note that juveniles are difficult to separate from immature Olivaceous/Bigua Cormorant, a species that has not been definitely recorded in the Falklands: Rock Shags have thinner necks and usually more red facial skin.

VOICE: Usually silent when alone. Groups gathered on resting places greet each other with a guttural *karrk*. In courtship both sexes utter a rapid rhythmic grunt *uk-uk-uk-uk* . . . Nestlings have a rasping *screep* which becomes louder and faster when parents return with food.

FOOD: Small fish caught by diving.

HABITAT, STATUS & BREEDING: Common breeding resident found in sheltered bays and harbours throughout the Falklands. Usually stays closer inshore than the

Imperial Shag, feeding amongst kelp patches. Uses jetties and hulks of beached sailing ships for resting and nesting. Usually nests colonially on ledges of steep cliffs in sheltered inlets at least 6m (20 feet) above the sea. Colonies vary from six to several hundred; sometimes nests singly and occasionally on cliff tops. Nests constructed from tussac grass, seaweeds and sometimes diddle-dee twigs, are renovated or built from late September. Two to five, usually three greenish-white eggs with chalky deposits are laid between early November and mid-December. Juveniles leave the nests mid-January to late February.

DISTRIBUTION ABROAD: The species *P. magellanicus* breeds on the coasts of South America from 37°S in Chile and 50°S in Argentina to Cape Horn and is particularly common around Tierra del Fuego. Continental birds are mainly sedentary but some occasionally wander as far north as 33°S in Chile and to 35°S on the coast of Uruguay.

53. Imperial Shag *Phalacrocorax atriceps albiventer* Plate 2

A. Viguá blanco or Cormorán real

c. Cormorán de las Malvinas

Local name: King Shag

Large to very large. 27–29in/69–74cm

IDENTIFICATION: Greater size, blue eye-ring, orange caruncles (knobs) above the base of the bill, continuous white underparts and foreneck distinguish adults of this species from the Rock Shag (52). Demarcation between black and white on the face is in line with gape. Bill grey-brown, legs and feet pink. *Adult breeding*: glossy black crown with forward-facing crest (August–December); shiny blue-black hindneck and back, glossy green-black wing-coverts and tail; small patch of white plumes behind eye (August–November); white wingbar formed by lesser coverts (October–May); thighs and underwing black. *Adult non-breeding*: lacks crest, wingbar and head plumes, caruncles smaller. *Immature*: similar in pattern to adult but dark brown above and lacks caruncles.

In flight, the fully extended neck appears totally white from a distance, broad pointed wings flap rapidly and tail is noticeably long. Often occurs in large flocks offshore when feeding, especially in winter.

VOICE: Calls are variations on a deep, guttural *kork*. Colonies are very noisy during nest-building in October.

FOOD: Fish and crustaceans obtained largely in open waters.

HABITAT, STATUS & BREEDING: Numerous breeding resident, found around all coasts. Appears to travel further offshore for food than the Rock Shag. Breeds in close-packed colonies, often in association with Rockhopper Penguins and Black-browed Albatrosses, usually on flat cliff top sites, which are also used as roosts in winter. Nest building or renovation continue till November; the nest is a column of mud, tussac grass and algae about 30cm (1 foot) high topped by a shallow cup and lined with grass. Two to four, usually three pale green-blue limy eggs are laid between late October and (mostly) in mid-November. Eggs hatch in December; most juveniles are flying by mid-February.

DISTRIBUTION ABROAD: Recent work on the Imperial Shag ('King Shag *P. albiventer*' and the 'Blue-eyed Shag *P. atriceps*') has shown that birds of intermediate type occur wherever these two 'species' are known to co-exist. This species group includes about eight geographical races, found on southern coasts and inland lakes of Chile and Argentina from about 40°S to Tierra del Fuego and at South Georgia, South Shetland and other Antarctic islands to about 65°S; also at Heard, Crozet and islands in the southern Indian Ocean. *P. a. atriceps* acquires a white dorsal patch in the early breeding season. The race *P. a. albiventer* always has a black back and is restricted to the Falklands.

54. Red-legged Shag   *Phalacrocorax gaimardi*   Plate 2
A. Cormorán lile
C. Lile
Very large. 28–30in/71–76cm

IDENTIFICATION: Grey plumage heavily chequered with silver-grey on the back, elongated white patch at each side of the neck (at all ages), bright red legs and feet, yellow bill and bare red facial skin all make this species easily recognised. When swimming may appear black but white neck patch is prominent and red legs usually visible as it jumps to dive. *Adult breeding*: underparts paler than upperparts; scattered white spots on foreneck and face. *Adult non-breeding* has uniform dark grey head. *Immature* is generally brown-grey; wing-coverts and underparts mottled with brownish white. More solitary than other shags though associates with them at sea. Flight is characteristically low and straight; voice is an unusually high-pitched chirp (Murphy 1936).

STATUS & RECORDS: Vagrant from continental South America recorded two or three times; one seen near West Point Island about January 1950; another in West Point Island harbour late April and May 1965; possibly a third in September 1965 (R Napier in Woods 1975).

DISTRIBUTION ABROAD: According to Blake (1979), the larger race *P. g. gaimardi* breeds on the Pacific coast from about 6°S in Peru to 46°S in Chile. A slightly smaller and lighter grey race *P. g. cirriger* breeds on the Atlantic coast of Argentina only in the region of Puerto Deseado (47°S); it is probably a rare vagrant to the Magellan Straits (53°S).

Herons & Egrets   *Ardeidae*
Herons and Egrets are large waterside birds with long legs, long dagger-shaped bills and long necks which they fold back in flight giving a thick-chested appearance. In flight their wings are broad and flap slowly and the feet project beyond the tail.

About 50 species in eight genera are distributed throughout the world, most of them occurring in tropical regions. South America has 22 species and 13 of them occur in Argentina. Of the six species recorded in the Falklands, only one breeds. Four species are irregular wind-drifted vagrants and one species, the Cattle Egret, occurs in large numbers each autumn as young birds disperse from South American breeding colonies.

Black-crowned
Night Heron

55. Cocoi Heron   *Ardea cocoi*   Plate 7
A. Garza mora
C. Garza cuca
Gigantic. 38–50in/97–127cm
IDENTIFICATION: A very large heron, twice the size of the resident Black-crowned
Night Heron (60); *adult* has grey back and wing-coverts, black flight feathers and
tail, white neck streaked with black down the centre and white underparts with
black sides to the body from shoulder to flanks. Head is black from forehead to
nape and extending below the eye. Bill very heavy, yellow with darker base; bare
facial skin greenish or bluish; iris yellow. Legs dull greenish or yellowish with
white feathers on tibia. *Immature* has grey underparts streaked with buff, a grey
neck and dark streaks on under tail-coverts.

STATUS & RECORDS: Irregular vagrant, though Wace (1921) felt it was a frequent
visitor. Bennett (1926) stated that it occasionally occured remote from habitations
and Cawkell & Hamilton (1961) recorded one in Hill Cove camp for several weeks
in summer 1955. One, probably of this species, was seen fishing up a small stream
in Island Harbour camp by W Sutherland in September 1960 (M Clark in Woods
1975); one probable Cocoi Heron flew down Stanley harbour at dusk, 1 May
1981 (Peatfield in Wolsey 1986c); one probable at North Arm on 28 March 1986
(P Hall pers. comm.). One, sometimes two at Teal Inlet during the past six to seven
years up to February 1987 suggests breeding, but there is no evidence (Wolsey
1987a). Between 29 March and 26 May 1987, at least one was seen on four
occasions at Stanley and San Carlos (Wolsey 1987b).

DISTRIBUTION ABROAD: Widely distributed in South America from Panama through
Chile, Brazil and Argentina to about 52°S, except in the high Andes. It is only
an occasional visitor to the Magellanic region.

56. Great White Egret   *Egretta alba*   Plate 7
A. Garza blanca
C. Garza grande
Immense to gigantic. 33–40in/85–102cm
IDENTIFICATION: Very large size, all white plumage with a noticeable kink in the
very long neck, yellow bill and black legs and feet distinguish this egret from the
Snowy and Cattle Egrets (57 & 59). At close range a black line from the gape
to well behind the eyes is a useful identification mark. In *breeding* plumage, *adults*
develop white plumes on the back and the bill becomes orange. *Immatures* have
a black tip to the bill.

STATUS & RECORDS: Irregular vagrant from South America, described by Wace
(1921) as a very rare visitor, but has been recorded singly at least nine times
on beaches, at streams, in marshy ground or on short grass. One reported by
Bennett (1926) in October 1913; near Lake Hammond mid-October 1958; on
rocks at Cape Pembroke 19 April 1960; at Fitzroy late May 1960; at Bluff Cove
for several weeks in June 1964; at Horseshoe Bay from 21 May 1959 to August
and, possibly the same bird, again in December 1959 (Woods 1975). At least
one seen between 20–24 April 1968 at Stanley, Fitzroy, Bluff Cove and Port Louis

(D Davidson pers. comm.). One seen at Bertha's Beach pond September 1985 (Wolsey 1986c). One seen on the San Carlos river 12 April 1987 (Wolsey 1987b).

DISTRIBUTION ABROAD: The species *E. alba* has an almost worldwide distribution, except in arctic regions. The race *E. a. egretta* is widely distributed through the southern United States and South America, breeding from Central America south to Santa Cruz (47°S), Argentina. It is an uncommon visitor to Tierra del Fuego.

57. Snowy Egret *Egretta thula* Plate 7
A. Garcita blanca
C. Garza chica
Medium-large to large. 22–26in/56–66cm
IDENTIFICATION: Resembles Great White Egret (56) in shape and all white plumage, but is much smaller. Bill black with yellow facial skin; legs black with yellow feet visible in flight. *Breeding adult* has conspicuous white plumes on nape, back and neck. *Immature* lacks plumes, otherwise similar. Distinguished from Cattle Egret (59) by longer, slender black bill, slightly larger size and more graceful stance.

STATUS & RECORDS: Vagrant from South America, first recorded on 3 May 1957, when a single bird was found dead below Cape Pembroke Lighthouse (Woods 1975). This occurence was apparently associated with an intense travelling anticyclone over Buenos Aires Province, Argentina, which produced strong northerly winds from eastern Argentina to the Falklands. In 1987, one was seen at East Cove on 20 April and two were seen nearby at Bertha's Beach on 26 April (Wolsey 1987b).

DISTRIBUTION ABROAD: Two races, *E. t. thula* and *E. t. brewsteri* which is slightly larger, breed from the southern United States to about 40°S in Chile and Argentina. Northward migration of southern breeding populations apparently occurs and vagrants have been recorded at Punta Deseado, Argentina (47°S) and the Magellan Straits (52°S).

58. Green-backed Heron *Butorides striatus* Plate 7
A. & C. Garcita azulada
Small-medium to medium. 15–19in/38–48cm
IDENTIFICATION: A small, dark, thickset heron, mainly glossy green above, often appearing black, with a scaly pattern of buff edges to flight feathers. Underparts grey, paler on throat; head looks heavy, capped with greenish black and showing a white mark below the eye. Bill fairly heavy, black with yellow at base of lower mandible. Legs and feet dull yellow. *Juvenile* differs by browner upperparts, spotted white on wing-coverts and buffish underparts heavily streaked with dark brown.

STATUS & RECORDS: Vagrant from South America: one record, an immature bird found dead at Carcass Island in June 1960 (Woods 1975).

DISTRIBUTION ABROAD: Widespread in warm temperate and tropical regions of the world; three races found in South America east of the Andes from Panama to central Argentina (38°S), where it occurs in marshy habitats with trees.

59. Cattle Egret   *Bubulcus ibis*   Plate 7
A. Garcita buyera
C. Garza boyera
Medium to medium-large. 19–21in/48–53cm
IDENTIFICATION: A small, stocky white heron with rounded head, short, thick yellow or orange-yellow bill and facial skin, yellow iris and dark green legs. *Adult breeding* has reddish-buff plumes on crown, nape, breast and mantle; bill and facial skin become orange to red and legs bright yellow. *Immature* may show traces of buff on head and breast; legs are blackish and soles of feet yellow. Smaller than Snowy Egret (57) with faster wingbeats.

STATUS & RECORDS: Non-breeding visitor, occurring annually, it prefers drier habitats than most other herons, often feeding on open grassland and frequently in association with grazing animals. First recorded at Stanley on 29 April 1976 (Strange 1979); since then has occurred during autumn period (March to May) in increasing numbers each year at many places in the Falklands. In the autumn of 1986, after northwesterly gales on 15 April, W Curtis saw about 450 off East Falkland on 16 April and it was estimated that up to 3,000 birds were seen throughout the Falklands (Wolsey 1986a). Sixty were seen at Volunteer Point and 36 at Pebble Island in early April 1987 (Wolsey 1987b). Most birds appear to be immature; few survive beyond June though there are unconfirmed reports of overwintering.

DISTRIBUTION ABROAD: Originating in central Africa, this species has spread widely in the Americas since first recorded in Surinam about 1880. Breeds from the Northwest Territories of Canada and Newfoundland through Central America and most of South America to about 40°S. Has occurred regularly in Tierra del Fuego during autumn since first seen in 1975.

60. Black-crowned Night Heron   *Nycticorax nycticorax*   Plate 7
A. Cuaco or Martinete
C. Huairavo
Local name: Quark
Medium-large. 21–23in/53–58cm
IDENTIFICATION: The only heron resident in the Falklands, it is grey and black above and heavily-built. *Adults* have a shiny black back and crown with a cream or white forehead and long white plumes extending from the nape; bill blackish; legs slaty in front, orange-yellow to pink behind with slaty toes and yellow soles; iris scarlet red. *Juvenile* and *first year* birds are dark brown above, heavily flecked with buff and buff below streaked with dark brown; iris orange, legs yellow-green. *Second year* birds resemble adults but have dark grey-brown forehead, dark brown crown, brown-grey breast, and brown inner wing-coverts flecked with buff. Probable *third year* birds have dark grey crown and grey-brown forehead. Plumage sequences have not been fully described. In flight uses slow flaps of its broad, rounded wings; feet project just beyond the short tail. Often seen resting motionless on beaches or cliff ledges during daylight or at high tide; active at dusk and later.

VOICE: Usual flight call is a very harsh *kwark* from which the local name is derived.

At breeding colonies uses variable threat-calls, *unk-unk-unk* or *rok-rok-rok*, a peculiar low advertising call like a bubble of mud bursting followed by a long wheeze, variations on the flight call and bill snapping. Nestlings use a persistent shrill ticking call.

FOOD: Takes small fish, aquatic insects and larvae in rock pools at low tide. Sometimes hunts from a perch on floating kelp up to 450m ($\frac{1}{4}$ mile) offshore. Suspected of taking Grey-backed Storm-Petrels on Kidney Island (Woods 1975) and has been known to catch Tussac-birds on the ground and nestling House Sparrows from nests on Carcass Island (K Bertrand pers. comm.).

HABITAT, STATUS & BREEDING: Fairly common resident around the coasts of the Falklands, often seen singly or in pairs on beaches with rock pools. Usually breeds communally, on steep low cliffs with shrubby plants or tussac grass, in rushes or tussac by ponds and on Carcass Island, in dense Monterey Cypress trees. The nest is a substantial flat platform of grass or sticks in which two to three, sometimes four smooth blue-green eggs are laid from late October. May have two broods in a season as eggs have been found in late January.

DISTRIBUTION ABROAD: Widespread in North and South America, Eurasia and Africa from about 53°N through the tropics to 55°S in Tierra del Fuego. Three races occur in the Americas: *N. n. obscurus* is resident in southern Chile and Argentina to Tierra del Fuego; the Falkland race *N. n. cyanocephalus*, is darker below and smaller.

Storks   *Ciconiidae*

The 17 species in this family are mainly tropical and subtropical birds of Africa and Asia. They are very large, long-legged, large-billed and broad-winged birds, mainly occurring in marshy places with trees and are usually solitary when nesting. Storks fly with slow wingbeats, often soaring at great heights. Three species breed in much of South America to about 40°S; one has probably occurred in the Falklands.

61. Maguari Stork   *Ciconia maguari*   Plate 8
A. Cigüeña americana
c. Pillo
Gigantic. 38–43in/97–110cm

IDENTIFICATION: *Adult* has all white body plumage and wing-coverts, black flight feathers and short forked black tail. In flight the long orange-red legs project well beyond the tail and the long neck is fully extended. Bill heavy, straight, orange-red; bare skin of throat and at base of bill is orange-red; iris yellow. *Immature* almost completely blackish.

STATUS & RECORDS: Vagrant from South America; one almost certain record; an adult at Horseshoe Bay, East Falkland on 24 August 1961 (Woods 1975).

DISTRIBUTION ABROAD: Widely distributed in South America from Colombia, Venezuela and the Guianas through Brazil and Argentina to about 42°S. Occasional birds reach southern Argentina and the Magellanic region.

Ibises & Spoonbills *Threskiornithidae*
Ibises and spoonbills are long-legged waterside or terrestrial birds with fairly long necks, short tails and broad, long wings. Ibises have long, slender and decurved bills while spoonbills have long and flattened bills. Adults have bare or partly bare heads and the sexes are similar except that males tend to be slightly larger. Unlike herons, they fly with the neck fully extended. Of the 29 species in this family which are found in tropical and subtropical parts of the world, seven ibises and one spoonbill occur in South America. Four ibises and this spoonbill are found in Argentina; one ibis and the spoonbill have occurred in the Falklands.

62. Buff-necked Ibis *Theristicus caudatus* Plate 8
A. & c. Bandurria común
Large to very large. 26–29in/66–73cm
IDENTIFICATION: Noisy and shy, about goose-size; *adult* has head, neck, mantle and upper breast orange-chestnut; black flight feathers and tail glossed dark green; grey-brown shoulders and back, with white secondary coverts showing as a prominent white band across the wing. Bill and bare facial skin black; legs and feet red. A grey band across the lower breast and black belly is visible when standing. *Immature* has paler head and back, a shorter bill and feathered throat. Flight strong; often utters loud, hard *kwa-kwa* or *clak-clak*.

STATUS & RECORDS: Irregular vagrant from South America, where it occurs on swampy and ploughed land. There are more than 10 records in the Falklands of singles and parties of up to seven at settlement greens, all in migration periods of March/April and October/November. Recent records include one seen at Eliza Cove, near Stanley on 1 April 1981 (Wolsey 1986c) and two at Beaver Island in mid-November 1986 (Wolsey 1987b).

DISTRIBUTION ABROAD: Four races inhabit most of South America; *T. c. caudatus* and *T. c. hyperorius* are blackish below and occur in lowland regions of northern and central South America; *T. c. branickii* has a grey wingpatch and is found in andean regions from Ecuador to northern Chile; *T. c. melanopis*, the form described above, breeds in Chile from about 25°S to Tierra del Fuego and in Argentina north to about 38°S; in winter migrates north to about 28°S.

63. Roseate Spoonbill *Ajaia ajaja* Plate 8
A. Espátula rosada
c. Espátula
Very large. 27–32in/69–81cm
IDENTIFICATION: Distinctive long spoon-shaped bill makes identification easy; *adult* has white neck, back and upper breast, and otherwise rosy pink body with crimson shoulder patch and rump; tail yellowish; head bare, greenish with broad black band from base of bill around nape; bill mottled green and black; legs dark red. *Immature* has feathered white head, paler pink plumage, dark brown wingtips and no red patches on wings and rump. Feeds by wading and sweeping the bill from side to side.

STATUS & RECORDS: Infrequent vagrant from South America; only four documented records. Abbott (1861) noted one in a pond near Kidney Cove in July 1860, Bennett (1926) stated that it was an occasional visitor and recorded one found dead near Stanley in 1922. One found at Rolon Cove near Stanley in 1953 and an adult found dead at Port San Carlos on 31 May 1962 (Woods 1975).

DISTRIBUTION ABROAD: Breeds from the southern United States through most of eastern South America to about 38°S in Argentina. Occurs as a non-breeding visitor rarely to about 52°S in Argentina and in central Chile.

Flamingos *Phoenicopteridae*

A distinctive group of large waterbirds, easily recognised by their pink plumage, long neck, massive downcurved bill and very long legs. Flamingos fly with neck and feet extended and can swim easily. Four species are found mostly in tropical regions of southern Europe, Africa, Asia and the West Indies; two species occur in the Andes between Peru and Tierra del Fuego. One South American species has occurred several times in the Falklands.

64. Chilean Flamingo *Phoenicopterus chilensis* Plate 8
A. Flamenco común
C. Flamenco chileno
Gigantic. 39–44in/100–112cm

IDENTIFICATION: Very large size, extremely long neck and legs and all black primaries and secondaries make this bird unmistakable in flight. *Adult* is generally white above tinged with pink; wing-coverts orangey-red; basal half of bill white and terminal half black; legs greyish with red joints and toes. *Immature* greyish-white; legs yellowish with blue-red joints; bill paler.

STATUS & RECORDS: Infrequent vagrant from South America, recorded at least three times between 1910 and 1932 (Woods 1975). One reported by P Richards in 1967/68 (no locality recorded) and one photographed at a pond in Albemarle camp, West Falkland by Gunner Robbins on 24 September 1985 (Wolsey 1986c).

DISTRIBUTION ABROAD: Occurs in South America from about 10°S in Peru, through Bolivia, Paraguay, southern Brazil and Uruguay, Chile and Argentina to Tierra del Fuego. Large flocks winter at lagoons in the Magellanic region between April and September.

Swans, Geese and Ducks *Anatidae*

Swans, geese and ducks are medium to gigantic birds that inhabit fresh or salt water or grassland. They have broad, flattened bills, webbed feet, fairly long necks and noticeably rounded heads, usually carried horizontally when swimming. Over 140 species have been described and they are found in all parts of the world. Twenty-one species have been recorded in the Falkland Islands; fifteen breed, including one introduced species, now living in the wild (feral). Five species are vagrants from South America. Another species, the Mallard originating from Europe, was said to have been introduced but has apparently failed to survive. All but one are powerful flying birds, with broad, sharp-pointed wings; they fly with necks extended and show a short tail. The four Falkland geese are in a group known as Sheldgeese, which have a glossy patch on the secondary coverts. These geese and the two Steamer Ducks have hard knobbly spurs on the bend of each wing, sometimes used in territorial disputes. The endemic Flightless Steamer Duck has short wings and a very heavy body and cannot achieve free flight. All of the breeding species in this family, except the Flightless Steamer Duck, also breed in southern South America. There is no firm evidence that Falkland breeding wildfowl migrate though continental populations of many species move north in winter.

65. Coscoroba Swan   *Coscoroba coscoroba*   Plate 8

A. Ganso blanco

c. Cisne coscoroba

Gigantic. 36–45in/90–114cm

IDENTIFICATION: A small swan with a duck-like bright pink-red bill, it is separated from the Black-necked Swan (66) by its all white neck, smaller size and black tips to the six outer flight feathers. *Adult male and female* are almost identical; legs and feet pink. *Immature* is generally marked with brown-grey. Becomes airborne more easily than the Black-necked and has relatively longer wings. When swimming, needs careful observation to distinguish from the white feral Domestic Goose (71).

Has a loud musical trumpeting call, *cos′-cor-oba*, uttered when disturbed and from which the name was derived.

STATUS & RECORDS: Status uncertain; probably bred in the nineteenth century; only one breeding record, of a pair and three small cygnets at Mare Harbour on 1 May 1860 (Abbott 1861). Abbott also remarked that he had seen this species only at Mare Harbour, where there were usually eight to ten birds. Wace (1921) considered it a frequent visitor while Bennett (1926) classed it as a rare visitor. Cawkell & Hamilton (1961) had reports of a pair near Fitzroy in 1953 and in 1951 an adult and immature spent three months in winter on floodwater near Stanley. A small flock (< 10) near Cape Dolphin in 1959 (Woods 1975) and a single bird at North Arm before 1986 are the most recent records. It has occurred at ponds and along shorelines but there have been no breeding records since the Breeding Birds Survey started in 1984.

DISTRIBUTION ABROAD: Southern South America from Tierra del Fuego, where it is much less common than the Black-necked Swan, to 45°S in Chile and through Argentina to southeastern Brazil, Uruguay and southern Paraguay (25°S). Southern populations migrate northward after breeding though it is considered a permanent resident in the Magellanic region (Venegas & Jory 1979).

66. Black-necked Swan   *Cygnus melancoryphus*   Plate 8

A. & c. Cisne cuello negro

Gigantic. 39–49in/99–124cm

IDENTIFICATION: The largest freshwater bird breeding in the Falklands, recognised by its great size and all white plumage, except for a black neck and head, with a white streak running back above the eye. Bill blue-grey with a large red knob at the base which is larger on the male than the female; legs and feet pink. *Immature* has grey flecks on the head and the white plumage is generally edged and spotted with grey; the bill has no red knob. Usually very wary of humans; may fly or swim to the centre of a pond when approached within ½km (¼ mile) and therefore rarely seen closely.

VOICE: Has a loud, plaintive whinnying call, *whee-her-her-her* and the male also utters a musical *hooee-hoo-hoo*.

FOOD: Takes mainly aquatic plant material from shallow waters in ponds, creeks and estuaries.

HABITAT, STATUS & BREEDING: Uncommon resident breeding species, probably more numerous in Lafonia, but also found on Pebble Island and on large ponds or lakes in West Falkland. Flocks gather in favoured estuaries during winter, particularly Swan Inlet, Lafonia and the River Murrell estuary near Stanley. There may be some interchange with the population of the Magellanic region of South America. Breeds between early August and mid-September, building a large nest of twigs and grass on an islet in a pond or near a lake; four to seven cream-coloured eggs are laid.

DISTRIBUTION ABROAD: Occurs from 30°S in Chile, southeastern Brazil, Paraguay, Uruguay and Argentina to Tierra del Fuego. Most breed in the southern part of this range; there is some northward migration after breeding.

67. Ashy-headed Goose   *Chloephaga poliocephala*   Plate 9
A. Cauquén cabecigris
C. Canquén
Local names: Coast/White-breasted Brant
Medium-large. 22–24in/55–61cm

IDENTIFICATION: Similar to Ruddy-headed (68); distinguished by grey head and neck with a white eye-ring, chestnut breast and mantle sometimes showing narrow dark bars, black and white barred flanks and white belly. *Adult male* and *female* are alike. Bill black; legs orange behind, black in front; feet orange and black. In flight shows black rump and tail, grey back, white forewing and secondaries divided by a broad metallic green bar (speculum) on the secondary coverts and a black outer wing. *Immature* duller, red-brown on breast with more noticeable dark bars and dark brown secondary coverts.

VOICE: Probably similar to the Ruddy-headed but no observations are available from the Falklands. In Tierra del Fuego, Humphrey (1970) noted a 'thin wheezy widgeon-like whistle' uttered by a male with its head thrown back.

FOOD: No records from the Falklands; probably grazes on grasses and takes berries.

HABITAT, STATUS & BREEDING: Rare breeding species and possible migrant from South America. Wace (1921) noted that many reached the Falklands in August 1920. Usually seen singly with Ruddy-headed or Upland Geese on short grass and may be overlooked. Cawkell and Hamilton (1961) noted breeding at two localities on West Falkland and on New Island in 1953. A pair with goslings were seen by R Cockwell at Port Howard in 1968 (Wolsey 1986c) and there was a possible breeding record from Crooked Inlet in 1985 (D Donnelly pers. comm.). Nest-sites and season are probably similar to Ruddy-headed Goose.

DISTRIBUTION ABROAD: Southern Chile and Argentina from about 37°S to Tierra del Fuego. Apparently much less numerous than Ruddy-headed and Upland Geese; occurs on andean grassland, in open woodland and on coastal islands. Migratory in the south and present in Tierra del Fuego from early September to April.

68. Ruddy-headed Goose   *Chloephaga rubidiceps*   Plate 9
A. Cauquén colorado
c. Canquén colorada
Local names: Brent, Brant
Medium-large. 20–22in/51–56cm

IDENTIFICATION: Resembles female Upland Goose (69) but much smaller; separated by sharp demarcation between rich chestnut upper neck and finely barred black and grey lower neck. *Male and female* alike though male larger. Head usually rich ruddy with paler forehead and narrow white eye-ring; some are much lighter but colour change on neck still obvious. Mantle, lower neck, breast and flanks closely barred black on grey, darkening to chestnut or deep buff on breast; lower belly and under tail-coverts clear rich chestnut, noticeable when swimming. Back grey-brown with narrow light edges. Bill black; legs and feet bright orange with variable black spots, much brighter than female Upland. Individuals with variable white on belly are seen occasionally. Wing pattern in flight as Upland and Ashy-headed. *Immature* duller than adult with black speculum. Usually seen in pairs, though flocks of flightless birds undergoing wing moult are seen between December and January.

VOICE: Male and female differ; female has very low, rasping guttural quack used singly in flight, or repeated on the ground when in confrontations with other pairs or Upland geese; male uses a short, musical *toonk* either singly or with rising pitch when repeated: also has double whistle *reeoo-woo* and a rapid vibratory low note in displays.

FOOD: Grazes on short grass and low plants throughout the year, takes berries of pigvine in autumn and winter and may eat green algae on shores when the ground is snow-covered (Summers & Grieve 1982).

HABITAT, STATUS & BREEDING: Resident, fairly common but less numerous than Upland Goose; apparently more restricted to coastal slopes. Nests from late September to early November, laying five to eight slightly shiny creamy-buff eggs in a grass nest lined with down; nest-sites may be well hidden in long grass or rushes, in an old Magellanic Penguin burrow, on top of a tussac grass clump or quite exposed amongst low diddle-dee. The female alone incubates while the male 'waits off', often at a considerable distance from the nest. He will return rapidly, however, if the female is flushed. When with small goslings, the male will perform a 'broken-wing' display and call loudly while the female leads the goslings to safety.

DISTRIBUTION ABROAD: Lowland grassland in extreme southern South America from 52°S to Tierra del Fuego. It is migratory in Tierra del Fuego, arriving in

September and leaving northward in April to winter in southern Buenos Aires province of Argentina. Formerly abundant but now becoming rare, possibly due to excessive shooting; the Falkland Islands are thought to hold the majority of this species' world population. There is no evidence of interchange between mainland and Falkland populations, though this is possible.

69. Upland Goose   *Chloephaga picta*   Plate 9
A. Cauquén común
C. Caiquén
Very large. 28–30in/71–76cm

IDENTIFICATION: Large, unusually tame goose of open grassland, familiar to all Falkland Islanders. *Male* looks mainly white from a distance; long black legs with noticeable white-feathered tibia distinguish it from male Kelp Goose (70). Head, neck and underparts white, barred black on flanks and mantle; back grey-brown and rump white; tail varies from all black to black with white outer feathers. *Female* has rusty-brown head and neck, merging into barred black and brown breast; flanks heavily barred black and white; back grey-brown; rump, under tail-coverts and tail black. Both male and female have a black bill; female has dark yellow legs. *Immature male* has grey shading on head and neck, black bars extending onto neck and sometimes barring on breast. *Immature female* duller than adult with yellow-brown legs. In flight, wing pattern is similar to Ashy-headed and Ruddy-headed (67 & 68); female separated from female Kelp Goose by black tail and from Ruddy-headed by larger size and dark under tail-coverts; male differs from all-white adult male Kelp Goose by black primaries and black/green speculum. Occurs in pairs or small groups loosely associated; immature birds and failed breeders flock near ponds and cannot fly for about a month between late November and early January due to wing moult.

VOICE: Very vocal when defending feeding or nesting territory; male has a weak whistling call *wheep* used when taking flight and the female has a low rattling *a-rrr* used in flight or on the ground. In displays, when pairs face up to each other, the male's call becomes a loud breathy multiple-toned whistling like a poorly played flute that rises in pitch and is repeated frequently; the female utters a loud vibratory, lower-pitched *crr-crroo* or a shorter *choonk-choonk*.

FOOD: Grazes mainly on short green grass; also takes grass seeds, including tussac grass and various berries especially diddle-dee. May graze on filamentous green algae on shorelines when ground is snow-covered.

HABITAT, STATUS & BREEDING: Resident, numerous and widely distributed, it is most common in coastal areas, especially on greens at settlements, around ponds and by creeks. The Upland Goose has been persecuted for nearly three centuries since it was a valuable source of food for early settlers and, later, around 1900 was blamed by sheep farmers for the decline in numbers of sheep. It has remained numerous due to the low human population, the inefficiency of culling, and, more recently, through the growth of enlightened attitudes towards a bird that can co-exist with sheep. Recent studies by the Grassland Trials Unit (now Agricultural Research Centre) in Stanley have been mentioned in the Introduction. Summers and Dunnet (1984) felt that Upland and Ruddy-headed Geese should perhaps be regarded as a tolerable nuisance and that farmers should site reseeded grassland areas away from ponds and green valleys. Upland Geese are still a good alternative source of food and fresh-laid eggs are enjoyed by many local people. Nests between early August and late November with the main laying season in October; lays five to eight large cream-coloured eggs in a grass nest amongst ferns, diddle-dee or white grass, or on a tussac grass clump up to 1½m (5 feet) above ground. The female incubates while the male 'waits off' at a distance. Both parents defend their young vigorously but many small goslings are taken by Kelp Gulls and Skuas.

DISTRIBUTION ABROAD: The Falkland Upland Goose *C. p. leucoptera* is larger than the race *C. p. picta* of southern South America which is found from Tierra del Fuego to about 38°S in Chile and Argentina. Males of this smaller continental race have two colour phases. The males of one phase, sometimes described as a distinct race *C. p. dispar*, have the underparts heavily barred black and white, from lower neck to belly. Males of the other phase are pure white beneath except for heavy black barring on the flanks. Barred '*dispar*' birds are apparently more common in the south of the range. Olrog (1979) noted the occurrence of birds of intermediate plumage. Some migrate northward from Tierra del Fuego and reach 35°S in Argentina; others stay in Tierra del Fuego through the winter. Harradine (1976) noted occasional occurrence of the continental race in the Falklands but there are no dated records. Wace (1921) felt that the Falkland race was semi-migratory and Mödinger (1986) stated that the white-breasted Falkland race was scarce at some localities in Tierra del Fuego and southern Patagonia, but no further information is available.

70. Kelp Goose *Chloephaga hybrida*   Plate 9
A. Cauquén caranca
C. Caranca
Large to very large. 26–29in/66–74cm
IDENTIFICATION: *Adult male* has completely white plumage, stout bright yellow legs and feet and black bill with a pink patch on the culmen. The most conspicuous bird of rocky shores, it can be confused at a distance with a Snowy Sheathbill (125) but is much larger with slower movements, or with the male feral Domestic Goose (71) which lacks the distinctive yellow legs and black bill. *Adult female* is smaller, differently coloured and easily overlooked; head dark brown with light brown cap and white eye-ring; back dark brown; neck, breast and flanks heavily barred black and white; rump, belly, under tail-coverts and tail white. Bill pink and legs bright yellow. *Juvenile male* has sooty black head and neck, white forehead, lores and eye-stripe, mainly black back, dark brown secondary coverts and primaries and variable black bars on neck and flanks. Dark feathers are lost gradually; by September *first year male* has only dark secondary coverts and primaries. Most dark flight feathers are lost by the following March though some two-year old males retain a few. *Juvenile and immature female* resemble adult, but lack the light brown cap; they have dark upper tail-coverts at first and dull yellowish bills. Immature male and female both have dull greenish-yellow legs.

Pairs remain together throughout the year and family groups are maintained until at least mid-winter. Loose flocks of up to 100 occur in late winter and spring, when much chasing and displaying take place. Birds in these groups after late October are probably non-breeders. Adults moult flight feathers in December and apparently become flightless temporarily but they are normally reluctant to fly far. Flight appears laboured and is usually close to the surface; female has similar wing-pattern to the other Falkland geese; separated from female Upland by the white tail. Almost indifferent to intruders and prefers to walk away; pairs with goslings take to the sea.

VOICE: Male and female have completely different calls; pre-flight and flight call of the male is a thin, repeated weak whistle; that of the female is a loud resonant honking. In territorial disputes and when pairing, the male uses a wheezing note and rapid repetitions of the thin whistling. The female utters repeated honking calls, higher-pitched than the flight call and a distinctive hooting *ooer* or *ooeroo*.

FOOD: Feeds largely on bright green papery 'Sea Lettuce' (*Ulva* sp.) and a Red Alga (*Porphyra* sp.) which grow in the intertidal zone of rocky beaches. In autumn, will eat ripe diddle-dee berries and sometimes grazes on short grass.

HABITAT, STATUS & BREEDING: Resident, common and widely distributed around the Falklands, mainly on rocky coasts and shingle beaches. Visits nearby fresh-water ponds for bathing and drinking. Nests between late October and early November, laying four to six, sometimes seven eggs of a light buff colour in a rough grass nest, well lined with down when the clutch is complete. Nests are near the shore, sheltered amongst tussac grass or rushes, sometimes on a low cliff ledge. The female incubates while the male stands guard close by. Immature males pair at one year but probably do not breed until at least two years old. Pairs breeding on Kidney Island appear to leave breeding territories between late March and mid-April and make a short migration to the more sheltered inlets of Stanley harbour for the winter, returning in September and October. A single colour-ringed female, marked in Stanley harbour in May 1957, was found breeding on Kidney Island in three out of the following five summers; each winter she was seen on dates between 1 March and 17 September along a 1.6km (1 mile) length of the southern shore of the harbour.

DISTRIBUTION ABROAD: The race *Ch. h. malvinarum* is confined to the Falklands, though Olrog (1979) stated that it occurred in autumn on the eastern coast of Tierra del Fuego. A smaller race, *Ch. h. hybrida* is abundant on coasts and islands of southern Chile from 42°S to Tierra del Fuego and less common on the coast of Argentina to about 50°S. It is resident in the Magellanic region, though some disperse northwards as far as 33°S in Chile and 39°S in Argentina.

71. Feral Domestic Goose *Anser anser* Plate 21

A. & C. Ganso

Very large. c30–32in/c74–81cm

IDENTIFICATION: At close range, obviously a 'Domestic Goose', with thick neck, heavy broad-based orange or orange-pink bill and more or less protruding paunch between the thick orange-pink legs. *Male* either pure white or white with variable grey-brown streaks on sides of the neck, back and flanks; *female* has white head with variable grey-brown streaks on side of neck, white breast, belly and under tail with sharply outlined grey-brown flank patch; back grey-brown with whitish edges to feathers forming narrow cross bars; tail white with narrow central dark brown band, noticeable in flight; wings very variable, may have all white primaries and grey-brown secondaries *or* all white secondaries *or* all dark wings above and below except for some white on outer two primaries. Some have all dark grey-brown heads and necks; on others, white is restricted to a variable patch bordering the bill.

When swimming, all white birds distinguished from Coscoroba Swan (65) by thick neck and horizontal or slightly uptilted carriage of head with heavy triangular bill. In poor light, birds with brown head and neck are distinguished from Black-necked Swan (66) by smaller size and thick straight neck. Distinguished from male Kelp Goose (70) by the heavy orange-pink bill and legs.

The population on West Point Island is more wary and difficult to approach than the native Upland and Ruddy-headed geese. Many will fly out over the sea and land about 200m (220yds) offshore before swimming back when the intruder has passed. A few with curly body and flight feathers (Sebastopol type) cannot fly. Those on Carcass Island are tamer and tend to walk away from an intruder.

VOICE: Has a variety of cackling and honking calls including a conversational *cuk-cuk-cuk* and a loud resonant *arng-ung-ung*. Both are used as pre-flight calls; in flight, a higher-pitched honking call is used.

FOOD: Grazes on short grasses, including young shoots of tussac and is known to strip seeds of tussac on West Point Island.

HABITAT, STATUS & BREEDING: Resident; breeding at a few settlements. Domestic geese were probably introduced early this century. A pair taken to West Point Island in 1935 from Johnson's Harbour laid eggs annually which failed to hatch. In 1944 a pair of the curly-feathered 'Sebastopol' breed were imported to West Point from Montevideo, Uruguay. These successfully hatched eggs in 1944. Interbreeding with the original pair occurred and by 1955 numbers had increased to about 50. The population remained stable for ten years, then increased, reaching over 130 by October 1983 when they were occupying lower coastal slopes on the eastern side of the island. Fifty-seven pure white, 68 brown/white smooth-feathered, three white Sebastopol and four brown/white Sebastopol birds were counted. The smooth-feathered birds appeared to be of the West of England type which were taken to America by the Pilgrim Fathers in 1620. Feral Domestic geese appeared on Carcass Island in the late 1950s, probably after being blown from West Point. They have survived and in 1983 at least 30 were present. R Napier reported that Weddell Island, Dunbar, Roy Cove, Hill Cove and Chartres settlements all had some feral geese. About ten birds bred at Sea Lion Island and others were reported in 1984 from Beaver Island and by Gipsy Cove near Stanley.

Nests from late September and lays up to at least nine large buff eggs in a grass nest, on top of a tussac clump hidden by overhanging leaves, on the ground sheltered in grass, or in dense low gorse. On Carcass in October 1983, four occupied nests were within 2m (6 feet) of each other in a circular gorse patch of about 25sq.m (30sq.yds). The first goslings were seen on Carcass 28 October with down that was either golden-yellow with a brown saddle across the back, or white with dark brown markings; bill and legs orangey-yellow.

DISTRIBUTION ABROAD: Wild geese of several species have been domesticated for at least 4000 years. It is thought that the European Greylag Goose *Anser anser* was the original species but probable that others have been captured and domesticated over the ages. They have been transported to many countries from their original places of domestication in Eurasia.

72. Crested Duck   *Lophonetta specularioides*   Plate 9
A. Pato crestón
C. Pato juarjual
Local name: Grey Duck
Medium-large. 20–24in/51–61cm

IDENTIFICATION: Easily recognised by its generally brown and buff mottled underparts and mantle, pale whitish neck and cheeks and dark brown patch encircling the eye, extending from crown to nape and ending in a short ragged crest. Appears long-bodied due to the black under tail-coverts and long, pointed black tail, usually held at an upward angle. *Male and female* are similar though male slightly larger and more brightly coloured. Bill mainly black, with some yellow near the base; iris varies from bright crimson to brick-red; legs and feet dark grey. *Juvenile and immature* birds resemble adults but have brownish necks and shorter tails. In flight appears uniform dark brown above and paler below, showing black rump and tail with a conspicuous white bar across the secondaries, bordered in front by black glossed with purple. Occurs in small parties, pairs and flocks of up to 80. Aggressive and territorial, it will attack others of its own and different species.

VOICE: A fairly noisy bird, especially when pairing in spring. Male and female have different calls; male uses a short buzzing *shweeoo* as a territorial call and during displays, also a repeated dry rattling call uttered when the displaying male is swimming backwards with tail raised and head up-stretched. He suddenly dips the bill down before shooting the head up high, with the crest protruding. Female uses a low barking *grruf* and, when feeding, a low nasal *quek-quek-quek*. In displays uses a harsh, guttural *querk-quak-quak* with the head thrown up, or utters a series of short rapid quacks.

FOOD: Feeds mainly by sieving liquid mud, also by upending in shallow water; takes small marine invertebrates including lice, shrimps and small bivalves.

HABITAT, STATUS & BREEDING: Resident, common and widespread in sheltered coves and creeks and on ponds near the sea. Often bathes and drinks where streams flow onto beaches. Territories may be held throughout the year; R Reid found that 1300m (1400 yards) of coastline on George Island held eight pairs in August 1961 (Woods 1975). The breeding season is extended; eggs or very small ducklings have been seen in every month between July and May, but the main breeding season is September to November; it is often double-brooded. The nest, sometimes close to water but often well inland, is lined with down amongst grass, tussac, diddle-dee or fern and is made of these materials. Five to seven cream coloured eggs are laid, though clutches of nine and 11 are known.

DISTRIBUTION ABROAD: Two races occur in separate parts of South America; *L. s. specularioides* (the Falkland race) is resident in the Andes from 36°S (Chile) and

38°S (Argentina) to Tierra del Fuego. It also occurs in coastal regions of Chile and Argentina from about 42°S to the Magellanic region; in winter ranges north to 37°S on the coast of Argentina. A larger race *L. s. alticola* occupies high andean regions of Peru, Bolivia, Chile (to 35°S) and Argentina (to 38°S).

73. Falkland Flightless Steamer Duck   *Tachyeres brachydactyla*   Plate 9
A. Pato vapor malvinero
Local names: Loggerhead, Logger
Large to very large. 24–30in/61–76cm
IDENTIFICATION: A large mottled grey duck with a long bulky body, rounded brown and white, or grey and white head, a heavy orange or yellow bill, a broad broken white bar across the back and a short spiky tail. The Logger is very common and is familiar to all local people with its large size, pugnacious behaviour and loud calls. *Adult male* has an almost white head with light grey cheeks, bright orange bill with black nail, orange-yellow legs and feet with dark grey webs; breast, flanks, back and rump dark grey with scaly light grey mottling on the back and red-brown on breast; belly and undertail white; wings dark grey with white secondaries that usually show as a prominent bar when swimming. *Adult female* smaller than male; head dark brown-grey with white eye-ring and white streak running back, fading down side of neck; indistinct diffuse glossy yellow ring at base of neck; bill greenish-yellow. *First-year male* resembles female but has heavier bill and prominent white head streak; with increasing age, the head lightens on crown and nape first and red-grey on the cheeks is retained for several years. General appearance very similar to Flying Steamer Duck (74); distinguished by bulkier body, heavier bill and tips of folded wings only reaching to the top of the rump.

Ducklings in down are earth-brown with a noticeable grey collar across the upper back, a black bill and a usually continuous broad white patch from behind the eye to the sides of the neck.

Incapable of sustained flight but makes full use of its disproportionately short wings for propulsion across the surface of water. In territorial chases, or when escaping from danger, it 'steams' rapidly over the water often for 50m (55 yards) or more, kicking up a great deal of spray with the combined effects of rapid wing-beats and strong paddling with its large feet. The whole body may lift clear briefly in very strong headwinds. Sometimes attacks intruding Kelp Gulls by submerging gradually, swimming underwater and suddenly surfacing by the gull. Immature birds have favourite loitering areas in coastal kelp patches; flocks of up to 200 occur in harbours and engage in communal diving. Freshwater ponds are used in the evenings, apparently for communal bathing and drinking and pairs are found at stream outlets onto beaches. Pairs with small ducklings will roost on beaches just above high water mark.

VOICE: A noisy bird, often heard calling in defence of territory by day or night. Male uses a loud explosive, descending and sometimes vibratory *cheeroo*, repeated regularly about once a second; a rapid repeated *kek-kek-kek* and a short low hooting note are probably alarm calls. Female utters a low creaking or grating note with the head thrown up vertically, in territorial disputes; a higher-pitched *crek-crek-crek* is also used.

FOOD: Takes marine invertebrates, including mussels, limpets, crabs and shrimps. Also takes offal occasionally and some pairs will grow accustomed to eating whole maize, as fed to domestic fowls. Obtains most food by upending in shallow water, or diving for up to 30 seconds at a time in deep water.

HABITAT, STATUS & BREEDING: Endemic resident, very common and widespread around coasts of the Falklands, especially where large offshore kelp beds occur in sheltered harbours and creeks. Pairs defend their coastline territory strip throughout the year against adjacent pairs and other species. Almost always on salt water in daylight, occasionally on coastal ponds. Ranges regularly to the outer edge of kelp beds and has been seen up to 5km (3 miles) offshore. Nests in short grass, diddle-dee, dry kelp or tussac grass or in old Magellanic Penguin burrows from a few metres above high water mark to about 400m ($\frac{1}{4}$ mile) inland. The nest is a depression scantily filled with grasses and lined with down in which five to eight, occasionally ten or 11 large cream-coloured eggs are laid between mid-September and December, though nests with eggs are known from all months. The female alone incubates while the male waits offshore, patrolling their territory. Mortality among newly hatched ducklings is high due to predation by Kelp Gulls and Antarctic Skuas, but full-grown birds have no predators except, occasionally, Sea Lions.

DISTRIBUTION ABROAD: *T. brachydactyla* is confined to the Falklands. A similar but larger flightless Steamer Duck *T. pteneres* inhabits the coasts of southern Chile from 37°S to Tierra del Fuego and north to about 46°S on the coast of Argentina. A recently described species, the White-headed Flightless Steamer Duck *T. leucocephalus* is restricted to the coast of Chubut province, southeastern Argentina (Humphrey & Thompson 1981).

74. Flying Steamer Duck *Tachyeres patachonicus*   Plate 9
A. Pato vapor volador
C. Quetru volador
Local name: Canvasback
Medium-large to large. 23–28in/58–71cm

IDENTIFICATION: Very similar to the Logger (73) in general coloration and easily mistaken for that species. Separated by its more slender build, much less heavy bill and longer wings which reach to the base of the tail when folded. *Male* larger than female; has a grey head with a white stripe behind each eye and a reddish brown throat patch; bill orange-yellow, bluish around nostrils; legs yellow, shorter and more slender than those of the Logger. *Immature male* has red-brown forehead, cheeks and throat and a yellow bill. *Female* very similar to female Logger but bill yellowish with blue cutting edge and a very small black nail. In flight is easily distinguished from other flying ducks by its heavy build and generally dark grey upperparts with clear white belly and large white wingpatch on secondaries. Much more shy than the Logger. Flies well but seems reluctant to take to the air and will land again within a few hundred metres. Will 'steam' across water like a Logger though the body often lifts clear of the surface and the wings barely touch, therefore producing much less spray.

VOICE: No published records of calls available.

FOOD: No records from Falklands available but in the Magellanic region apparently takes fewer bivalves and more crustaceans, such as prawns and crabs, than the local flightless species.

HABITAT, STATUS & BREEDING: Breeding resident occurring in coastal regions and on freshwater ponds; population size unknown due to much confusion with Logger but it appears to be uncommon. The status of this species in the Falklands needs clarification. Nests from October, possibly earlier, laying five to eight buff eggs, much smaller than those of the Logger. Nest-sites similar to the Logger; recent records (J Hutchings, Carcass Island) of nests in a small gorse bush about 3m (10 feet) diameter and in a large rush patch, up to 350m (400 yards) from the sea. Sitting females exploded from both nests when disturbed by a dog and flew out into the harbour; eggs were chipping in one nest on 5 November.

DISTRIBUTION ABROAD: Inhabits inland lakes, rivers and coastal waters of southern South America from 37°S in Chile and about 44°S on the coast of Argentina to Tierra del Fuego. Also found inland in Argentina to about 38°S.

75. Mallard *Anas platyrhynchos*   Not illustrated
A. & C. Not recorded
Medium-large to large. 20–26in/50–66cm
IDENTIFICATION: *Male* in breeding plumage easily identified by bottle-green head, white ring round neck and ruddy-brown breast; back and underparts pale grey; white band in front of black under tail-coverts, black upper tail-coverts and white tail with two central black feathers that curl upwards. Bill greenish-yellow, legs and feet orange-red. *Male in eclipse* after breeding, resembles female but has darker crown and breast, more yellow bill and generally heavier build. *Female* dull mottled brown and blackish above with paler head and neck, dark crown and streak through each eye; underparts paler; tail whitish; bill dull orange with blackish ridge and tip. *Immature* resembles female but is duller with underparts more streaked. In flight, recognised at all ages by bright blue speculum on secondaries, edged both sides with white.

STATUS & RECORDS: Introduced to East Falkland in the 1930s and said to be breeding in very small numbers (Cawkell & Hamilton 1961). Although the 1953 Bird Protection Ordinance listed it as a protected species there are no recent records of feral Mallard. Some domesticated ducks seen in Stanley in 1983 showed evidence of Mallard ancestry.

DISTRIBUTION ABROAD: Very common throughout the northern hemisphere and well-known because of its adaptability to almost any shallow aquatic environment with fringing vegetation and by its readiness to take artificially supplied food. Has hybridised with several other species of duck, producing a great variety of plumage forms.

76. Spectacled Duck *Anas specularis*   Not illustrated
A. Pato anteojo
C. Pato anteojillo
Medium to medium-large. 18–22in/46–55cm

IDENTIFICATION: Similar in size to the Chiloe Wigeon (78), this freshwater duck is recognised by its blackish-brown head and back, a prominent large white oval in front of the eye and a clear white foreneck extending onto sides of the neck. Underparts light brown with heavy black spotting on the flanks. Wings mainly black with metallic bronze speculum and white tips to secondaries; rump and tail grey-brown; underwing dark except for white axillaries. Bill dark slaty grey; legs and feet orange. *Male and female* are alike, though male is slightly larger. *Immature* is similar to adult but has little white on face.

STATUS & RECORDS: Vagrant, recorded once on 24 January 1979; a pair were seen on a freshwater lagoon at Bleaker Island by R Stranek (Nores & Yzurieta 1981).

DISTRIBUTION ABROAD: Inhabits rivers, streams and mountain lakes, mainly in wooded areas of Chile and Argentina from about 37°S to Tierra del Fuego. Some migrate north to about 30°S in winter but it is a permanent resident, though uncommon, in the Magellanic region.

77. Speckled/Yellow-billed Teal *Anas flavirostris* Plate 10
A. Pato barcino
C. Pato jergón chico
Local names: Teal, Duck
Small-medium. 15–16in/38–41cm

IDENTIFICATION: The smallest duck breeding in the Falklands, it is recognised by its dark brown upperparts, speckled and streaked with buff, buff underparts speckled and mottled black, a darker brown head with blackish streak through the eye and a bright yellow bill with black ridge. *Male and female* are alike, though male is larger. Legs and feet blue-grey. Swims with a characteristic down-at-the-front attitude; noticeably more tame than other ducks; gregarious, rarely seen singly. Sometimes seen in flocks of at least 200 in winter. In flight recognised by dark appearance with no marked head pattern and black and green speculum narrowly bordered with buff in front and white behind.

VOICE: Male has a short musical trilling call, often heard from flocks. The female has a high-pitched quacking.

FOOD: Takes minute aquatic animals, including insects and their larvae, fish eggs and small crustaceans. Feeds by straining surface water and in dives lasting about five seconds. It also eats berries of diddle-dee and pigvine.

HABITAT, STATUS & BREEDING: Resident, common and widespread, found throughout the Falklands on fresh water from the smallest peaty ponds to large lagoons. In winter it may be found in sheltered bays and creeks. Nests from mid-August onwards, often rearing two broods; ducklings have been seen as late as April. Lays five to eight reddish-cream eggs in a well-hidden grass nest near water or up to 1.6km (1 mile) from a pond.

DISTRIBUTION ABROAD: Four races inhabit South America. *A. f. altipetens* and *A. f. andium* occur in Andes of Venezuela, Colombia and Ecuador. *A. f. oxyptera* is found in andean regions of southern Peru and northern Chile and Argentina to about 30°S. The Falkland race *A. f. flavirostris* is widespread in southern South America from 30°S to Tierra del Fuego. Most southern birds migrate northward from April towards Uruguay, Paraguay and southeastern Brazil and return during August; some remain in Tierra del Fuego in winter. A small population of about 50 birds was found in 1971 at Cumberland East Bay, South Georgia (Prince & Payne 1979).

78. Chiloe Wigeon *Anas sibilatrix* Plate 10

A. Pato overo
c. Pato real
Local names: Black & White Wigeon, Wigeon
Medium to medium-large. 19–21in/48–53cm
IDENTIFICATION: At a distance, appears very dark above, with black head and neck, apart from white forehead and front of the face and white patch on the ear-coverts. Underparts also appear dark, except for a white rear. *Male and female* are alike though male is larger and often brighter. The head has variable green sheen behind the eyes, the bill is blue-grey tipped black and the feet are black. Breast finely barred black and white; remainder of underparts white with variable orange patch on flanks; back and scapulars black, streaked with white. In flight is easily identified by a large white crescent on each forewing contrasting with dark flight feathers, white front to head, white rump and black tail. *Immature* has much less white on the face. Usually seen in pairs or small groups, alone or with teal, and sometimes in flocks of up to 40 in winter. Compare with Spectacled Duck (76).

VOICE: The male has a distinctive whinnying alarm call *hoo-wee-ee-oo* also used in courtship and a rapid chattering whistle. Female uses a repeated high-pitched *quek-quek-quek* in flight. A soft whistling *huweet* has also been noted. It often calls when feeding at night.

FOOD: Few records available but it appears to feed mainly on freshwater plants in ponds and has been recorded grazing on short grass.

HABITAT, STATUS & BREEDING: Resident, widely distributed on larger ponds and lakes; nowhere very common but locally numerous in parts of Lafonia. Also occurs in coastal kelp patches and on green pasture near shores. Nests from September to December, laying five to eight white eggs in a well-hidden grass nest often a long way from the nearest water. It may sometimes be double-brooded.

DISTRIBUTION ABROAD: Common in Chile from 40°S and in Argentina from 34°S to Tierra del Fuego; less common north to 28°S in Chile. Some southern breeding birds migrate north in winter (April to September) and reach Paraguay, Uruguay and southeastern Brazil, while others remain in Tierra del Fuego. Vagrants have been identified twice at South Georgia, in January 1972 and winter 1974 and at the South Orkney Islands in 1966 (Prince & Payne 1979).

79. White-cheeked Pintail *Anas bahamensis* Not illustrated

A. & C. Pato gargantillo
Medium to medium-large. 18–21in/46–50cm
IDENTIFICATION: Larger than the Silver Teal (81), which has a similar head pattern, this species has white cheeks and throat contrasting sharply with dark brown forehead, crown and hindneck. Underparts and back light red-brown spotted with

black, particularly noticeable on the flanks. Rump black; under and upper tail-coverts and long pointed tail pale buffy white. Bill blue with a red spot near the base; legs and feet grey. *Male and female* similar, though female is paler with a shorter tail. In flight distinguished by long buff tail, blackish back, rump and wings with green speculum broadly bordered either side with buff.

STATUS & RECORDS: Vagrant from South America; one specimen was obtained before 1860 by Captain Pack (Abbott 1861). There are no recent records.

DISTRIBUTION ABROAD: Three races have been described from South America, occurring in Venezuela and the Guianas, southern and eastern Brazil, Paraguay and Uruguay to Argentina (40°S). The race *A. b. rubrirostris*, recorded in the Falklands, also occurs in central Chile occasionally and has been seen at least once in Tierra del Fuego.

80. Yellow-billed Pintail   *Anas georgica*   Plate 10
A. Pato maicero
C. Pato jergón grande
Local names: Grey Teal, Coast Teal
Medium to medium-large. 19–21in/48–53cm

IDENTIFICATION: Similar to the Speckled Teal (77) but larger; paler above with a noticeably longer, slender neck and round head. *Male* has head and neck nearly uniform light brown with dark red-brown crown; back dark brown well streaked with buff; breast more rufous, spotted with dark brown. The pointed light brown tail is not noticeable at a distance. Bill fairly long, deep yellow with a black central stripe and blue-grey tip; legs and feet dark grey. *Female* similar but slightly smaller with paler bill and lighter neck. In flight, distinguished from Speckled Teal by larger size, light head, longer bill, grey-brown shoulder and whitish patch on belly. Wings above, brown with black speculum conspicuously bordered fore and aft with buff and, on the male, glossed with green. *Juvenile* has duller bill and greyer breast.

VOICE: Relatively silent compared with other Falkland ducks. The male has a short repeated whistle used in flight and the female has varied quacking notes.

FOOD: No records of food taken in the Falklands; probably feeds on shrimps and insect larvae by dabbling and upending.

HABITAT, STATUS & BREEDING: One of the least common Falkland ducks, it is found on freshwater ponds with emergent vegetation and frequents sheltered coastal waters in winter. It occurs in all suitable parts of the Falklands and is locally more common in Lafonia. Probably overlooked sometimes because it closely resembles the common Speckled Teal. Possibly migratory; Abbott (1861) stated that it was resident but all personal records are from the September to March period. Nests between September and December, laying seven to ten cream coloured eggs in a grass nest hidden amongst coarse grass or rushes.

DISTRIBUTION ABROAD: One of the commonest ducks in Argentina and Chile, the Falkland race *A. g. spinicauda* ranges from Tierra del Fuego through Chile to south-western Colombia and east of the Andes, to Bolivia, Paraguay and southeastern

Brazil. Migratory in the south of its range, arriving in Tierra del Fuego in August/September and leaving in March/April. The race *A. g. niceforoi* is rare in the Colombian Andes. A smaller, darker race, *A. g. georgica*, is endemic at South Georgia.

81. Silver Teal *Anas versicolor*   Plate 10
A. Pato capuchino
C. Pato capuchino austral
Local name: Pampa Teal
Medium. 17–18in/43–45cm

IDENTIFICATION: Wide dark brown cap extending below the eyes, contrasting pale cream cheeks and barred black and white flanks distinguish this small duck. *Male and female* are similar, though female is smaller and duller. Bill mainly pale blue with an orange basal patch. Breast buff spotted with brown; under tail-coverts, rump and tail finely barred black and white, appearing grey from a distance. Back and wings dark brown, streaked buff on scapulars; legs grey. In flight, shows grey-brown shoulder and broad glossy green speculum bordered fore and aft with white; underwing white with brown leading edge. A fairly shy duck, it occurs singly or in small groups with Speckled Teal and Chiloe Wigeon.

VOICE: Usual call, probably of the male, is a high-pitched whistle *weeoo*. A distinctive descending rattling call, from an adult suspected of having hidden ducklings, was possibly produced by the female.

FOOD: Feeds by upending or dabbling below the surface and takes clams and shrimps, probably also insect larvae (Weller 1972).

HABITAT, STATUS & BREEDING: Resident, found in small numbers on larger freshwater ponds with emergent vegetation, sometimes in flocks in winter. Little information on breeding is available; nesting probably occurs from October and up to at least five eggs are laid; adults apparently with small ducklings have been seen in late January.

DISTRIBUTION ABROAD: The Falkland race *A. v. fretensis* occurs in southern Chile from 42°S and Argentina from about 40°S to Tierra del Fuego; southern populations migrate north in winter. A smaller race *A. v. versicolor*, also migratory, occurs from central Chile and southeastern Brazil to northern Argentina.

82. Cinnamon Teal *Anas cyanoptera*   Plate 10
A. & C. Pato colorado
Local name: Red Teal
Medium. 16–19in/41–48cm

IDENTIFICATION: *Adult male* in full plumage is unmistakable; head, neck and underparts are a rich glossy chestnut, browner on the belly, with a black crown, blackish tail and black under tail-coverts; back blackish-brown with long buff stripes. Bill fairly long and black; iris yellow to orange; legs and feet yellowish. *Male in eclipse* plumage, assumed probably from December to February, resembles female. *Female* is mainly dark brown above, flecked with light brown; head and neck buff streaked brown, underparts light brown heavily mottled darker. Female and eclipse male are separated from Yellow-billed Pintail (80) by the black bill, yellow legs and dark under tail-coverts; from Speckled Teal (77) by the larger size and black bill. In flight, both sexes show black primaries, a pale blue forewing and a white line separating it from a glossy green (male) or blackish (female) speculum on the secondaries.

HABITAT, STATUS & BREEDING: Probably a rare resident breeding species, reputed to nest at Bull Point, Lafonia; possibly also at Speedwell Island, in Pond Flats camp east of Port San Carlos, on Sea Lion Island and Pebble Island. A pair were seen on Stanley Common in November 1979 and two males near Surf Bay through the 1981 winter (Peatfield 1981, Wolsey 1986c). Ten were seen on Saunders Island, 7 April 1987 by S Wolsey.

DISTRIBUTION ABROAD: Five races occur from western North America to southern South America. The Falkland race *A. c. cyanoptera* is found from southern Peru, through central Chile, Bolivia, Paraguay and southeastern Brazil to Argentina. It is an uncommon visitor to Tierra del Fuego.

83. Red Shoveler *Anas platalea* Plate 10
A. & C. Pato cuchara
Medium to medium-large. 18–21in/46–53cm

IDENTIFICATION: Huge spoonlike black bill, longer than the head, gives this duck a distinctive down-at-the-front carriage when swimming. *Male* has a greyish-buff head speckled with black, red-brown underparts heavily spotted with black, a white patch at the base of the tail and black under tail-coverts. Shoulders buff heavily blotched with black; back and rump mainly black streaked whitish; tail fairly long, dark in the centre with whitish sides. Iris pale yellow; legs and feet orange-yellow. *Female* is mainly dark brown streaked buff above and buff heavily mottled dark brown below. Iris brown; bill brownish-black; legs and feet dull yellow. *Male in eclipse* resembles the female. In flight resembles Cinnamon Teal (82) but appears long-necked and shows white on tail; male has blue forewing and a white bar above a glossy green speculum; female has greyish-blue forewing, a narrow white bar and blackish speculum.

STATUS & RECORDS: Vagrant from South America; undated record by Hamilton at Swan Pond, Cape Dolphin (Cawkell & Hamilton 1961); Bennett (1926) and Wace (1921) remarked that it was an accidental visitor and that specimens had been collected but no dated records were given. The only recent record is of one seen on Swan Pond, Seal Bay, East Falkland on 20 and 24 October 1985 (Wolsey 1986c).

DISTRIBUTION ABROAD: Inhabits lowland ponds, coastal lagoons and marshes with dense reedbeds from southern Peru, Bolivia, southeastern Brazil, Paraguay and Uruguay through southern Chile and most of Argentina to the Straits of Magellan; uncommon in Tierra del Fuego and migratory in northern and southern parts of its range.

84. Rosy-billed Pochard   *Netta peposaca*   Plate 10

A. Pato picazo

c. Pato negro

Medium to medium-large. 19–22in/48—55cm

IDENTIFICATION: A distinctive stocky duck with a bulbous knob at the base of the bill; *male* has a purple-glossed head and neck, black back, breast and tail with flanks and belly closely streaked grey; under tail-coverts white; bill and knob bright rosy red; legs and feet yellow; iris red. *Female* mainly reddish-brown, darker on crown; chin and throat, breast and belly whitish; under tail-coverts white; bill and smaller knob blue-grey; legs and feet yellowish-grey. In flight both male and female show a prominent white speculum tipped with black, with whitish streaks on primaries and dark forewing.

STATUS & RECORDS: Vagrant from South America; flock of about 30 seen in 1920 (Bennett 1926) from which five specimens were shot; a male was seen at Sedge Island and a pair on Carcass Island in September 1966 after a period of very strong westerly winds; one seen on Pebble Island in January 1981 and one at Sea Lion Island on 13 October 1981 (Wolsey 1986c).

DISTRIBUTION ABROAD: Found in marshy areas with small pools covered in water-weeds from about 28°–53°S in Chile, in Paraguay, Uruguay, southeastern Brazil and lowland Argentina to about 42°S. Migrates northward in winter from southern parts of its range.

85. Lake Duck   *Oxyura vittata*   Plate 10

A. Pato zambullidor chico

c. Pato rana de pico delgado

Small-medium. 15–16in/38–40cm

IDENTIFICATION: Belongs to a group known as 'Stiff-tails'; separated from other ducks by their small size, short neck and dumpy body with long tail often held nearly vertically. This species is the smaller of two found in the Americas. *Male breeding* has all black head and hindneck; bright blue bill; chestnut breast, flanks and back; mottled whitish and brown belly; dark brown wings and fan-shaped tail; red-brown iris, and grey legs and feet. *Male in winter and female* blackish-brown above with red-brown streaks; head has broad buff or white bar from bill to nape below eye, bordered by a dark line; whitish throat and foreneck; white underparts mottled brown; blackish bill, dark grey legs and feet.

The closely related Peruvian Ruddy Duck *Oxyura jamaicensis ferruginea* is larger with a broader bill; *male* has black head and upper neck and more extensive chestnut on breast. *Female* has dark crown and patch through eye, no clear facial bars and darker underparts. Stiff-tailed ducks swim buoyantly with tail either flat or vertical; they dive frequently and rarely fly; wingbeats are rapid and whirring.

STATUS & RECORDS: Vagrant from South America; several specimens collected from 'a number' observed in 1916–17 during a long period of drought in Argentina (Bennett 1926). There have been no recent records.

DISTRIBUTION ABROAD: The Lake Duck *O. vittata* is found on lowland ponds with thick vegetation from central Chile and northwestern Argentina (28°S) to about

52°S and breeds in small numbers in Tierra del Fuego. It winters north to southeastern Brazil, Paraguay and Uruguay. The Ruddy Duck *O. jamaicensis ferruginea* occurs in andean regions to Tierra del Fuego, where it is a breeding summer visitor; it is probably more likely to occur in the Falklands than the Lake Duck.

86. Black-headed Duck   *Heteronetta atricapilla*   Not illustrated
A. Pato cabeza negra
C. Pato rinconero
Small-medium. 14–16in/36–40cm
IDENTIFICATION: The adult male, female and immature plumages of this small short-tailed duck, the size of a Speckled Teal (77), are noticeably different. *Adult male* has glossy black head and neck, brownish-black back, wings and tail narrowly barred and speckled with red-brown; secondary coverts and secondaries have white tips, showing as two narrow bars in flight; underparts brown, closely mottled white on flanks and lower neck, appearing silvery from a distance. Bill blackish or blue-grey with pale red patch at base of upper mandible; legs and feet grey-brown. *Adult female* resembles male but head is mottled brown and whitish, darker on crown; the bill shows less red. *Immature* similar to female but is more red-brown above and has a distinct light eye-stripe. Female and immature can be confused with female Cinnamon Teal (82) but lack the blue shoulder and glossy speculum of that species.

STATUS & RECORDS: Vagrant, apparently recorded before 1917 as a rare visitor (Wace 1921), but not included in Bennett's (1926) list nor in Cawkell & Hamilton (1961). There have been no recent records.

DISTRIBUTION ABROAD: This is the only fully parasitic duck; it makes no nest but lays eggs in the nests of coots, Brown-hooded Gulls, Night-Herons and even ground-nesting birds of prey. It breeds in marshlands between about 20° and 40°S in Paraguay, southeastern Brazil, Uruguay, central Chile and northeastern Argentina. There is apparently some northward migration in winter to about 15°S.

Vultures   *Cathartidae*
The New World vultures are large, generally blackish soaring birds that usually feed on carrion. Most appear to locate food by sight, though Turkey Vultures can do so by smell. There are seven species in the family; five are known as vultures and two larger species as condors. They occur from islands south of Tierra del Fuego to southern Canada, with most species and largest numbers in the tropical and subtropical regions. Vultures are unusual in being silent except for low hissing or grunting noises. One species occurs widely in the Falkland Islands; there is also at least one unsubstantiated sighting of the Andean Condor Vultur gryphus.

Turkey Vulture

87. Turkey Vulture   *Cathartes aura*   Plate 11
A. Jote cabecirrojo
C. Jote de cabeza colorada
Local names: Turkey Buzzard, Turkey
Large. 26–28in/66–71cm

IDENTIFICATION: Easily recognised at a distance by the very broad, long wings, conspicuously 'fingered' at the tips, fairly long round-ended tail and small head. Plumage generally black-brown above and slightly glossy with buff edges to secondary flight feathers; black-brown body and under wing-coverts contrasting with pale grey underside of flight feathers. *Adult* has a bare bright red head and pale creamy, strongly hooked bill, and dull greyish-crimson legs and feet. *Juvenile* similar but the head is dull grey with a collar of whitish down briefly after fledging and the legs are brown. *Immature* gains red head slowly from one year old. Flies in a leisurely manner, flapping slowly or with wings held a little above body level and typically rocking slightly as it scans the ground. On the ground, looks bulky and has an ungainly waddling gait. Hunts singly or in small parties; many gather where food is plentiful and up to 90 have been seen at ponds where they bathe.

VOICE: The only Falkland bird with no calls except for low hissing noises produced by the young in the nest and, rarely, by adults.

FOOD: Usually takes carrion from carcasses of sheep, cattle, seals and birds and seal faeces. Reputed to maim fallen sheep by taking the eyes and ripping the belly; it probably only attacks very weak animals.

HABITAT, STATUS & BREEDING: Common resident occurring in most parts of the Falklands, though it is still being persecuted. Apparently absent from some islands, *eg* Beauchêne Island, where the pugnacious Striated Caracara may occupy a similar feeding niche.

Nests between early September and late November; the main season is mid-September to late October. It lays two, occasionally three white eggs which have variable red-brown spots and lines. The nest is a scrape on the ground beneath overhanging tussac grass or a rock, sometimes in a cave or an old shanty. Flying juveniles are seen from mid-January.

DISTRIBUTION ABROAD: Six races have been recognised, occurring between southern Canada and Tierra del Fuego. The Falkland race *C. a. falklandica* is found along the Pacific coast from Ecuador and Peru to southern Chile. A slightly larger and darker race *C. a. jota* occurs in the Andes from Ecuador and Peru through to southern Argentina. It is possible that this race occasionally crosses to the Falklands (Cawkell & Hamilton 1961).

Hawks & Eagles   *Accipitridae*
This family includes many broad-winged diurnal birds of
prey, ranging from the size of a Thrush to over 1m (39in)
in some eagles. They occupy all kinds of habitats and occur
throughout the world except in Antarctica. Some common
features are strongly curved and hooked bills with a bare

Red-backed Hawk

fleshy base (cere) in which the nostrils are situated, powerful feet with strong and sharp claws and the tendency for females to be larger than males. They hunt live prey in the air, on the ground or water, and take birds, mammals, insects or fish.

Fifty-seven species occur in South America, 41 of them in Argentina, but only three have been recorded in the Falklands. One is a widespread breeding species, another formerly bred and the third is a rare vagrant.

88. Sharp-shinned Hawk   *Accipiter striatus*   Plate 11
A. Esparvero chico
c. Not recorded
Small to small-medium. 10–14in/25–36cm

IDENTIFICATION: A small slender hawk, with short, rounded wings and a fairly long, white-tipped tail. *Adult* plumage is generally dark slaty grey or brown above and paler below. Underparts vary from reddish flecked with white to mainly chestnut brown or mainly white with rufous tibia feathers. The tail is dark brown with four or five broad blackish bars and a narrow white tip. Undersides of wings heavily barred brown on white. Bill dark with a pale cere; legs and feet bright yellow. *Immatures* are flecked with buff above and the underparts are white, heavily striped with buff or brown. Flies usually at low levels taking small birds by surprise as it twists and turns between trees.

STATUS & RECORDS: Vagrant recorded once; an immature was present in the Stanley area for about three weeks in May/June 1981. On one occasion it was seen to pursue and kill a House Sparrow (Peatfield 1981).

DISTRIBUTION ABROAD: About ten races are fairly common in woodland and scrubby regions in most of North America, Central America and northern South America. It also occurs in southern Brazil, Uruguay, Paraguay and northern Argentina to about 38°S.

89. Red-backed Hawk   *Buteo polyosoma*   Plate 11
A. & C. Aguilucho común
Local names: Hawk, Blue Hawk
Medium to medium-large. 18–22in/46–56cm

IDENTIFICATION: Distinguished from the Caracaras (91–93) by the short, square whitish tail with a broad subterminal black band, this large hawk has broad 'fingered' wings and a rounded head. It glides with wings held flat, moving steadily forward, but can swoop rapidly and often hovers, with wings slightly flexed and tail fanned, sometimes as high as 60m (200 feet) above ground. Male is smaller than the female. Both sexes have variable body plumage colours, but the *female* has a rich chestnut-brown mantle and back in all colour phases. All *adults* show a very pale tail which is white with fine grey bars, with a broad black subterminal bar and narrow white tip. *Light* individuals are white beneath with fine brown bars on flanks and undersides of wings; crown, nape and wing-coverts are dark brown with slate-brown flight feathers. *Dark* birds are generally red-brown below and slate-brown above, or slate-grey above and below; *light males* are slate-grey above and white below. *Juvenile* is mainly dark brown above, streaked and flecked with buff and mottled variably with chestnut on mantle and wing-coverts, often showing whitish patches on the nape and having a grey tail with many narrow blackish bars. *Immatures* are even more variable as they gradually acquire one of the light or dark adult plumage patterns. All adults have bright yellow legs and feet with black claws; the bill is blue-grey with a black tip and yellow-green cere. Nesting pairs can be very aggressive, swooping close to intruders with talons extended and calling loudly.

VOICE: Generally silent outside the breeding season, though sometimes calls when hunting. The call, most frequently heard from pairs near the nest, is a series of loud screams, *keeeeow-kyow-kyow-kyow* . . ., higher-pitched in the male.

FOOD: Takes small mammals and birds, including hares, rats, mice, rabbits, goslings and snipe. Sometimes feeds on carrion and may take domestic fowls.

HABITAT, STATUS & BREEDING: Resident breeding species that can be seen over most parts of the Falklands, it is not numerous and is usually seen singly. Nests on ledges of high crags are used annually and renovations with twigs of diddle-dee lead to large accumulations of material. Two to three almost elliptical whitish eggs, variably marked with red-brown are usually laid during October, sometimes in late September.

DISTRIBUTION ABROAD: Widely distributed in southern South America, particularly in andean regions, this species is found from central Colombia to Tierra del Fuego. It occurs in lowland areas of Argentina from about 32°S and, in winter, extends north into southeastern Brazil and Uruguay.

90. Cinereous Harrier   *Circus cinereus*   Plate 11
A. Gavilán ceniciento
C. Vari común
Medium. 16–20in/41–51cm
IDENTIFICATION: Long narrow wings, long tail, slender body and an owl-like head are characteristics of all Harriers. Their graceful flight is distinctive, flapping and gliding low over open ground, often turning and changing direction. *Female* is dark brown above, marked with buff or white on crown, nape and shoulders; rump white; tail grey with four broad dark bands; underparts brown on breast, barred red-brown and white on belly. *Male* is smaller, pearl-grey on head, neck and upperparts except for a white rump and a black subterminal bar on the tail; sides of the tail are white barred with black; underparts below neck like the female. Both sexes have black wingtips, conspicuously 'fingered', a collar of feathers around the face, long yellow legs, yellow iris and cere and blue-black bill. *Immatures* resemble the female but are darker above with a buff collar; underparts are whitish, heavily streaked with red-brown and the iris is reddish. Shape of the wings and tail and flight action are good distinguishing marks at long range and should separate males from the light phase male Red-backed Hawk (89).

VOICE: Generally silent outside the breeding season; when nesting, uses chattering and squealing notes, but there are no records in the Falklands.

FOOD: Takes small animals and birds from the ground or low bushes and sometimes feeds on carrion. Darwin noted in 1833 and 1834 that it fed on molluscs, insects and small quadrupeds; Abbott (1861) saw them swooping at rabbits.

HABITAT, STATUS & BREEDING: Former breeding species, probably lost through destruction of natural grassland and through shooting. It was stated to be extremely tame for a bird of prey and to follow people when they were hunting rabbits (Gould & Darwin 1841; Abbott 1861). Bennett (1926) classed it as an accidental visitor; Cawkell & Hamilton (1961) had one report in 35 years suggest-ing breeding and there have been a few sight records since 1961 (Woods 1975; Peatfield 1981). It is unlikely that this species breeds though not impossible.

DISTRIBUTION ABROAD: The Cinereous Harrier occurs in open grassland and marshy areas from Colombia and Peru through Chile and western Argentina to Tierra del Fuego. Southern populations are partly migratory though Fuegian birds remain through the year. It is considered by some authors to be a southern race of the Hen Harrier *Circus cyaneus* (Cramp & Simmons 1979).

Caracaras & Falcons   *Falconidae*
In many ways similar to the Hawks Accipitridae, *the family* Falconidae *contains about 60 species in four subfamilies. Two subfamilies are represented in the Falklands. The Caracaras* Daptriinae *include about nine large, long-legged and broad-winged birds of prey resembling buzzards, occurring mostly in tropical and subtropical America. They are omnivorous and often eat carrion, spend much time on the ground, can run rapidly and unlike true falcons, build their own nests. Two species are resident in the Falklands; the Crested Caracara or Carancho, is widespread and moderately common, the Striated Caracara or Johnny Rook, noted for its tameness and audacity, was very common until a century ago but is now mostly restricted to Beauchêne Island and offshore islands around West Falkland. A third species, common in South America, has occurred three times as a vagrant.*

True Falcons, subfamily Falconinae *have a worldwide distribution. They vary in body-length from 15cm to 60cm, have sharply pointed wings and are extremely agile and accomplished fliers, frequently killing other birds or insects in the air. One species, the Peregrine Falcon, is resident and fairly common in the Falklands where it often preys on Thin-billed Prions. The smaller American Kestrel has been observed several times but its status is uncertain; it is probably a vagrant but it may breed.*

91. Chimango Caracara   *Milvago chimago*   Plate 11
A. Chimango
C. Tiuque
Small-medium to medium. 15–17in/38–43cm
IDENTIFICATION: Much smaller than the two resident Caracaras (92 & 93), the Chimango is generally dull brown above, with a large whitish patch at the base of the darker primaries, a narrow white rump and a whitish tail marbled with

brown with a broad black subterminal band and white tip. The head is dull brown, darker on crown, sides and hindneck; underparts whitish on chin, belly and under tail-coverts, otherwise mottled red-brown and buff. Sexes are alike, except that *male* has blue-grey legs and *female* has dull yellow legs; both sexes have dull yellow bills. *Immature* birds are more rufous and often blotched whitish and tail markings are less distinct. Hudson (1920) described the flight as 'easy and loitering' and noted that 'they spend hours a day soaring like Martins'. He also remarked that it was 'loquacious and sociable, frequently congregating in parties of 30–40.'

STATUS & RECORDS: Vagrant, recorded two or three times; one dead bird found in Grave Cove camp about 1942 (R Napier pers. comm. and noted in Cawkell & Hamilton 1961); one at West Point Island in the 1950s (R Napier); another bird, probably this species, seen by G Stewart at Beaver Island in June 1960 (Woods 1975).

DISTRIBUTION ABROAD: Common in open country and some forested parts of southern South America, from Bolivia and southeastern Brazil through Uruguay, Argentina and central Chile to Tierra del Fuego. Two, possibly three races are recognised: *M. c. chimango* occupies most of the range to the central Magellanic region; a darker race, *M. c. temucoensis* is found in forest regions of southern Argentina and Chile from 37°S to northern Tierra del Fuego and migrates north to about 25°S; a larger race *M. c. fuegiensis* has been described from Tierra del Fuego (Goodall, Johnson & Philippi 1957).

92. Striated Caracara   *Phalcoboenus australis*   Plate 11
A. Matamico estriado or Matamico grande
c. Carancho negro
Local names: Johnny Rook or Jack Rook
Medium-large to large. 23–25in/58–63cm
IDENTIFICATION: Generally dark brown or black plumage, rounded head, small pale patch on the wings and an all brown or white-tipped tail, separate this species from the Crested Caracara (93). It is well known in the Falklands for its inquisitive nature and tameness. Female is a little larger than male, otherwise the sexes are alike.

Adult mainly black with a broad collar of fine white or buffish streaks on nape, mantle, sides of neck and throat, extending down the breast as small white spots; belly and front of tibia bright rufous-buff; tail black with broad white tip; wings above slightly shiny black with small pale buff patch on bases of inner primaries and small white tips. In flight overhead, shows mainly dark brown underside with elongated buff patches on central wing-coverts and in the centre of the belly. Bill blue-grey with orange cere and facial skin; legs and feet orange-yellow, claws black; iris brown.

First year immature is dark brown with streaked collar of buff-brown across mantle, fading on side of neck, sometimes streaked lightly on upper breast; tibia feathers dark brown; tail buffy-brown with dark brown sides to feathers and no bar; primaries and secondaries brown with darker edges; in flight shows a large triangular patch of buff-orange across inner half of primaries. Bill black with cream to pink cere and facial skin; legs and feet grey-white.

Second year immature distinguished by orange-yellow cere and gape, creamy-yellow legs and feet, lighter brown secondary coverts and a more extensive light buff collar, reaching further down mantle and just onto breast; tail as first year.

Third year immature is generally darker black-brown with a collar of narrow streaks on breast and heavier streaking on mantle; flanks lightly spotted buff, tibia dark brown with some red-buff tips on inner side, centre of belly has a buff-red patch and the tail is buff-brown with broad dark brown edges. Bill blue-grey at base, slaty towards tip; cere, gape and facial skin orange-yellow; legs bright yellow, feet orange-yellow.

In flight it appears much more agile than the Crested Caracara; on the ground it can run quickly but typically walks and examines the ground carefully. Where present, numbers are soon attracted by carrion; on West Point Island, a whole leg of beef put on a hillside drew about 25 birds away from the grass airstrip. Later, some fed within 5m (16 feet) of an observer. When gorged, the crop which is orange-yellow on adults and whitish on immatures, protrudes prominently from the neck feathers.

VOICE: Calls are variable; they include a wailing *waa-aow*, resembling the howling of a domestic cat, a strident *keee-ar*, a loud hoarse *kar* or *kaw* and very high-pitched strangulated shrieks. In courtship, the male utters a low guttural trill.

FOOD: Takes all kinds of carrion, including dead sheep and lambs and kills goslings. Groups of five or more have been seen to attack adult female Kelp and Upland Geese, immature Gentoo Penguin and Crested Duck. One Caracara flew from behind and knocked the bird over with its feet, before the others descended and started pecking (R Hutchings pers. comm.) It is reputed to kill lambs and to take the eyes and tongue from fallen sheep. On Beauchêne Island scavenges dead penguins and catches Wilson's Storm-Petrels, Diving Petrels and Fairy Prions at night. The young are mainly fed on Rockhopper Penguin chicks (Smith & Prince 1985).

HABITAT, STATUS & BREEDING: Resident, locally common on islands west of West Falkland, in the southern end of Falkland Sound, at Sea Lion Island and Beauchêne Island. Smaller numbers occur on coasts of West Falkland. Until at least the 1860s, this species was 'exceedingly numerous' (Darwin in 1833/4) or 'one of the commonest birds in East Falkland' (Abbott 1861). Ramsay (1913) stated that in 1903 it was quite familiar in the vicinity of Stanley. Cobb (1910) remarked that it 'has decreased in numbers in the Falkland Islands of late years,' and mentioned that it was 'on the list of birds for whose destruction a reward is offered, on account of damage done to sheep and lambs'. Cobb was writing when an Ordinance was enacted, classifying this species, the Crested Caracara and the Turkey Vulture as pests for which a bounty would be paid. Although the Striated Caracara was removed from the list in the 1920s, some unlawful killing continued for at least 40 years. This persecution led to extinction on East Falkland and near-extinction on West Falkland. In the past 20 years the population appears to have increased slightly.

The nest is built of twigs or grass on cliff-ledges, under large rock slabs or on the tops of tussac grass clumps. Two to three cream coloured eggs, heavily marked with dark red, are laid in late October or early November.

DISTRIBUTION ABROAD: The world distribution of this species is very restricted; apart from the Falklands, it is found only on islands south of the Beagle Channel and the southern coasts of Tierra del Fuego. The population in the Tierra del Fuego region is reputed to have declined seriously in recent years due to shooting.

93. Crested Caracara   *Caracara plancus*   Plate 11
A. Carancho
C. Traro
Local name: Carancho
Medium-large to large. 21–25in/50–63cm
IDENTIFICATION: Easily recognised when perched by its flat-headed appearance; the heavy black cap extends as a ragged crest at the nape and contrasts with pale cheeks and the very deep pale bill. In flight it is equally distinctive. Wings are long, broad and 'fingered', with a large whitish patch on primaries; they appear parallel-sided and show little backward curve; tail is long and square, whitish with a broad terminal black bar. Flying action is leisurely, with short butterfly-like flaps between glides when the wings are held flat or slightly down-bent and the long yellow legs droop slightly. *Adult male and female* alike; dark brown above and below with fine buff bars on back and breast and pale edges to flight feathers, uniform dark brown belly and feathered tibia; pale sandy buff sides of head, throat and under tail-coverts. Bill cream or yellowish with variable green tinge; cere and bare facial skin to eye varies from bright orange to dull pink, possibly a difference between the sexes. *Juveniles* are darker than adults and heavily streaked with buff above and below. Bill blue-grey or yellowish; facial skin varies from pale pink to dull crimson; legs dull yellow.

Crested Caracaras walk and run well on their long legs. Generally rather shy, though flocks of immatures (up to 25) in winter are inquisitive. Usually seen singly or in pairs. Often mobbed in flight or on the ground by South American Terns, Blackish Oystercatchers and Antarctic Skuas.

VOICE: Usual call, from which the name is derived, is a very harsh, loud *kruk*, uttered singly or repeated. When perched, the call may be given rapidly several times, suddenly followed by a loud purring sound uttered with the head laid back on the shoulders and followed by more *kruk* calls as the head returns to its normal position. In aerial courtship displays, when pairs swoop on each other, a shrill screaming *keeer* is used.

FOOD: Takes carrion of many kinds, including dead penguins, sheep and cattle and has been recorded eating a stranded octopus. Attacks fallen sheep and probably kills lambs. May carry food long distances; a resting ledge near a nest on Kidney Island, East Falkland had three legs of a hare on it in December 1960. The nearest population of hares was at least 800m ($\frac{1}{2}$ mile) away on the mainland.

HABITAT, STATUS & BREEDING: Resident, widespread around coasts and inland crags but not numerous. It is probable that the population of this species increased as sheep farming developed during the last quarter of the nineteenth century. Early writers on Falkland birds (Pernety 1771, Darwin in 1833/4, Abbott 1861) failed to mention the Crested Caracara. If it was present, this is strange because of its large size and distinctive appearance. Garnot (1826) used one of the early synonyms for this species, *Falco brasiliensis*, but his description of the bird's boldness matches the known behaviour of the Striated Caracara rather than the present species. Brooks (1917) noted that it was 'now uncommon as it is shot at every opportunity'; Bennett (1926) remarked that it was a resident but not common; Cawkell & Hamilton (1961) also stated that it was not common and 'wary, doubtless through persecution'. In southern Argentina and Tierra del Fuego, Darwin and others noted its presence and widespread distribution before 1840. Possibly it has never been common in the Falklands; the size, dark colour, fierce appearance and scavenging habits would all tend to make farmers see it as a menace to their livestock.

It builds a large nest of diddle-dee twigs, bones and grass lined with wool, on a cliff-ledge and adds to the structure annually; two or three brownish-red eggs, or cream blotched with dark red, are laid between late August and October.

DISTRIBUTION ABROAD: Widespread from Central America through South America to Tierra de Fuego. Three races have been described; the Falkland race *C. p. plancus* is larger and darker than the others and it occurs from south of the Amazon in Brazil through most of Chile and Argentina to Tierra del Fuego. The other two races *C. p. audubonii* and *C. p. cheriway* are found in Central America and northern South America respectively.

94. Peregrine Falcon   *Falco peregrinus*   Plate 11
A. & C. Halcón peregrino
Local names: Sparrow Hawk, Black Hawk
Small-medium to medium. 15–19in/38–48cm
IDENTIFICATION: Broad-based, sharply pointed and swept back wings, tapered tail and generally very dark plumage distinguish this fast-flying species from other Falkland birds of prey. *Female* noticeably larger and often darker than male. *Adult* dark slate-grey above with prominent sooty-black head extending to the cheeks like a helmet; throat red-buff, breast and undersides of wings and tail whitish or red-buff, heavily barred dark brown; eye-ring, cere and legs bright yellow, bill slaty-blue. *Immature* usually darker than adult and heavily streaked on breast and belly; cere and eye-ring bluish or greenish, legs blue-grey. Flies with quick shallow wingbeats and glides, sometimes hovers briefly and always looks powerful and agile. When hunting, stoops at great speed with wings half-closed, striking prey in the air; also chases birds in level flight.

VOICE: Calls infrequently outside the breeding season, occasionally uttering a sharp *kek*, sometimes repeated. In courtship flights uses harsh chattering notes, those of the male being higher-pitched.

FOOD: Usually kills birds in flight, ranging in size from House Sparrow to Upland Goose and commonly takes Thin-billed Prions near colonies. In recent years there have been at least seven reports of individuals killing prions and Wilson's Storm-Petrels up to 56km (35 miles) offshore during the autumn and using ships as feeding stations (Ross 1986, Wolsey 1986c). Bourne & Curtis (1987) noted that all records of this behaviour were in the period 16 March to 18 April, suggesting that the falcons were on migration.

HABITAT, STATUS & BREEDING: Resident, widespread and likely to be seen singly anywhere over the Falklands; pairs may be noisy and aggressive near nest-sites on coastal cliffs. Lays two to four heavily marked red-brown eggs, between late September and late October, in a scrape-nest or large hollow, usually on an inaccessible ledge. In the past it has been persecuted for reputed attacks on domestic fowls; the population appears to be stable at present and there has been no indication of a decline due to pesticide ingestion.

DISTRIBUTION ABROAD: This species occurs in most parts of the world. The Falkland race *F. p. cassini* inhabits southern South America from about 28°S in Chile and 42°S in Argentina to Tierra del Fuego. In winter, continental populations range north as far as southern Colombia and Uruguay.

95. American Kestrel   *Falco sparverius*   Plate 11
A. Halconcito común
c. Cernícalo
Small. 9–11in/23–28cm

IDENTIFICATION: Much smaller than Peregrine Falcon (94) and about the size of a Thrush, it is recognised by the variegated pattern on head and face and chestnut back and tail. *Adult male* has a chestnut back lightly barred black; chestnut tail with subterminal black bar and white edge; inner half of wing blue-grey marked with black, outer half blackish. Underside of wing whitish with fine black spots. Head grey on crown with a central chestnut spot, white cheeks with double black vertical bar and buff sides of neck with a black spot in the centre. Underparts whitish to buff spotted black on breast and flanks. *Adult female* has similar head markings, though crown is streaked black and the back and inner half of wings and tail are chestnut barred with black. *Juvenile male* resembles adult but head markings are less bright and breast is streaked black, not spotted. *Juvenile female* is not easily separated from adult female. Both sexes and all ages have yellow eye-ring, cere and feet, brighter in adults and a bluish-grey bill. Flight is buoyant, graceful and rapid; it often hovers to sight prey on ground or stands on high perches. Calls frequently, a loud, shrill *killy killy killy*.

STATUS & RECORDS: Vagrant or very rare breeding species; status uncertain. Not recorded by early writers but there are three nineteenth century specimens from the Falklands in the British Museum. There have been at least ten records this century from West Falkland, West Point Island and the vicinity of Stanley. One bird spent most of 1924 around Stanley (Bennett 1926), two birds were present in the Stanley area from March to about July 1980 (Peatfield 1981). Few records have the month or season recorded. No adults with juveniles have been seen and only one record involved two birds. Cawkell and Hamilton (1961) stated that the suspected breeding place was the northeastern corner of West Falkland. It appears likely that records are of vagrants that had survived for varying periods rather than residents; the possibility of breeding, perhaps in Port Howard camp, needs investigation.

DISTRIBUTION ABROAD: Widespread and common in the Americas from the arctic tree line to Tierra del Fuego in open country and urban habitats, though absent from northern and eastern Brazil. About 16 races that vary in size and depth of colour have been recognised. The birds recorded in the Falklands were presumed to be of the race *F. s. cinnamominus*, which is found from southeastern Peru and Bolivia, Paraguay, Uruguay and extreme southeastern Brazil through Chile and Argentina to Tierra del Fuego.

Rails and Coots   *Rallidae*

Rails are small to medium-large, ground-dwelling birds of swamps or open water. They are well adapted to living in dense aquatic vegetation having laterally compressed bodies, fairly long legs and toes and soft plumage. They have short, rounded wings and some species migrate long distances; others have lost the power of flight since colonising remote oceanic islands. Rails walk with bobbing heads and flirting tails. Many are very secretive and little known. Coots are a distinct genus, more adapted to life on open water with dense waterside vegetation, where they dive for food.

About 130 species in 18 genera are distributed in all continents and many islands from the Arctic to the sub-Antarctic. Forty-four species are known from South America, 25 have been recorded in Argentina and five (or six) species have occurred as vagrants in the Falklands where there is no current evidence of breeding.

96. Plumbeous Rail   *Rallus sanguinolentus*   Not illustrated
A. Gallineta común

c. Pidén

Small-medium. 14–16in/36–40cm

IDENTIFICATION: A secretive, long-legged, brown marsh bird with a long ($2\frac{1}{2}$in/55–69mm) dull green and slightly downcurved bill. Plumage is greenish-brown above with a dark slate-grey crown, dark brown wings, a short tail and slate-grey underparts. Legs and feet are red or dull green; iris red.

STATUS & RECORDS: Vagrant, apparently recorded once according to Olrog (1959), de Schaunsee (1970), Daciuk (1975) and Blake (1979) but the date and place of sighting is not stated.

DISTRIBUTION ABROAD: Inhabits South America from Peru and southeastern Brazil through most of Argentina to Tierra del Fuego and islands near Cape Horn. Occurs in humid marshes and around lakes where it is difficult to observe due to its skulking habits. On islands south of Tierra del Fuego, Reynolds (1935) described it as common along beaches, particularly in dense woody growths of the shrub *Hebe elliptica*, known as 'Box' in the Falklands. Breeds in Tierra del Fuego and migrates north in winter; little is known of its movements.

97. Speckled Crake   *Coturnicops notata*   Plate 12
A. Burrito menor

c. Not recorded

Tiny. $5\frac{1}{2}$in/13–14cm

IDENTIFICATION: Rotund, short-tailed and very secretive; blackish-brown above, spotted with white; head heavily spotted, throat and breast mottled white and black, flanks barred white. Short bill, legs and feet greenish-black; iris red. Male and female similar.

STATUS & RECORDS: Vagrant; a bird, thought to be this species, was caught alive on the banks of a small stream near Stanley 25 April 1921 (Bennett 1926). It died but the skin was not kept, therefore identification has not been confirmed.

DISTRIBUTION ABROAD: Only 16 specimens of this very secretive species are known from tropical and subtropical South America (Blake 1979). It apparently has a patchy distribution in the north (Colombia, Venezuela and Guyana) and southeast (Paraguay, Uruguay, southeastern Brazil and southeastern Argentina), where it inhabits dense, low vegetation in marshes and cultivated fields.

98. American Purple Gallinule *Porphyrula martinica* Plate 12
A. Polla de agua azul
c. Tagüita purpúrea
Small to small-medium. 10–14in/26–36cm
IDENTIFICATION: *Adult*: iridescent dark blue head, neck and underparts; back tail and wings above brownish green; whole undertail white; bill red, yellow tipped, frontal shield pale blue; iris brown. *Immature*: greenish-brown above; head, neck and flanks buff-brown, most of belly and whole undertail white; bill dull grey-green, frontal shield grey. In flight, long neck, short tail with conspicuous white underside, long, dangling yellow or greenish legs and rapidly beating rounded wings are noticeable features at all ages. Rarely strays far from cover but flies readily and usually utters a loud cackling *kek kek kek* on flying.

STATUS & RECORDS: Vagrant, recorded three times: 23 September 1934, one long-dead near Mile Pond, Stanley Common (Bennett 1935); mid-June 1960, a first-year bird caught by a cat at Port Louis (Woods 1975); February 1983, a dead immature bird found by Lord Buxton near Stanley was identified at the British Museum.

DISTRIBUTION ABROAD: Breeds in tropical and subtropical South America and southeastern states of the USA; winters south to Buenos Aires province of Argentina. Usually found in aquatic habitats such as pools, freshwater marshes and slow-moving streams. Highly migratory; many long distance records of vagrants, at South Georgia and the islands of Tristan da Cunha, Ascension and St Helena.

99. Red-gartered Coot *Fulica armillata* Plate 12
A. Gallareta piquirroja
c. Tagua común
Medium. 16–21in/41–53cm
IDENTIFICATION: Largest of the three Coots recorded which all have sooty or velvet-black heads and fairly long necks, with slate-black bodies and wings. It is distinguished by a bright red 'garter' on the leg above the ankle joint, sometimes visible when swimming. Frontal shield oval, yellow or red with yellow border; bill yellow with red patches at base. In flight, the black wings have a barely visible narrow white outer edge to the outer primary and small white patches under the tail. *Immature* birds have pale grey underparts and duller, less well developed frontal shields.

STATUS & RECORDS: Uncertain, probably a vagrant; Cawkell & Hamilton (1961) felt that it may breed but there is no evidence. It has occurred at least five times: a male caught near Stanley 23 May 1923 (Bennett 1926); one seen near Stanley in the 1940s; one shot of three seen near Calm Head, Port Stephens in early 1951; one shot near Stanley 4 May 1953 (Cawkell & Hamilton 1961). One adult was shot near Stanley on 14 December 1960. The stomach of this specimen contained about 30% green plant material including grass pieces about 5mm (¼in) long and about 70% sand and minute fragments of mollusc shells (Woods 1975).

DISTRIBUTION ABROAD: Common on large pools and open lakes in southern South America from Paraguay, southeastern Brazil (20°S), Uruguay, Argentina and Chile (30°S) to Tierra del Fuego, but does not occur in the high Andes. Apparently a partial migrant from southern parts of its range though some remain on salt-water lagoons in Tierra del Fuego throughout the year.

100. White-winged Coot *Fulica leucoptera* Plate 12
A. Gallareta frentiamarilla
C. Tagua chica
Small-medium to medium. 14–17in/35–43cm

IDENTIFICATION: Smallest of the three Coots; bill lemon-yellow to ivory-white; large, round-topped frontal shield bright yellow or orange. In flight shows a faint white line along leading edge and a narrow white band on tips of secondaries; mainly white under tail.

STATUS & RECORDS: Vagrant; has occurred two or three times. One, probably this species, at Goose Green late February to early March 1960 (M Shaw in Woods 1975); one rather worn bird on a pond at Sea Lion Island seen by S da Prato from 1–6 September 1983 and one, in good condition, seen on a pond at Carcass Island by R and J Hutchings and R Woods, 30–31 October 1983 (Wolsey 1986c). This bird fed by upending in the pond and by grazing short waterside vegetation.

DISTRIBUTION ABROAD: Breeds from eastern Bolivia, southeastern Brazil, Paraguay and Uruguay throughout Chile (18°–55°S) and all Argentina (23°–53°S) from saline waters by the coasts to high andean lakes. It is resident and common in Tierra del Fuego on lakes and marshes, including temporary wetlands and sometimes grazes well away from water.

101. Red-fronted Coot *Fulica rufifrons* Plate 12
A. Gallareta frentirroja
C. Tagua de frente roja
Small-medium to medium. 15–19in/38–48cm

IDENTIFICATION: Intermediate in size between Red-gartered Coot (99) and White-winged Coot (100). Frontal shield long and narrow, pointed at the top and all red; bill yellow with blood-red base. In flight shows all black wings and white undertail with black centre.

STATUS & RECORDS: Uncertain, probably a vagrant; Wace (1921) stated that it had bred in the Falklands but was very scarce and possibly extinct. Abbott (1861) recorded a coot, 'probably *F. chloropoides*' shot in Stanley harbour in 1859. Wace mentioned this record under *F. rufifrons* and noted that a specimen was obtained by the British Antarctic Expedition (1839–43). Bennett (1926) thought that it may have bred and stated that several were seen in 1915 and one was shot in October of that year. Another was kept alive in Stanley in November 1924. There are no recent records.

DISTRIBUTION ABROAD: Found in Paraguay (rarely), coastal Uruguay, Argentina (30°–54°S), Chile (25°–40°S) southeastern Brazil (20°–24°S) but does not inhabit high andean lakes. In eastern Argentina, favours dense or partly open marshland with shallow or deep water and will graze on nearby slopes (Weller 1967). Has occurred only once in Tierra del Fuego. Probably migratory in southern parts of its range.

Oystercatchers   *Haematopodidae*
Oystercatchers are a distinctive small group of black and white or black waders, with long red bills specially adapted for opening shellfish and probing sand. They fly rapidly with shallow wingbeats. Their piercing calls are used frequently in flight and are often heard at night. Eleven species inhabit the coasts of most continents except tropical Africa, southern Asia and the coldest regions. Three species occur in South America and two are resident in the Falklands.

102. Blackish Oystercatcher   *Haematopus ater*   Plate 13
A. Ostrero negro
c. Pilpilén negro
Local name: Black Curlew
Medium. 19–20in/48–50cm
IDENTIFICATION: Larger than the Magellanic (103) but is easily overlooked on rocky beaches because the dark plumage gives it excellent camouflage. *Adults* are sooty-black on head, neck and underparts and dark brown above; the long and heavy bill is red, the iris yellow with a red eye-ring; legs and feet are pale pink and appear incongruously thick. *Immatures* dark brown, flecked with buff above; bill is blackish, streaked with orange and legs and feet are grey. In flight, the all dark plumage, long bill and long wings with quick shallow wingbeats make it easily recognised. Usually seen in pairs or small parties, though sometimes associates with Magellanic Oystercatchers in winter flocks. In the breeding season is often active at dusk and can be heard calling until well after dark; antagonistic behaviour towards both Striated and Crested Caracaras has been observed when adults have small chicks. Adults usually walk away quietly if someone approaches a nest but will stand nearby and call loudly if the person remains near the eggs. Injury-feigning has been seen when chicks were present.

VOICE: The flight-note is a loud clear *keep* or *keeup* with an abrupt ending, quite different from the Magellanic's usual call. Produces rapid, ear-piercing vibratory whistles in aerial courtship displays and on the ground.

FOOD: Limpets and mussels form the main part of the diet. Limpets are removed from rocks by a sharp jab of the bill and a quick levering movement without breaking the shell. Mussels are wedged into rock crevices before being opened.

HABITAT, STATUS & BREEDING: Resident, well distributed around all Falkland coasts, it is possibly more numerous on the eastern side of East Falkland. It is thought to be less common than the Magellanic Oystercatcher. Found most frequently on rocky beaches; also occurs on sandy beaches, in bays where mussels abound, and small parties of mostly immature birds congregate in sheltered creeks in winter. Pairs seem to remain in or near breeding territories throughout the year.

The breeding season starts later than that of the Magellanic species. Two, sometimes only one, grey-buff or buff eggs spotted and streaked below and on the surface with yellow-brown and purple-brown, are laid from late October. Eggs have been found as late as 27 January; these were probably replacements for a lost clutch. The nest is a scrape on sand or is on bedrock, often containing a few small shells or fragments of dead kelp. It is usually sited close to the shore, though nests have been found on a rock stack 10m (35 feet) above sea level and on a shingle bank over 91m (100 yards) from a sandy shore.

DISTRIBUTION ABROAD: *H. ater* has an exceptionally wide latitudinal distribution being resident on the western coast of South America from 7°S in Peru along the whole Chilean coast to the Magellanic islands and Cape Horn. It is also resident on the coast of Argentina from Tierra del Fuego and Staten Island to about 43°S and occurs as far north as the mouth of the River Plate in winter. The breeding birds of the Magellanic region migrate north and east to the continent of South America in winter.

A hybrid between this species and the Magellanic Oystercatcher was obtained in 1973 at 49°S on the estuary at San Julián, Argentina (Jehl 1978). This locality is near the northern limit for *H. leucopodus*, where hybrids between *H. ater* and the American Oystercatcher *H. palliatus* are not infrequent and all three species occur together. No hybrids between *H. ater* and *H. leucopodus* have been reported in the Falklands.

103. Magellanic Oystercatcher   *Haematopus leucopodus*   Plate 13
A. Ostrero del Sur
c. Pilpilén austral
Local names: Black & White Curlew; Pied Oystercatcher
Medium. 17–18in/43–46cm

IDENTIFICATION: A conspicuous bird of sand-beaches and creeks, this oystercatcher is handsomely pied with shiny black head, breast and back and white belly. The long, bright orange-red bill, striking orange-yellow iris and yellow eye-ring contrast sharply with the stout pink legs and feet. In flight it shows a distinctive triangular white patch on the inner half of the wing and a white tail with a broad black outer half. *Male and female* are indistinguishable by colour but the female is slightly larger, particularly in the length of the bill. *Immatures* are similarly patterned but have buff flecks on the black feathers and a dull orange bill with a black tip.

Flocks of up to 100 gather between January and August, sometimes with Blackish Oystercatchers (102). When nesting, antagonistic behaviour is shown towards other species of birds and people; birds with eggs in the nest will fly at an intruder but will attempt to draw attention from chicks by creeping away, feigning injury and calling plaintively.

VOICE: The most frequent call, used in flight or on the ground, is a long-drawn, plaintive whistle *peeeeee*, often wavering and rising in tone towards the end and noticeably higher in pitch than the Blackish Oystercatcher. Birds calling together in flocks produce a peculiarly discordant sound because one sex uses slightly higher notes than the other. Particularly noisy early in the breeding season when pairs display with bills lowered and tails raised high and fanned while they produce a series of whistles, rising in pitch and speed.

FOOD: Takes marine worms from the intertidal zone of sand-beaches and small crustaceans, limpets and mussels from rocky beaches. Limpets are taken by breaking a small section from the edge then levering the shell from the rock.

HABITAT, STATUS & BREEDING: Resident, common and widely spread around coasts, particularly where sand-beaches are backed by low grassy slopes. It is apparently more numerous than the Blackish Oystercatcher, though this impression may be due to its conspicuous colouring and habit of flocking. It visits freshwater ponds in winter, apparently for roosting.

Nesting occurs about a month earlier than in the Blackish Oystercatcher; the main laying season is from late September to late October, with early clutches from the second week of September and late clutches through to mid-December. Two dark olive-brown or greenish eggs, heavily marked with black blotches, are normally laid in a scrape on sand, short turf or dead kelp. Nests may be partly sheltered amongst diddle-dee or sand-cabbage plants, from high water mark to at least 91 m (100 yards) inland.

DISTRIBUTION ABROAD: *H. leucopodus* is common in the Magellanic region of southern South America. It occurs on beaches, inland lagoons and sometimes in meadows and semi-desert areas from Chiloe Island (42°S) and occasionally Valdivia (40°S) in Chile to Cape Horn, through Tierra del Fuego and Staten Island to Chubut (43°S) in Argentina.

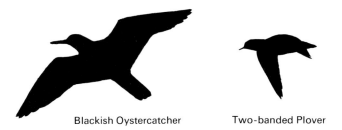

Blackish Oystercatcher   Two-banded Plover

Plovers   *Charadriidae*
Plovers are small to medium sized, round-headed birds with large eyes and shortish bills, that live on shores or open ground. They run and fly swiftly. The family comprises about 65 species that occur in most parts of the world. Twenty-four species in the genus Vanellus, *known as lapwings, are mainly tropical. The 37 plovers in the genus* Charadrius *include birds that occupy a great variety of habitats from the Arctic to tropical deserts. The remaining species differ in several ways from the* Charadrius *group. Most are classified in single-species genera.*

Of the 17 species in this family known in South America, 13 are resident and four are wintering migrants from the Northern Hemisphere. Fourteen occur in Argentina, of which nine species breed. The two Falkland breeding Charadrius *species show distinctive dark and light head patterns which become dull in winter. The larger Southern Lapwing is a vagrant, with very conspicuous black and white plumage and loud calls. The fourth species, Tawny-throated Dotterel, is a rare vagrant to the Falklands.*

104. Southern Lapwing   *Vanellus chilensis*   Plate 14
A. Tero común
c. Queltehue
Local name: Teru
Small-medium. 13–14in/33–36cm

IDENTIFICATION: Larger than the two resident plovers, the Southern Lapwing is easily recognised by its striking black, white and grey plumage and its loud, penetrating cry. *Adult* has dark grey head, with wispy black crest at nape, and a narrow black patch from forehead and base of bill runs down the centre of the neck to join an extensive black area on the breast; thin vertical white line in front of eye to side of bill; belly and under tail-coverts white; back brown-grey with bronzy patch on scapulars. Bill is dark red with a black tip; legs fairly long, dark crimson; eye and eye-ring crimson. Each wing has a sharp red spur at the carpal joint, sometimes visible when flying.

In flight it has a very striking appearance, showing shiny black outer wing, diagonal white and grey patch on secondary coverts, white rump and tail with broad black subterminal bar and narrow white tip. Underwing pattern is also distinctive; black flight feathers and breast contrast with all white under wing-coverts and belly. Flying action deliberate with slow beats of its broad rounded wings, holding them downcurved and raising them little above horizontal at each stroke. *Juvenile* duller than adult, brown rather than black with buff edges to feathers. *Immature* has paler primaries, yellowish bill and no crest. A wary and noisy bird that calls when flushed, a loud harsh, almost nasal *parp-peup-peup-peup*.

STATUS & RECORDS: Vagrant, most likely to be seen around settlements during spring and autumn migration periods. Occurs irregularly; at least 11 records since Abbott shot the first near Stanley in 1860. Dated records are in March (two) and September/October (three); two records of three together in 1953 at San Carlos and Walker Creek (Cawkell & Hamilton 1961). One survived at least a fortnight around Stanley in September/October 1962. The most recent records are of one at West Point Island on 10–11 October 1983 (Wolsey 1986c) and one at Stanley golf course from 5 February to early March 1987 (Wolsey 1987a).

DISTRIBUTION ABROAD: Widespread in open country through much of South America east of the Andes and in Chile and Argentina from about 20°S to Tierra del Fuego. Four races have been described; *V. c. chilensis* is common in most of Argentina. *V. c. fretensis*, which breeds from about 45°S to Tierra del Fuego, is slightly smaller but otherwise almost identical. Falkland vagrants are probably from this southern population, which reaches Tierra del Fuego in late August and migrates northward in late March and April.

105. Two-banded Plover *Charadrius falklandicus* Plate 13
A. Chorlitejo doble collar
C. Chorlo de doble collar
Local names: Plover, Two-barred Plover
Very small. 7–7½in/18–19cm

IDENTIFICATION: Smaller than the Rufous-chested Dotterel (106), this plump brown, white and black plover is typical of Falkland sand-beaches. It is usually quite tame and often prefers to run rather than fly when disturbed. *Adult male in breeding* plumage is light grey-brown above with pure white forehead, lores and underparts, a broad black crescent on the breast and a narrow, sometimes incomplete black bar across the neck. A black line crosses the front of the crown, passes through the eyes and meets the neck band, separating white foreneck from bright chestnut hindneck and nape; top of head brown. *Adult female breeding* has lighter chestnut only at sides of nape and less extensive black bands, otherwise resembles male. In *non-breeding* plumage, between late summer and autumn, both male and female have duller brown bars on head and breast and lose most of the chestnut on head. *Juvenile* resembles non-breeding adult; the brown breast and neck bands are lighter and the upperparts are flecked with buff. Adult plumage is attained the following summer. Bill and legs black.

In flight shows a faint white bar across the primaries and a dark tail with white sides, similar to Rufous-chested Dotterel but easily separated from White-rumped Sandpiper (119). Flocks gather at sand-beaches from mid-December onwards; maximum numbers recorded in January of about 150 at Surf Bay near Stanley. Flocks as large as 50 can easily be overlooked on a beach when resting or during periods of strong winds, as they sit quietly in the lee of small boulders, piles of dead kelp or sand hummocks above high water mark.

VOICE: Frequent call-notes are a liquid *prink* or *prit* used as flight-notes and a thin squeaky *tseet* when running. A low harsh *chut* and an explosive tittering *prrrit* are uttered mostly by males chasing each other within flocks. When an intruder is near eggs or small young, a very low buzzing note is uttered during injury-feigning display by the female, and sometimes the male, as the adult creeps away with wings spread and bent forward and tail fanned and depressed.

FOOD: Feeds on small invertebrates picked from the surf edge, heaps of rotted kelp or short grass and sand areas. Also feeds and bathes around freshwater pools behind beaches, at mussel beds covered with seaweed and at rock pools.

HABITAT, STATUS & BREEDING: Resident, locally common around coasts and islands at sand-beaches and muddy creeks, often accompanied by White-rumped Sandpipers during summer. Between September and December, it occurs on dry slopes of short grass and diddle-dee, up to 1.6km (1 mile) from the shore. Nests between late September and mid-January, though later clutches after November are probably replacements. The nest is a scrape sometimes lined with wisps of grass, in short grass, diddle-dee or ferns and often on a small hummock. Some pairs nest on beaches between dry heaps of kelp. Lays two to three, occasionally four greenish or buff eggs, blotched and spotted with brown mostly at the larger end. A colour-ringing study on the Cape Pembroke peninsula and at Lake Point south of Stanley between 1957 and 1959, showed close attachment to one area throughout the year. Examination of trapped birds also showed that moult and replacement of flight feathers was prolonged and could be found on individuals between early December and early April (Woods 1975).

DISTRIBUTION ABROAD: Common in coastal regions of southern Chile and Argentina from about 35°S to northern Tierra del Fuego. Southern populations are strongly migratory, ranging north to about 22°S in Chile and to southeastern Brazil. However, some remain in the Magellanic region through the winter. There is no evidence that Falkland birds migrate to the continent. It is possible that they form a distinct race of the species.

106. Rufous-chested Dotterel   *Charadrius modestus*   Plate 13
A. Chorlo pechicolorado
c. Chorlo chileno
Local name: Dotterel
Small. 8–9in/20–23cm

IDENTIFICATION: Larger, taller and more wary than the Two-banded Plover (105), this handsome species is recognised by the broad white head stripe extending from the forehead to above and behind the eye. *Adult* in *breeding* plumage (mid-August to December) has blue-grey face and throat, bright chestnut breast with broad black band below; white flanks and belly except for a small orange patch behind the leg. Crown, nape and all upperparts darkish grey-brown with faint red-brown fringes on the back in fresh plumage. Bill black; legs grey-green. *Male and female* similar but female is slightly duller. *Juvenile* has no head stripe, is dark brown above with a scaly pattern of buff streaks and spots, and brown on the breast. Adults start moulting by mid-December into non-breeding plumage which is fully assumed by the end of March; head stripe is buff and all the neck and breast are brown. Some adults retain traces of the black breast band through winter. *Downy chicks* are golden-buff blotched with black above; a prominent cinnamon patch on the hindneck separates them from Two-banded Plover chicks.
    It has very rapid flight, shows broad white sides to the blackish tail and white shaft streaks on the outer primaries; the white head stripe is prominent in breeding birds. When nesting it is always alert and active, one of the pair often standing guard on a small mound uttering a distinctive plaintive call at intervals.

VOICE: Calls whenever flushed, uttering a loud and often tremulous whistle, *peeoo*. Has several variations on this call, including a rapid repetition and a longer version used by adults on guard near the nest. In courtship flight, one bird (probably male) flies with a slow-motion wing action and glides with wings raised up to 30m (100 feet) above the territory. It utters a low, regular *tik-tik-tik* alternating with a loud whirring and rattling call. The male also uses a loud wheezy *wheear* followed by the rattling call when he pursues the female or both chase other dotterels. Adults show anxiety by calling when chicks are disturbed but they have no injury-feigning distraction display like the Two-banded Plover.

FOOD: Appears to take insects, including burrowing larvae from grassland and probably feeds on small invertebrates from intertidal beaches and mudflats.

HABITAT, STATUS & BREEDING: Widespread and common breeding species that occurs in a variety of habitats from coastal mudflats, sand and boulder beaches and creeks to flooded grassland, eroded clay slopes and hard diddle-dee camp and to at least 200m (700 feet) above sea level. Often associates with Two-banded Plover on mudflats in spring and autumn. In late summer, flocks of up to 100 have been recorded on eroded ridges of clay and boulders; these were probably pre-migration gatherings, though some birds winter in the Falklands. Small parties have been recorded between April and July on grassland near the coast; they behave quietly, are in dull plumage and therefore not conspicuous, in sharp contrast to their behaviour during the breeding season. Abbott (1861) stated that all left by the end of April while Bennett (1926) and Cawkell and Hamilton (1961) stated that although most migrated, some remained through the winter. Flocks have been seen mounting high and heading westward from Stanley Common and West Point Island. Pettingill (1960) felt it unlikely that it regularly departed in autumn against the prevailing winds. It could be that more birds winter in the Falklands than was previously suspected and this deserves further study.

It breeds on drier slopes where white grass, diddle-dee and rushes are abundant, nesting between late September and mid-January with the main laying period in October; December clutches are probably replacements. The nest-site is merely a scrape sheltered by overhanging low vegetation. It lays only two olive-brown eggs, heavily blotched with black, though reddish eggs have been found.

DISTRIBUTION ABROAD: Widespread and common in the Magellanic region, Tierra del Fuego and adjacent islands; also breeds less commonly to about 42°S on the Chilean coast. After breeding some migrate to low ground between about 40°S and 27°S in Argentina, Chile and Uruguay, occasionally further north. In the Magellanic region, many remain through the winter and migrate locally from inland breeding areas to coastal habitats (Venegas & Jory 1979).

107. Tawny-throated Dotterel *Eudromias ruficollis*   Plate 14
A. Chorlo cabezón
c. Chorlo de campo
Small. 10–11in/25–28cm

IDENTIFICATION: A slim, tall plover with a thin bill as long as the head, it shows some resemblance to the Rufous-chested Dotterel (106) with orange neck and pale eye-stripes. *Male and female* similar: head blackish-grey on crown and nape; a narrow black bar extends from the bill through the noticeably large eye; a broad creamy stripe curves over the eye from forehead to nape; chin, throat and below eye also creamy. Below the orange neck, the breast is dark grey-brown fading to buff on belly, tinged reddish on flanks and with a distinctive circular black patch in the centre of the belly. Lower belly white and under tail-coverts cream. Sides of the neck, hindneck and mantle grey-brown; rest of back and wing-coverts blackish heavily streaked buff and chestnut-brown. Tail grey with a narrow black subterminal bar showing at the sides because long upper tail-coverts hide the central feathers. Legs pink with very short thick toes and black claws; bill black slightly downcurved at tip.

In flight shows a narrow clear white stripe across inner webs of primaries; when overhead, clear white under wing-coverts and dark belly patch are conspicuous. Hudson (1920) noted that it was very active and could run faster than other plovers; he also remarked on its shyness, swift and high flight and on a distinctive tremulous call with a falling inflection, always uttered when it took flight.

STATUS & RECORDS: Vagrant, reported at least three times. Wace (1921) noted that it was recorded by the English Antarctic Expedition (1842); Bennett (1926) indicated a specimen of local origin in the Stanley Museum and felt that this species was 'an occasional visitor and may even breed'; Cawkell and Hamilton (1961) had no records since Bennett's list. Two were seen on West Point Island on 28 August 1961, one dead (Woods 1975); an adult was seen near Cape Pembroke Lighthouse on 3 and 4 September 1979 (Peatfield 1981). As the two dated records are in spring, it seems probable that this species occurs as a vagrant on migration.

DISTRIBUTION ABROAD: Breeds in andean regions of Chile from about 18°S to Tierra del Fuego; southern populations arrive late August/early September and leave in March and April. Winter distribution extends northward to about 30°S in Argentina, where it is found on lowland grassland. A smaller, paler race *E. r. pallidus* has been described from Peru.

Magellanic Plover *Pluvianellidae*
This species is placed in a family on its own as it does not appear to be closely related to any other wader family. It may not be properly called a 'plover'. This name has been retained until its relationships have been more carefully examined.

108. Magellanic Plover *Pluvianellus socialis*   Plate 14
A. & C. Chorlo de Magallanes
Small. 8–8½in/20–21cm

IDENTIFICATION: A squat, pale grey and white wader with short bright pink legs, it is very well camouflaged on shingle beaches, its usual habitat. *Male and female similar, though males are slightly larger: head and upperparts pale grey, darker on lores; broad grey-brown band across breast, darker at the lower edge on males; rest of underparts pure white. Tail and rump black in centre with broad white sides, conspicuous in flight; inner wing pale grey, primaries darker grey-brown with clear white central bar; underwing pure white. Bill shortish and stout, black with small pinkish patches at the base in summer, but yellowish in winter; iris bright pink. Immature similar but has orange-yellow legs, and larger yellowish basal spots on the bill, a streaked breast and upperparts finely flecked with white.* On beaches it usually waddles but can run quickly and is more wary than the Two-banded Plover (105). The flight is often erratic and fast.

STATUS & RECORDS: Vagrant, apparently recorded twice; Zotta (1944) reported its occurrence in the Falklands, presumably a winter record before 1935 (Jehl 1975); one probable immature remained at Salvador settlement from March to June 1959 (Woods 1975).

DISTRIBUTION ABROAD: Only known to breed on the shores of ponds and lakes from northern and eastern Tierra del Fuego, along the southern side of the Straits of Magellan and on the southern half of coastal Santa Cruz province, Argentina. Some birds are resident but others migrate northward to about 45°S, wintering in sheltered bays and river mouths along the coast of Argentina (Jehl 1975).

Godwits, Sandpipers and Snipes   *Scolopacidae*

A large family of 85 species in 27 genera, the Scolopacidae *vary from very tiny to medium-large (12–60cm, 5–23in) in body-length. Most species breed in moorland or tundra habitats in the Northern Hemisphere and many are highly migratory, wintering far into the Southern Hemisphere. Generally they have long slender bills with flexible tips, used for probing in soft mud or shallow water and for picking insects from low vegetation. Most species have long legs, long and pointed wings, long necks and short tails. Their plumage is usually patterned grey, brown or reddish above and streaked on white below when breeding; winter plumage is more uniform. Flight is rapid and flocks perform aerial evolutions, especially over feeding grounds.*

Thirty-three species have occurred in South America, of which 27 are known in Argentina where all except four species of snipe are migrants from the Northern Hemisphere. Fourteen species have been recorded in the Falklands where the Common (Magellan) Snipe is the only regular breeding species and the Cordilleran Snipe may breed. The other 12 species are migrants from arctic regions; three appear to occur regularly and nine are only known as vagrants.

Common Snipe — White-rumped Sandpiper

109. Hudsonian Godwit   *Limosa haemastica*   Plate 14
A. Aguja or Becada de mar
c. Zarapito de pico recto
Small-medium. $14\frac{1}{2}$–$15\frac{1}{2}$in/37–39cm
IDENTIFICATION: Similar in size to the Magellanic Oystercatcher (103), though taller and slimmer, this rare vagrant wader in *winter plumage* is generally grey-brown above and on the head, with a narrow white-eye stripe from the bill to just behind the eye, and paler grey beneath fading to white on the belly. The slightly upcurved bill is nearly twice as long as the head, blackish with pinkish base; the long legs are dark grey. In flight it shows dark upperparts with a narrow white central wingbar, a white rump and slightly wider terminal black tail band; feet project beyond the tail. The underwing pattern is distinctive; grey flight feathers with white central bar and grey-white body contrast with all black under-wing coverts and axillaries (where the wing joins the body). *Breeding plumage* is less likely to be seen in the Falklands; male has underparts mostly dark chestnut and upperparts marked with buff while female is paler below. *Juvenile* similar to winter adult but has buff edges to back feathers and is brownish below.

STATUS & RECORDS: Vagrant from wintering grounds in South America; the first specimens were collected in autumn 1833 or 1834 (Gould & Darwin 1841). Two specimens given by Fitzroy are in the British Museum, one in winter plumage and one in breeding plumage. McCormick collected one at St. Salvador Bay in September or November 1842 (in Bennett 1926). Sclater (1860) and Bennett (1926) refer to specimens obtained about 1860 by Captain Pack. Abbott (1861) collected two specimens with 'red-barred breast' (breeding plumage) at Port Louis on 20 May 1860 and noted the presence of 'flocks ... seen at Mare Harbour in the month of May 1860'. Bennett (1926) noted that it was an accidental visitor and Cawkell and Hamilton (1961) stated that they had no knowledge of this species in the Falklands. There were no records for 120 years after 1860 until one was seen at the Northwest Point of Carcass Island by J Hutchings on 31 December 1983. It was also seen on 2 January 1984 by K Shackleton and was present in the area until at least 18 January 1984; a field description confirmed the identity. Another was seen by S Francis at Ronda, Salvador on 17 November 1984.

DISTRIBUTION ABROAD: Breeds in Arctic America and migrates to southern South America, wintering on the eastern side from southeastern Brazil through Uruguay and Argentina to Tierra del Fuego. Formerly thought to be very rare, possibly reduced by hunters since the mid-nineteenth century but recently found wintering in large numbers in San Sebastian Bay, Tierra del Fuego (Marchant *et al* 1986).

110. Whimbrel *Numenius phaeopus*   Plate 14
A. Zarapito trinador
c. Zarapito
Medium. 16–18in/40–46cm

IDENTIFICATION: A tall brown and buff wader with a very long downcurved bill, it is recognised by the broad buff stripe over the eye, a dark line through the eye and dark sides to the crown. A narrow buff central stripe over the crown is less easily seen. Sexes similar in *breeding and winter plumage* though females usually larger. Upperparts including wings and rump, dark brown flecked with buff; tail closely barred brown and buff; underparts warm buff, lightly streaked brown on face, neck and breast becoming clear warm buff on belly and under tail-coverts. *Immature* similar, upperparts more spotted on wing-coverts and worn flight feathers are lighter brown. Bill blackish with pink basal half or less; legs blue-grey. In flight, very long brown wings, darkest on primaries, long curved bill and red-brown underwing and axillaries are distinctive. Often calls when flushed, a very distinctive rippling whistle on one note, *bibibibibibibi*. Usually silent when feeding and inconspicuous on the ground as the plumage colours merge into the brown and buff background of a sand-beach with boulders.

STATUS & RECORDS: Vagrant or non-breeding visitor, first recorded at Carcass Island on 7 December 1962 by K Bertrand (Woods 1975). Since then, an increase in numbers or more awareness amongst observers have produced several records. One 'probable' reported by C Gallimore at Northwest Point, Carcass Island on 19 November 1969 (Wolsey 1986c); two seen at Christina Bay, Cape Pembroke on 2 January 1974 by A Carey (S Booth pers. comm., who also reported hearing Whimbrel calling over Stanley more than once, usually at dawn or dusk). One was reported as shot before 1980 on Pebble Island; five to about 30 were seen at Ronda, Salvador between 1 November 1980 and 24 February 1981; one near the Grassland Trials Unit, Stanley on 13 November 1981; at least two were present at Northwest Point, Carcass, from May to October 1983 (their breeding season) and five to eight were seen in the same area between 16 October 1983 and mid-February 1984; one on 19 and 22 December 1985 at Port Louis (Wolsey 1986c) and two to five at Hill Cove on 3 & 4 April 1986 (W Curtis). Increased records since 1970 suggest that it winters regularly in the Falklands and that individuals may be present in all months.

DISTRIBUTION ABROAD: Breeds in northern temperate and arctic regions; four races are recognised that pass non-breeding seasons in the tropics and Southern Hemisphere. *N. p. hudsonicus* breeds in Arctic North America and winters from southern United States and most coasts of South America to northern Tierra del Fuego. Non-breeding birds are present in continental parts of the Magellanic region through the year (Venegas & Jory 1979).

111. Eskimo Curlew   *Numeninus borealis*   Not illustrated
A. Zarapito polar
C. Zarapito boreal
Small-medium. 12–14in/30–36cm
IDENTIFICATION: Resembles the Whimbrel (110) in shape but is much smaller with a shorter and less downcurved bill; sides of head darker brown with narrow buff eye-stripes and obscure central crown stripe, therefore head pattern is less contrasting. Upperparts dark brown heavily mottled buff, including rump and tail. Underparts cinnamon-buff strongly barred brown on neck and breast with large dark Y-shaped marks on flanks. More easily distinguished in flight by the strongly cinnamon underwing and unbarred dark brown primaries. Superficially similar to the Upland Sandpiper (112) but separated by larger size, much longer curved bill, wingtips projecting beyond tail when folded, blue-grey legs and buff underparts. Call note in flight described as a 'fluttering *tr-tr-tr*' or 'a melodious whistle *bee, bee*' (Witherby 1940).

STATUS & RECORDS: Vagrant from wintering areas in South America; one specimen was collected before 1861 by Captain Pack (Abbott 1861) and there were two possible sightings by E Cawkell, at Johnson's Harbour in November 1950 and near Surf Bay in February 1951.

DISTRIBUTION ABROAD: Until about 1886, bred in Arctic Canada (Mackenzie) and migrated in huge flocks through eastern United States to wintering grounds between Chile and southern Argentina. Migrating birds were hunted excessively and the species was thought to be extinct early in the twentieth century but occasional birds continue to be reported on migration, including 23 in Texas in May 1981 (Marchant *et al* 1986).

112. Upland Sandpiper   *Bartramia longicauda*   Plate 14
A. & C. Batitú
Small. 11–12in/28–30cm
IDENTIFICATION: This sandpiper resembles the Whimbrel (110) in colour but is much smaller. The head is small and rounded, dark brown on the crown with

an indistinct buff central stripe; the large, dark eye is prominent on the pale buff face; neck thin and particularly noticeable when the bird is alert; neck and under-parts buff-white, finely spotted brown on neck; breast and flanks heavily streaked dark brown; belly and under tail-coverts whitish. Back and wings dark brown, heavily marked with buff on back and wing-coverts; lower back, rump and tail centre blackish with sides of tail barred brown and buff. Bill slender, yellow with dark culmen; legs, dull yellow, long and appearing fairly thick.

In flight the long tail is noticeable and the long pointed wings show blackish primaries contrasting with mottled secondaries and coverts, but no light bars, while the neck is retracted. Unusual in that it prefers open grasslands and does not frequent shores with other waders. Runs with jerky head movements, like a rail, and feeds by walking and tilting the body like a plover. When flushed, typi-cally utters a liquid whistle *hulee-hulee-hulee* or a quieter *quip-ip-ip*.

STATUS & RECORDS: Vagrant from regular wintering grounds in South America, recorded twice. On 29 May 1938 two birds were seen in Stanley, one was carried off by a cat, the other collected and found to be in a starved condition (Bennett 1938); one at Stanley football field survived from 26 to 31 October 1961 (Woods 1975). It attracted the attention of resident Falkland Thrushes and the sandpiper displayed at them with bill open and tail fanned and slightly depressed.

DISTRIBUTION ABROAD: Breeds from the central United States (39°N) to north-western Alaska (70°N) and migrates through central America to winter in southeastern Brazil, Paraguay and Argentina to about 42°S.

113. Lesser Yellowlegs *Tringa flavipes* Plate 14
A. Archibebe patiamarillo menor
C. Pitotoy chico
Small. 9–10in/23–25cm

IDENTIFICATION: The grey-brown upperparts and whitish underparts of this slim wader are unremarkable but it has very long bright yellow or orangey legs, a slender dark bill, just longer than the head and a pale head stripe reaching from bill to above the eye. In *non-breeding plumage*, head and underparts are white, lightly streaked brown on neck and breast; mantle and scapulars are grey-brown with whitish spots and flecks. In flight, the dark back contrasts with a square white patch on rump and upper tail-coverts and the finely barred black and white tail appears grey; primaries and secondaries are uniformly dark; axillaries and under wing-coverts closely barred white and brown; the long yellow legs project beyond the tail. In *breeding plumage*, the back is a darker, blackish-brown. Individuals reaching the Falklands may have more contrasting plumage than des-cribed for non-breeding birds because moult is halted until birds are in winter quarters. *Immatures* resemble non-breeders but are buff tinged above and have a greyish breast. Moves gracefully and feeds by picking from the surface of mud or ground, or by shallow probing.

This species is difficult to distinguish from the 25% larger Greater Yellowlegs *Tringa melanoleuca*, which could also occur as a vagrant. The Greater has a slightly upturned bill $1\frac{1}{2}$ times longer than the head and in flight, shows brownish notches on webs of secondaries (plain on Lesser Yellowlegs). See also Wilson's Phalarope (122).

STATUS & RECORDS: Vagrant, recorded three times; a female was shot near Stanley on 5 May 1924 (Bennett 1926), one was seen at Chata Creek near Teal Inlet on 1 January 1982 (R Hutchings pers. comm.) and another near Fitzroy in March 1984 (Wolsey 1986c).

DISTRIBUTION ABROAD: Breeds in tundra or open woodlands in northern North America from about 50°N to Alaska. Migrates through the United States and winters from Central America throughout South America to about 55°S in the Magellanic region. Non-breeding birds often remain in winter quarters throughout the year.

114. Ruddy Turnstone   *Arenaria interpres*   Not illustrated
A. Vuelvepiedras común
C. Chorlo vuelvepiedras
Small. $8\frac{1}{2}$–9in/22–24cm

IDENTIFICATION: A distinctive robust shorebird with short orange legs, a stubby but sharp-pointed bill and generally black and white appearance. *Adult* in *breeding* plumage has white sides to the head, black ear-coverts, white lores, white throat and most of the breast black with white patch extending into black from lower hindneck to sides of breast. Rest of the underparts pure white. Back and scapulars show extensive chestnut with dark brown inner wing-coverts. *Adult non-breeding* is duller with a mainly brown head but white throat and broad dark brown breast patches remain. *Immature* similar to non-breeding adult, with buff fringes on upperparts.

Flight pattern is unmistakable; dark wings show broad white bar across and a second white wedge on lesser coverts; dark back has a broad white bar up centre from rump; black patch on upper tail-coverts, tail otherwise white with broad black subterminal bar. An active feeder on rocky coasts or sand, where the strong bill is used to flip stones or dead kelp for crustaceans. It is noisy and squabbles often occur in flocks. Call-notes are a short guttural rattling sound and a clear short whistle.

STATUS & RECORDS: Unconfirmed vagrant from southern end of non-breeding range, noted by Wace (1921) as a rare visitor but not included by Bennett (1926) or Cawkell & Hamilton (1961).

DISTRIBUTION ABROAD: Breeds in arctic regions and as far south as 55°N on Baltic coasts. American Arctic breeders winter on coasts of North and South America from about 30°N to about 40°S; several recent records from coastal Tierra del Fuego (Venegas & Jory 1979) suggest that it could occur on Falkland coasts, particularly during the southern summer.

115. Common (Magellan) Snipe   *Gallinago (gallinago) paraguaiae*   Plate 13
A. Agachadiza común
C. Becacina
Local name: Snipe
Small. 10–11 in/25–28cm
IDENTIFICATION: A small ground-loving wader with a very long bill (2–$2\frac{1}{2}$in/50–

70mm), it appears generally sandy-buff with dark markings as it runs low between grasses or diddle-dee. *Male and female* are similar. When seen close on the ground, the upperparts are blackish, heavily spangled and streaked chestnut and buff, with two long, broad buff lines either side of the back. The head has a narrow central buff stripe, a broad buff stripe over the eye and dark lores, with diffuse buff and brown bands across the face. The eye is noticeably large, dark and set high on the head. Underparts are grey-white, heavily mottled or spotted with brown on neck, breast and flanks; the belly is pure white; tail barred whitish and dark brown with a chestnut subterminal band. Bill mostly pale brown with a dark tip; legs fairly long, yellow-green. *Immature* resembles adult but has a dark bill and blue-grey legs.

In flight, the very long bill, short tail and broad, angled and pointed wings with dark brown flight feathers and its behaviour are distinctive. When flushed it flies erratically, tilting to either side and usually pitches within a few metres. It is unusually tame, much prefers to run when disturbed and will approach an intruder within 2–3m (6–10 feet) when young chicks are present.

VOICE. The alarm note when flushed and the usual flight-note is a short, harsh *skerp*. Between early August and early November, less often to mid-January and occasionally in June, the male performs a nocturnal display-flight, circling high over its territory. A musical bleating sound is produced from the spread rigid outer tail feathers as the bird repeatedly dives and climbs. This 'drumming' is usually heard soon after dusk, before dawn and occasionally in mid-afternoon. During the breeding season the male uses a loud *chippa-chippa-chippa* call from the ground. Adults with small young utter a peculiar ventriloquial *tik-tok-tik-tok*, which carries a long way, also a quieter *tip-tip-tip*. An adult anxious about small chicks will utter *tik-tok* notes more rapidly and may also display with wings slightly dropped, tail held vertical, fanned and twisted sideways through almost 90°; a wailing *wow* is also used. Small chicks have a weak *see-see-see* call, also used by an injured adult.

FOOD: Mainly invertebrates, including earthworms and insect larvae.

HABITAT, STATUS & BREEDING: A widespread and fairly common breeding species, probably more numerous many years ago before hundreds were shot each autumn on Lively Island where they apparently used to gather before migration (Cawkell & Hamilton 1961). The population may also have been reduced by excessive grass-burning in the nesting season. It is found on wet camp with rank grass or rushes, on dry ground with diddle-dee cover, on eroded and replanted slopes up to at least 300m (1,000 feet) above sea level, in open tussac grass paddocks and on beaches with rotted kelp heaps. There is no recent evidence of migration; some birds are certainly present in winter, when they rarely call and are very incon-spicuous. Lays two, sometimes three, pear-shaped olive-green eggs which are spot-ted and blotched with black, in a slight grass-lined nest amongst grasses or low diddle-dee. Eggs or young have been found in all months between July and February though the main breeding season is probably August to October.

DISTRIBUTION ABROAD: Authors disagree about classificaiton of the small South American snipes. Some class them as races of the Common Snipe *G. gallinago*, others treat them as a distinct species *G. paraguaiae*, with three or more races occurring throughout most of South America, which is the system used here The Falkland breeding race *G. p. magellanica* also occurs from central Chile and Argentina to Tierra del Fuego. Southern continental populations migrate north-wards as far as Uruguay in winter.

116. Cordilleran Snipe   *Gallinago stricklandii*   Plate 13
A. Becasina grande
c. Becacina grande
Local name: Jack Snipe?
Small-medium. 12–14in/30–35cm
IDENTIFICATION: Larger, more brightly coloured and having a longer bill (3–3½in, 76–90mm) than the Common Snipe (115), this species is recognised by its rich reddish-brown back and wing-coverts which are barred and streaked with black but do not show clear buff lines as on Common Snipe. The tail is barred black and red-brown and the underparts rich buff, mottled or barred with dark brown except in the centre of the belly. The long, heavy-based and slightly drooping bill is brown with a blackish tip; legs are greyish-yellow. In flight, the wings are broad and strongly rounded, the dark flight feathers lacking a white trailing edge.

STATUS & RECORDS: A little known species, said by Bennet (1926) to be rare and 'sometimes breeding'; he listed a local specimen in Stanley Museum. Cawkell and Hamilton (1961) noted that Hamilton had seen one and Cawkell remarked in 1964 that Hamilton had received vague reports of a few pairs breeding near Third Corral, east of Port San Carlos. There are no documented breeding records and no recent sightings. The status of this species and the possible occurrence of the Giant Snipe need investigation.

DISTRIBUTION ABROAD: Breeds in southern Tierra de Fuego and islands of the Cape Horn and Magellanic regions, southern Chile to about 37°S and andean part of southern Argentina to about 45°S. There is some evidence of migration to north ern Tierra del Fuego in winter but it appears to be mainly sedentary. On islands near Cape Horn it frequents marshes and peaty ground with stunted scrub (Reynolds 1935, Humphrey 1970).

The Giant Snipe *Gallinago undulata gigantea* (16½in/42cm) is listed by Wace (1921 as a migratory species with specimens in the local collection. Zotta (1944) records it as occurring from Brazil to northern Argentina, accidentally further south and in the Falklands. Bennett (1926) was apparently unaware of its occurrence or as seems more likely, identified the local specimens as *G. stricklandii* rather than *G. undulata*. Unfortunately these skins were destroyed in the Town Hall Fire Marchant *et al* (1986) describes the Giant Snipe as massive, with barred flight feathers (unique among snipe), a long bill that is very deep at the base and a curious flat-headed appearance. Very little is known about behaviour.

117. Red Knot   *Calidris canutus*   Not illustrated
A. Correlimos gordo
c. Playero ártico
Small. 9–10½in/23–26cm
IDENTIFICATION: Much larger than the White-rumped Sandpiper (119) with a

shortish straight black bill and short greenish legs, it has a rounded, bulky appearance. In *winter plumage* it is mainly grey on head and back, whitish below washed with grey and lightly flecked darker on neck and breast. In flight, shows a narrow white wingbar, blackish primaries, a whitish rump and grey tail; legs do not project beyond the tail. In *breeding plumage*, underparts are deep chestnut and the back is marked black and chestnut. The call-note is a low *knut* or a liquid *quick-ick* when taking flight.

STATUS & RECORDS: Vagrant from its usual wintering areas; one probable record at Sea Lion Point, Ronda, Salvador on 15 and 19 November 1984 (S Francis).

DISTRIBUTION ABROAD: Breeds in several arctic regions, particularly northeastern Canada. North American races winter from coasts of southern United States to southern Chile and Argentina and irregularly to northern Tierra del Fuego.

118. Sanderling *Calidris alba* Plate 13
A. Correlimos blanco
c. Playero blanco
Small. 8–8½in/20–21cm
IDENTIFICATION: A plump little grey and white wader, slightly larger and more heavily built than the Two-banded Plover (105) with a longer black bill. *Adult in non-breeding* plumage is easily recognised; it has a white face and underparts and pale grey back with the black carpal joint sometimes showing as a 'shoulder patch'. In flight it can be immediately separated from Two-banded Plover and White-rumped Sandpiper (119) by the long, broad white bar across the blackish wings. The tail is dark with white sides, similar to the Two-banded Plover. *Immatures* show variable dark and light spangling on the back. Sanderlings seen in the Falklands are usually in non-breeding plumage; some in April/May could be darker above with some chestnut appearing on the neck as they assume *breeding plumage*, which is mostly chestnut above and on neck and breast. It is extremely active and often feeds along surf edges, scampering over the sand left by receding waves. Call-notes resemble the short *prit* of the Two-banded Plover.

STATUS & RECORDS: Uncommon non-breeding visitor from the Northern Hemisphere, first recorded certainly about 1936 and first collected by Hamilton in November 1937 at Cape Dolphin (Cawkell & Hamilton 1961). Garnot (1826) noted the presence of 'Sanderlings *Charadrius calidris*' as being no different from those of Europe; this may be a much earlier record. Sanderlings have been seen on or near extensive sand-beaches between September and May/June, often in association with White-rumped Sandpiper and Two-banded Plover. Most occurred as singles or small parties of up to four, but about 70 were present at Bertha's Beach, East Falkland in January 1963 (Woods 1975). Numbers at Surf Bay near Stanley have apparently increased since the 1960s to maxima of about 40 in April 1981 (Peatfield 1981) and 36 in April 1985 (Wolsey 1986c).

DISTRIBUTION ABROAD: Breeds on arctic islands of Canada and northern Greenland, also at Spitsbergen and in Siberia. North American birds migrate through North and South America to winter from the southern United States to about 52°S in Chile and southern Argentina.

119. White-rumped Sandpiper *Calidris fuscicollis* Plate 13
A. Correlimos lomoblanco
B. Playero de lomo blanco
Very small. 6–7in/15–18cm
IDENTIFICATION: A very small, slender and inconspicuous shorebird; in *non-breeding* plumage, it is grey-brown on head and back with dark streaking and has a dark eye-stripe with an indistinct white streak above. Mainly white below, streaked brown on the breast. Separated from juvenile Two-banded Plover (105) by much longer, slender and slightly downcurved black bill, more slender shape and greyer appearance. Easily identified when it takes flight by a white patch above the all dark tail, characteristic mouse-like squeaky call-note *jeet* and narrow white wingbar. Flight is rapid on long wings, which project well beyond the tail when at rest. Moult into *breeding plumage* commences in March when the back and crown gain variable buff margins and the white underparts show clearer streaking on the breast and large dark streaks on the flanks. Separated from Baird's Sandpiper (120) by greyer upperparts, white upper tail-coverts and different call.

STATUS & RECORDS: Common non-breeding visitor from arctic breeding grounds, present between September and April on sandy shores of creeks, sand-beaches with brackish pools and stranded kelp and at grassy margins of freshwater ponds near beaches. Usually occurs in parties and flocks of up to 100; about 350 were recorded at Bertha's Beach, East Falkland in January 1963 (Woods 1975). Often seen with Two-banded Plover and Rufous-chested Dotterel in autumn. At Surf Bay, east of Stanley, observations from 1957 to 1963 showed that numbers gradually increased from September to December, maintaining the high level until March. On southward migration, adults leave first and juveniles much later, probably not reaching their wintering areas until December (Cramp & Simmons 1982).

DISTRIBUTION ABROAD: Breeds on arctic coasts of North America and migrates south through West Indies to South America east of the Andes between Paraguay, Uruguay and Tierra del Fuego; a few occur in Chile between 25°S and 55°S.

120. Baird's Sandpiper *Calidris bairdii* Plate 14
A. Correlimos unicolor
C. Playero de Baird
Tiny to very small. 5½–7in/14–18cm
IDENTIFICATION: Closely resembles the White-rumped Sandpiper (119) in shape but appears generally buff with a less distinct pale streak above the eye and has a very slender tip to the bill. Upperparts dark brown, with broad buff fringes, often appearing scaly; underparts buff, streaked narrowly with brown on the breast; belly white. In flight, shows similar wing pattern to the White-rumped; separated by blackish rump, upper tail-coverts and central tail feathers with whitish sides to rump and upper tail. Flight note is a low, rasping *kreeep* or *krrt*. Tends to occur in drier habitats than the White-rumped and away from shores.

STATUS & RECORDS: Vagrant visitor from South American wintering areas, recorded at least seven times since 1920. Bennett (1926) reported one and Cawkell saw one at Hearnden Water near Stanley on 2 January 1955 (Cawkell & Hamilton 1961). Four were seen near Eliza Cove on 14 October 1979 (Peatfield 1981), one at Eliza Cove on 30 October 1981 and one or two near Yorke Bay on 14 November 1981 (Wolsey 1986c). One was at Ronda, Salvador on 17 November 1984 (S Francis) and a possible bird of this species was seen at Swan Pond, Fitzroy on 29 November 1986 (Wolsey 1986d).

DISTRIBUTION ABROAD: Breeds in Arctic America and migrates to South America where it winters, between the Equator and 55°S in Chile and throughout Argentina to Tierra del Fuego.

121. Pectoral Sandpiper *Calidris melanotos* Plate 21
A. Correlimos patiamarillo
C. Playero pectoral
Very small to small. $7\frac{1}{2}$–9in/19–23cm

IDENTIFICATION: Noticeably larger than the White-rumped Sandpiper (119), the Pectoral Sandpiper is recognised in all plumages by the greyish breast heavily streaked dark brown, contrasting sharply with white belly and yellowish legs. The shortish dark bill is slightly downcurved. Upperparts in *non-breeding* plumage are brown with dark centres to feathers, appearing scaly; head streaked dark brown with indistinct pale stripe above the eye. *Juveniles* look more scaly above, showing clear white V-marks on mantle feathers and have more noticeable pale eye-stripes. In flight, shows dark wings with a very faint white bar and mostly dark tail with white sides. Flight note is a loud, harsh *churk*. Occurs on coasts and wet grasslands and often feeds away from water.

STATUS & RECORDS: Vagrant, recorded three times. Two were photographed near Stanley early November 1971 (Prince & Payne 1979), one seen at Bull Point by K Standring in the summer of 1981/82 and one, probably this species at Ronda, Salvador in December 1984 (Wolsey 1986c).

DISTRIBUTION ABROAD: Breeds in Arctic North America and Siberia. Winters mostly in South America from about 10°–40°S on the western side and between 22°S and 50°S on the eastern side to southern Argentina.

122. Wilson's Phalarope *Phalaropus tricolor* Plate 21
A. Falaropo tricolor
C. Pollito de mar de tricolor
Small. $8\frac{1}{2}$–$9\frac{1}{2}$in/22–24cm

IDENTIFICATION: A distinctive small wader, easily identified by its long, needle-like black bill, small head, long neck, yellow legs and generally grey and white *non-breeding plumage*. It can be separated from the Lesser Yellowlegs (113) by its paler underparts including clear white under wing-coverts, pale grey back and the thinner bill. In *breeding plumage*, the female is much brighter than the male; head grey above with a broad black band curving from bill through eye down side of neck; narrow eye-stripe is white, as are chin and throat; hindneck and mantle grey; sides of neck, breast, scapulars and edge of mantle chestnut-red, paler on breast; belly white. The legs are black in the breeding season. *Juveniles* have a scaly pattern on the back. In flight, dark wings lack any light bar, the tail is grey with a large white rump patch and the legs project beyond the tail. When feeding, it walks rapidly and picks food almost frantically from the surface of mud. It also swims readily, picking morsels from the surface of ponds (see Lesser Yellowlegs 113).

STATUS & RECORDS: Vagrant, probably recorded at least twice; Sclater (1894) noted its occurrence; Bennett (1926) stated that it was a very occasional visitor and indicated the presence of a local specimen. One was seen and photographed on a pond near Eliza Cove on 6 November 1981 by N Keenlyside (Peatfield 1981).

DISTRIBUTION ABROAD: Breeds in the temperate prairie region of North America and migrates to South America, wintering from Peru and western Brazil through Uruguay to about 42°S in Argentina and in central Chile. A few birds reach the Magellanic region and there is one record for northwestern Tierra del Fuego.

Seedsnipes   *Thinocoridae*
The four species in this strictly South American family resemble doves in their plump bodies, short legs and small heads, have stout curved bills like a partridge but in flight their long wings are similar to those of waders. Their relationships are not clear but they bear little resemblance to snipe except for the rasping calls uttered when they take flight. Two species have been recorded, one of which is probably a vagrant and the other may be a very rare breeding species.

123. White-bellied Seedsnipe   *Attagis malouinus*   Plate 14
A. Agachona patagónica
C. Perdicita cordillerana austral
Small. $10\frac{1}{2}$–$11\frac{1}{2}$in/26.5–29cm
IDENTIFICATION: Much larger than the Least Seedsnipe (124), this species has a buff head and neck finely spotted brown, buff breast showing black crescents and a white belly with large dark crescents on the flanks. Upperparts are richly scalloped with chestnut and buff edges to dark brown feathers. In flight the wings and rounded tail appear uniform brown above, while the underwing is pure white. Bill dark brown and legs dull grey or brown. *Immature* birds show more white markings above and look more scaly while neck and breast are paler. Call note when flushed is a sharp repeated *tu-whit* and in flight it uses a plaintive *tooee*. When disturbed it usually flies rapidly away, twisting like a snipe.

STATUS & RECORDS: Vagrant from South America, recorded only three times. There is a possibility that it breeds in the Wickham Heights on East Falkland or the Hornby Mountains or Mount Adam region in the north of West Falkland. The type-specimen from which Boddaert named the species in 1783 was apparently collected in the Falklands. Abbott (1861) shot a seedsnipe 'probably of this species' on the beach at Mare Harbour in early October 1859. Two were seen on 26 April 1981 feeding, unconcerned by human presence only 3m (10 feet) away, on the southern side of Cape Pembroke (J and S Booth pers. comm.) These were possibly an adult and a juvenile, as the smaller bird was generally more buff-coloured.

DISTRIBUTION ABROAD: Breeds in high moorland and mountains of southern Chile and Argentina, from about 40°S to the islands south of Tierra del Fuego, where it feeds on berries and vegetation. Migrates locally to lower ground in winter.

124. Least Seedsnipe   *Thinocorus rumicivorus*   Plate 14
A. Agachona chica
C. Perdicita
Very small. 6–7in/15–18cm
IDENTIFICATION: About the size of a Black-throated Finch (182), this curious bird resembles a diminutive game-bird on the ground but in flight, with long pointed wings, resembles a plover. The male and female have similarly coloured upperparts, dark brown thickly mottled and fringed with sandy-brown and white. The *male* is streaked buff and dark brown on crown, nape and hindneck; sides of neck grey; throat white enclosed by a black band which extends down centre of neck to join a broad black breast band, separating grey sides of the upper breast from the white belly which shows some brown markings below the black breast band. *Female* has buffish neck streaked with dark brown and an indistinct dark neck and breast pattern recalling that of the male. The short, curved and broad bill is yellow-brown with a dark tip, the short legs yellow. In flight shows very narrow, pointed dark brown wings with a faint white bar; the tail is dark with white sides and, except on the central feathers, a broad white tip. Flight is fast and erratic but it often prefers to freeze when disturbed or to run away rapidly. When flushed it uses a scraping call. Song consists of hooting and repeated staccato notes given from the ground or in steeply diving display-flight.

STATUS & RECORDS: Possibly a very rare breeding species though more likely to be a vagrant from southern South America. Seven dated records: one in May 1922, one in 1923 and two in the summer of 1924 (Bennett 1926); one near Stanley in summer 1955 (Cawkell & Hamilton 1961); a probable female near Surf Bay 7 April 1974 and a male at Rolon Cove beach in January 1982 (J & S Booth pers. comm.).

DISTRIBUTION ABROAD: Occurs on open dry plains, coastal dunes and cultivated ground in South America. Three races have been described, though they are very difficult to separate; *T. r. rumicivorus* is found from northern Tierra del Fuego to 27°S in Chile and about 40°S in Argentina. Breeding birds of Tierra del Fuego apparently migrate northward for winter, when the species reaches about 30°S in Argentina and Uruguay. The other races inhabit lower andean regions of northern Argentina, Peru and Bolivia.

Sheathbills   *Chionididae*
Sheathbills are the only Antarctic shorebirds without webbed feet. Two species of these all-white, pigeon-like scavengers are known. One is restricted to a few islands in the southern Indian Ocean, the other species breeds on sub-Antarctic islands of the Atlantic Ocean and on the Antarctic continent to 65°S.

125. Snowy Sheathbill   *Chionis alba*   Plate 15
A. & C. Paloma antártica
Small-medium. 15–16in/38–41cm
IDENTIFICATION: All white plumage, busy, pigeon-like movements and short stout bill make this unusual shorebird easily recognised. The bill is yellowish with a black ridge and tip and has a horny sheath around the base; bare skin below

and around the eye and at the base of the bill is pink and on *adults*, is wattled. The thick legs are blue-grey with a well developed hind toe. *Male, female and immatures* have similar plumage. Can be confused with male Kelp Goose and Domestic Goose (70, 71) at long range but separated by much smaller size and quicker movements on the ground. In flight, wingbeats are quick and shallow and head and tail appear short. Usually silent, though birds quarrelling over food utter short, harsh calls. In summer, scavenges at albatross, penguin, shag and seal colonies, taking eggs, spilt food or seal faeces. In winter, feeds along shores taking green algae and limpets.

STATUS & RECORDS: Present around Falkland shores throughout the year but does not breed. Occurs in summer at seabird colonies, singly or in small parties. In winter, migrants from the Antarctic are present in flocks of up to 200–300. One ringed at George Island by R Reid in August 1961 was found at Signy Island, South Orkneys in January 1962 and a few ringed birds from the South Orkneys have been seen in the Falklands. No colour-ringed adults from Signy Island have been reported in the Falklands so it is probable that most Falkland birds are immature. Migrants seem to reach the Falklands in May and leave in October. Single birds are seen far from land and are possibly attracted to ships.

DISTRIBUTION ABROAD: Breeds at islands of the Scotia Arc between South Georgia and the South Shetlands and also on coasts of the Antarctic Peninsula to about 65°S. Many migrate to the coasts of the Falklands, Tierra del Fuego and Patagonia, sometimes reaching Uruguay. Non-breeders are also present through the year on the coast of Tierra del Fuego.

Skuas or Jaegers *Stercorariidae*

Skuas are strongly built dark brown or cream and brown, piratical and predatory seabirds. About six species are recognised in two genera, but there is still disagreement over classification of the genus Catharacta. *The larger* Catharacta *species resemble big gulls in shape but are much more agile in flight and show conspicuous white flashes across the bases of primary flight feathers. They have a bipolar breeding distribution and are pelagic over most oceans out of their breeding seasons. Three species have been recorded; the Antarctic Skua breeds, the Chilean Skua has been seen occasionally and may breed and the South Polar Skua has been identified a few times. The three smaller* Stercorarius *species (known as Jaegers in America) resemble falcons or large terns, have long, pointed wings and adults develop elongated central tail feathers. They all breed in northern, mainly arctic, regions and winter in southern oceans. The Long-tailed Skua has been recorded at least five times and the Arctic Skua three times since 1982.*

126. South Polar Skua *Catharacta maccormicki*   Not illustrated

A. Págalo antártico
c. Salteador polar
Medium-large. 21in/53cm
IDENTIFICATION: Similar in shape to Antarctic Skua (127) but plumage colours are more variable from dark brown to almost white underparts; recognised in *pale and intermediate forms* by pinkish-brown or buffish-brown head with paler

collar round hindneck contrasting with almost uniform blackish upperparts and pale buff or whitish underparts. *Darker* birds have pale base to bill, otherwise head, upperparts and underparts are dark brown to blackish. *Adult* bill and legs grey-black. *Juvenile* greyer on head and body; bill pale blue with black tip, legs and feet blue. Appears to have a smaller head and more slender bill than the Antarctic Skua. Flight similar to Antarctic with shallow wingbeats, showing a noticeable contrast between dark under wing-coverts and pale body.

STATUS & RECORDS: Probably a regular passage migrant to Falkland waters, recorded eight times. One, probably this species, seen in Stanley harbour 'in late summer' (Hamilton 1945a) and one on 27 October 1981 (J Peatfield); single birds were seen near Rolon Cove on 26 March 1983 (S da Prato), in Port William on 21 February 1986, at Hill Cove on 3 April 1986, at West Point Island on 5 April 1986 and in Falkland Sound on 20 April 1986 and 15 in Choiseul Sound on 31 March 1987, ten days after strong westerly gales (Bourne & Curtis 1987).

DISTRIBUTION ABROAD: Breeds on the Antarctic Peninsula where birds of the dark form predominate and has a circumpolar distribution on Antarctic continental coasts. Migrates into the North Atlantic and North Pacific oceans.

127. Antarctic Skua   *Catharacta antarctica*

Plate 15

A. Págalo grande
c. Salteador común
Local name: Sea Hen
Medium-large. 20–23in/53–58cm

IDENTIFICATION: A dark brown seabird with heavily built body, broad and pointed wings showing a large white flash at the base of the primaries and a short, slightly rounded or wedge-shaped tail. Separated at long range from immature Kelp Gull (134) by shallower and faster wingbeats and uniform black appearance. *Adult* is dark brown flecked with buff on neck and back, lighter grey-brown beneath, sometimes flecked chestnut on flanks and breast. Plumage varies considerably; some birds are generally lighter, show a yellow-brown hindneck and a dark, down-ward slanting cap. *Juvenile* darker with few light flecks above and more red-brown underparts. Under wing-coverts and axillaries very dark brown or black. Bill black, stout and hooked; legs and feet black though many have mottled white and black tarsi. When chasing other seabirds to make them disgorge, flight is very rapid and powerful and shows considerable agility. Notoriously aggressive when nesting; both parents may swoop close overhead, calling angrily and sometimes striking people or dogs with their feet.

VOICE: Various harsh guttural calls are used near the nest or when disputing another's claim to food, otherwise usually silent. In displays at breeding grounds, guttural calls are accompanied by wing-raising.

FOOD: Obtains much of its food by piratical attacks on other seabirds. In the Falklands, Imperial and Rock Shags are terrorised; a skua will fly nearby when a shag is diving and then crash-land at the spot where the shag surfaces. Also takes many goslings, young penguins and eggs of penguins and geese and readily feeds on offal or from sheep carcasses.

HABITAT, STATUS & BREEDING: Common and widespread summer resident, present between early October and late April/mid-May. Occurs over coastal waters, mainland coasts and on offshore islands, rarely over 1.6km (1 mile) inland. Nests colonially on mainland points or on open slopes of smaller islands, up to 1km ($\frac{2}{3}$ mile) from the sea; isolated nests are sometimes found. The scrape-nest is scantily lined with grass or diddle-dee pieces; one to three, usually two, eggs of variable colour, greyish, pale green or dark olive-brown spotted and blotched with dark brown are laid between late November and mid-December.

About 200 birds were ringed between 1961 and 1963, mainly at Dunbar Island and Carcass Island; no foreign recoveries have been reported. A pair colour-ringed at Kidney Island in 1961 returned to the same site the following year.

DISTRIBUTION ABROAD: Thought to be restricted to the Falklands until Devillers (1978) described typical *C. a. antarctica* individuals at colonies on the coast of Patagonia between 45°S and 47°S. At Puerto Deseado (47°S) Antarctic Skuas breed alongside Chilean Skuas and hybrids were described by Devillers. In winter the Antarctic Skua is pelagic, apparently ranging north to about 20°S in southern oceans. Two other races are recognised by Harrison (1983), *C. a. lonnbergi* which has a circumpolar distribution on sub-Antarctic islands and the Antarctic Peninsula and *C. a. hamiltoni* which breeds at Tristan da Cunha and Gough islands.

128. Chilean Skua   *Catharacta chilensis*   Not illustrated
A. Gaviota parda
c. Salteador chileno
Medium-large. 21–24in/53–61cm
IDENTIFICATION: Superficially similar to but generally less bulky than the Antarctic Skua (127) with narrower wings, it is recognised in *all plumages* by the dark horizontal cap, red-brown to cinnamon axillaries and under wing-coverts and usually a marked dark breast band below a pale cinnamon or buff throat and mainly reddish underparts. The bill is light, grey or blue with a dark tip. *Immature* birds show more cinnamon markings above and usually brighter reddish underparts. At breeding colonies was generally shy and not found to be aggressive towards intruders (Devillers 1978).

STATUS & RECORDS: Uncertain; may be an irregular vagrant or uncommon breeding species. Wace (1921) described it as a rare visitor, possibly more common in the west. There are three records; Hamilton (1937) obtained two specimens at Eagle Point, East Falkland on 26 November 1930 and saw two others, one of which was apparently mated to an Antarctic Skua. Hamilton obtained another specimen at Stanley on 29 October 1936. One was seen at Carcass Island on 9 December 1975 (Devillers 1978). Antarctic Skua colonies are worth examining closely as the Chilean Skua may be breeding in the Falklands.

DISTRIBUTION ABROAD: Breeds on the west coast of South America from about 35°S to southern Tierra del Fuego and Cape Horn and on the coast of Argentina between Puerto Deseado and Rio Gallegos. Ranges north in winter to the coast of northern Peru and probably to waters off Brazil.

129. Long-tailed Skua *Stercorarius longicaudus*   Not illustrated
A. Salteador rabudo
c. Salteador de cola larga
Small-medium. 12–15in/30–38cm (without tail streamers)
IDENTIFICATION: The smallest and most slender of the *Stercorarius* Skuas (Jaegers),
it is about the size of a South American Tern (140) and has a similar flying action.
In shape it resembles a small falcon or shearwater with long, narrow and pointed
wings, small head and elongated rump and tail appearing somewhat wedge-
shaped. *Adult breeding* has central tail streamers, projecting up to 10in/25cm but
these are only visible at close range and often broken irregularly; *immatures* have
much shorter streamers.

Adult in winter is generally grey-brown above on back and inner wing with
dark primaries, lacking a white flash, and a narrow dark trailing edge to
secondaries; rump barred brown and white. Underparts more or less barred brown
and white, usually with a dark breast band and dark belly; head brown above
with slightly paler cheeks. *Adult* in *breeding* plumage (April to August) has blackish
cap, whitish or yellowish cheeks, whitish breast darkening to grey-brown belly
and undertail. Bill blackish and legs bluish. *Immature* similar to winter adult,
strongly barred beneath and on rump, with noticeable small white wing flash.
Juveniles vary more, from whitish on head, breast and belly with heavily barred
underwing and undertail to largely brown underparts with dark breast band.
Separated from Arctic Skua (130) by slighter build, longer narrow wings, usually
without a white flash, and greyer upperwing with dark trailing edge. Flies with
buoyant action and easy changes in height, sometimes shooting over waves like
a shearwater; rarely attacks other seabirds but is attracted by carrion on the sea
surface.

STATUS & RECORDS: Vagrant at southern limit of non-breeding range, recorded at
least five times. W Curtis saw one immature in Port William and Stanley Narrows
on 11 November 1982, two adults and an immature 15km (9 miles) east of Volunteer Point, East Falkland on 29 November 1982 (Wolsey 1986c) and three east
of Cape Pembroke on 23 March 1987 (Wolsey 1987b). W Bourne saw four 320km
(200 miles) east of Stanley on 26 February 1985 and noted that it had been seen
in Falkland waters early in January 1985 (Bourne & Curtis 1987).

DISTRIBUTION ABROAD: Breeds in arctic regions of Europe, Asia and America; pelagic
in non-breeding season, occurring through Atlantic and Pacific Oceans to about
55°S between November and April.

130. Arctic Skua *Stercorarius parasiticus*   Not illustrated
A. Salteador común
c. Salteador chico
Medium. 16–18in/41–46cm (without tail streamers)
IDENTIFICATION: More heavily built, with broader wings and a relatively shorter
tail section than the Long-tailed (129), this skua looks like a large falcon, mostly
dark brown above with a clear white wing patch and short central tail streamers
up to 5in/12cm when adult. Bill and legs blackish-grey. Plumage very variable;
occurs in *light, dark and intermediate phases*, the dark phase being more common.

Birds in breeding plumage are unlikely to be seen in Falkland waters. *Adult in winter (dark)* is generally dark reddish-brown above and below with slightly darker cap and primaries showing a white flash and sometimes barred above and below the tail. *Adult (light and intermediate)* has dark cap merging into whitish cheeks, almost uniform reddish-brown back and wings lightly flecked with buff, brown and white bars above and below tail, brown breast and white belly, barred only on flanks. *Immature (dark)* differs from adult in having indistinct buff bars on dark brown upperparts and heavily barred brown and buff underparts, including axillaries and under wing-coverts. *Immatures (intermediate and light)* very variable, usually paler beneath with noticeable dark cap and paler greyish face, throat and hindneck; underside of wings, under and upper tail-coverts barred; breast often showing dark band. *Adults* in *breeding* plumage lack bars around tail base; light birds are mainly white beneath with yellowish face and variable brown on breast; dark birds show yellowish cheeks and collar.

Flies with powerful falcon-like wingbeats, often gliding and changing direction. Harries terns or gulls by sneaking in low, or suddenly turning to pursue them closely until food is disgorged (see Wallace 1986).

STATUS & RECORDS: Vagrant in Falkland inshore waters, at southern limit of pelagic winter range, recorded three times. W Curtis watched an adult on 15 November 1982 in Port William and saw two off Fox Point, Choiseul Sound on 17 February 1987; W Bourne saw a dark bird 80km (50 miles) east of Stanley on 5 April 1985 (Bourne & Curtis 1987).

DISTRIBUTION ABROAD: Breeds in arctic and northern temperate moorland and tundra regions, south to about 55°N and winters in southern oceans between about 30°S and 50°S particularly off coasts of South America and South Africa.

Gulls *Laridae*

Gulls are coastal birds with long pointed wings and slow flapping flight. They are generally white below and darker, grey or black, above and have fairly stout, slightly hooked bills. About 45 species occur throughout the world though few are found in the tropics. They feed in marine and coastal habitats and many species commonly take advantage of human activities by scavenging. Twelve species are found in South America and eight occur in Argentina. Six species have been recorded in the Falklands; three are breeding residents and three are rare vagrants.

131. Dolphin Gull *Larus scoresbii*   Plate 15
A. & C. Gaviota austral
Medium. 16–18in/40–46cm
IDENTIFICATION: Much smaller than Kelp Gull (134), with which it often associates, the *adult* in *breeding* plumage has a mainly grey body, heavy dark red bill, red eye-ring and red legs. Back and wings are slate-black with a broad white trailing edge to most primaries and the secondaries; tail white. Head from July to February, neck and underparts pale grey, including under wing-coverts. Between mid-March and early July adults gradually assume a dark grey hood, with variable, intermediate mottled appearance.

Juvenile has dark slate-brown head, throat and upper breast fading through brownish breast to whitish belly. Back dark brown with slate-brown wing-coverts; outer four or five primaries all black, small white tip on 6th, inner primaries and secondaries tipped white; rump and tail white with black subterminal band; bill blackish, legs dark brown. *First winter* bird has sooty-grey head, mottled white on throat, mottled grey and brown breast and retains black tail bar. Bill is dull pink-brown with broad black tip; legs dark pink-brown. In *first summer* after hatching, head becomes mottled with brown; bill shows more pink with $\frac{1}{3}$ or less black at the tip.

Second winter bird has near uniform sooty-grey head, sometimes flecked grey; mainly pale grey underparts; white tail; a pink bill with broad black subterminal bar and dark brown legs showing a variable orange or red tinge. Outer three primaries all black, noticeable white tips on 4th, 5th and 6th, larger tips on remaining primaries and all secondaries. In *second summer*, head is mottled dark grey and brown on light grey, bill is pink or light red with traces of subterminal black bar and legs are pale red-brown or orange-red.

Third winter and *adult non-breeding* plumage similar, though the bill of a third winter bird is light red with a darker tip and legs dull red-brown. Adult plumage is assumed in the third summer when only the outer primary is all black, though older birds show a faint white tip; all other primaries show progressively increasing white tips. More daring and much tamer than the Kelp Gull, it will stoop at intruders while screaming loudly, even in winter.

Between June 1959 and January 1963, 239 were ringed at Stanley, Kidney Island, West Point Island, Carcass Island, George Island and Bleaker Island; of these, 74 were colour ringed at Stanley or Kidney Island. Examination in the hand showed that average wing-length and tail-length increased with advancing age to maturity. Data from 67 birds (14 first year, 15 second year and 38 adults) gave mean wing-lengths of 323, 329 and 334mm respectively; tail-lengths were 121, 130 and 132mm. The greatest longevity shown was nine years.

VOICE: Flight-note is a distinctive short *kyik*, much sharper and higher-pitched than most calls of the Kelp Gull. A screaming, rapidly repeated *keear-keear-keear* is used when breeding or protesting at intruders.

FOOD: The diet is very varied; eats seal faeces and vomited penguin remains at sea lion rookeries, takes offal at slaughterhouses, regurgitated fish at Imperial Shag colonies and penguin eggs. Mussels collected on shores are dropped from heights between 1.5–7.5m (5–25 feet) in order to crack the shells. It also eats stranded jellyfish and small black flies on sand-beaches. Occasionally harries Rock Shags, forcing them to fly from a perch and vomit food; pesters adult Gentoo Penguins feeding their chicks or collects scraps around Rockhopper Penguin colonies.

HABITAT, STATUS & BREEDING: Resident breeding species, widespread around coasts though much less common than the Kelp Gull. Particularly attracted to seal, penguin or shag colonies and flocks gather in winter where sheep or cattle have been killed. Breeds in close-packed colonies, usually associated with Kelp Gulls, South American Terns or Brown-hooded Gulls on sand or shingle beaches and headlands, by ponds in grass or on rocky ridges with low tussac grass. Lays in December two to three olive-buff or grey-green eggs, well marked with dark brown blotches. The nest is a hollow, lined with grass and dead kelp pieces, often decorated with green plant material.

Returns and sight-recoveries of ringed birds showed that juveniles from the Lagoon near Bluff Cove dispersed to the northeast and southwest; adults were shown to move between Kidney Island or the Lagoon and wintering areas in Stanley. One Lagoon-bred fledgling (ringed February) was in Stanley between June and December and on Kidney Island the following April.

DISTRIBUTION ABROAD: Restricted to southern South America; breeds from about 42°S on coasts of Chile and Argentina to Tierra del Fuego and the Beagle Channel. In winter occurs north to about 37°S. No Falkland-ringed birds have been reported in South America.

132. Grey Gull *Larus modestus*   Plate 15

A. Gaviota gris

c. Gaviota garuma

Medium. 18in/46cm

IDENTIFICATION: Similar in size to the Dolphin Gull (131) and somewhat resembling first year birds of that species, has dull grey underparts and back; black primaries; a grey tail with a black subterminal bar and white tip; black legs tinged reddish and a much slimmer blackish bill. In flight the wings are very dark except for a white trailing edge to the secondaries. *Adult* in *breeding* plumage has a whitish head. In *non-breeding* plumage the head is dull brown. *Juvenile* has grey-brown head, paler on forehead and cheeks with dark streaks on nape. Body brown-grey flecked buff and tail blackish with narrow buff tip. *Immatures* become more uniform grey above and the grey tail has a broad black band. Adult plumage is attained by the third winter after hatching. Behaves more like a sandpiper than a gull, having a strong preference for sandy ocean beaches, where it feeds on crustaceans; also attends fishing trawlers off Chile and Peru.

STATUS & RECORDS: Vagrant from Pacific coast of South America; one record of a single bird at Stanley, August 1953, which associated with Kelp and Dolphin Gulls in gardens (Cawkell & Hamilton 1961), probably feeding on offal put out for domestic fowls.

DISTRIBUTION ABROAD: Breeds only in high desert regions of northern Chile and western Peru between about 20°S and 25°S, up to 50km (31 miles) inland. Disperses northward to the coast of Ecuador and southward at least as far as Valparaiso on the coast of Chile.

133. Band-tailed Gull *Larus belcheri*   Not illustrated

A. Gaviota colanegra or Gaviota Simeón

c. Gaviota peruana

Medium. 19–22in/48–56cm

IDENTIFICATION: Between Dolphin and Kelp Gulls (131, 134) in size, this black-backed gull is recognised in *adult breeding* plumage by the white head and body; white tail with a broad black subterminal band, widest in the centre; black primaries lacking white tips and heavy yellow bill with a black subterminal bar and red tip. Legs and feet yellow or yellow-green. In *winter* plumage, *adult* has mottled grey-brown hood extending to the neck and a white eye-ring. *Juvenile* has dark brown hood, heavily mottled brown and buff back, white upper tail-coverts and black tail with narrow whitish tip. Wings are black-brown with white tips to secondaries; underparts brown on breast fading to white on lower belly, bill dull yellow with a black tip and legs are grey. In *first winter*, head is darker and underparts and mantle more grey. In *second winter* resembles adult with dull yellow bill but still has a blackish tail with white tip. The adult of the smaller west coast race *L. b. belcheri* is lighter on the mantle and has a pale grey hindneck and breast and brighter yellow legs.

STATUS & RECORDS: Vagrant, recorded twice; a winter plumage adult seen by W Curtis at Albemarle on 6 April 1986, was probably *L. b. belcheri* (Bourne & Curtis 1987). A second winter immature was seen in Stanley harbour during three weeks from 24 March 1987 by A Henry (Wolsey 1987b).

DISTRIBUTION ABROAD: Two races occur on coasts of southern South America. The smaller race, *L. b. belcheri* breeds on Pacific coasts of northern Chile and Peru between about 25°S and the Equator. *L. (b.) atlanticus* 'Olrog's Gull', was first described in 1958 and is known to breed at San Blas Island near Bahia Blanca, Argentina; winter distribution is not well known though it may occur between 35°S and about 45°S.

134. Kelp Gull   *Larus dominicanus*   Plate 15

A. & C. Gaviota dominicana
Local names: Big Gull, White Gull; Grey Gull (1st year)
Medium-large. 22–24in/56–60cm

IDENTIFICATION: The largest gull breeding in the Falklands, it is familiar around Stanley and all settlements. *Adult* in *breeding* plumage has sooty-black mantle, back and wings above with a white mirror (patch) on the outer primary and white tips to remaining primaries and secondaries. Head, neck and underparts including under wing-coverts, rump and tail white; bill orange-yellow with bright red gonys patch; eye-ring red; legs and feet pale green/grey-yellow or orange-yellow. Adults with orange-yellow legs have deeper orange bills, possibly ageing. *Adult in winter* (mid-April to mid-September) as above except for very variable dark brown streaking on crown and nape. *Juvenile* appears very dark; dark brown above heavily edged buff and mottled brown with white below. Wings are dark brown; tail blackish variably barred brown, rump paler, whitish marked with brown; bill black; legs pink-brown and iris dark brown. By the end of the *first winter*, plumage becomes faded above and the head appears dirty white.

In *second winter* shows variable white on head, underparts and rump, variable slaty feathers on back and has a white tail with black bar. Bill is mainly black but cream at the base and tip and legs are grey-brown. In *second summer*, the back becomes darker and underparts show more white.

In *third winter*, resembles non-breeding adult; back and wings mainly slaty-black; tail white with variable traces of black remaining; bill pale yellow with traces of orange, usually a small red gonys patch and variable narrow black sub-terminal bar across both mandibles; legs pale green/blue-grey.

Fourth winter birds are not easily separated from non-breeding adults though they usually have paler bills and duller legs.

Although it is common around settlements it is usually very wary. Often seen in flocks, up to several hundred strong, on beaches in autumn.

VOICE: A noisy bird, with many variations on its call-notes. Usual flight-note is a wailing *keeyoo* repeated frequently, sometimes almost a scream with accent on the first syllable. A contact note used in flocks is a 'laughing' *kyok-eeyok-eeyok-eeyok*. A rapid, low-pitched 'conversational' note *uk-uk-uk-uk* is used by a bird investigating a human presence. Juveniles have a vibratory descending whistle with a plaintive quality.

FOOD: A successful scavenger, ready to take advantage of any weakened or dying animal; it also performs a useful service by feeding on sheep carcasses and offal. In winter, young birds particularly are a nuisance at hen-runs where they take meat thrown out for the fowls. Other foods taken include eggs of shags or ducks, ducklings and goslings, crustaceans such as krill and crabs, and molluscs and starfish from intertidal zones of beaches. In spring it apparently takes moth larvae from grassland and from early September, Stanley is deserted for a few weeks as the gulls patrol the camp at lambing time.

HABITAT, STATUS & BREEDING: A resident breeding species, it is abundant and wide-spread, occurring on low-lying coasts with off-shore kelp beds, around settlements and over the camp well inland. In autumn, adults and juveniles disperse from breeding grounds and they tend to gather where food is plentiful in winter. It also occurs regularly to about 16km (10 miles) offshore, occasionally further, around fishing fleets, and was recorded twice 320km (200 miles) to the east in the winter of 1982 (Bourne & Curtis 1987).

Historical records indicate that Kelp Gulls were present at the time of first human settlement and that the species has probably gained considerable benefit through the development of sheep farming. Pernety (1771) noted the presence of 'White Gulls' at Port Louis between February and April 1764. Garnot (1826) indicated that 'Black-backed Gulls' were present but found them unremarkable. In 1833/1834 Darwin noted this species in South America but did not record it in the Falklands (Gould & Darwin 1841). Abbott stated (1861) that the 'Saddle-backed Gull' was a common resident though he felt that many left in the winter, because he saw few and these were all old birds. Forty years later, with a sheep population of over 700,000, Vallentin commented (1904) that the 'Black-backed Gull' was, 'The commonest gull in the whole archipelago and universally distributed.' Cobb (1933) described the 'Big Gull' as the worst enemy among birds, of the sheep farmer, 'an excellent scavenger, but when he attacks live sheep and lambs, one forgets his good points,' and he commented on, 'their vast numbers'. This species is certainly thriving whether it is beneficial or not.

It nests in colonies of up to several hundred pairs, though single nests are found. Colonies are formed on shingle beaches, sandy ridges or diddle-dee and grass slopes near the sea. Nests are bulky untidy structures of grass, diddle-dee and dry kelp, irregularly spaced and rarely less than 2m (6 feet) apart. During the first half of December it lays two to three eggs, very variable in colour, from olive-green to blue-grey or rich buff heavily spotted and blotched with dark brown. Juveniles desert colonies with their parents early in March.

Over 1,300 were ringed between 1959 and 1964, most (>900) in Stanley and others at Darwin, Carcass Island and the Lagoon near Bluff Cove. No foreign recoveries were reported, again suggesting that the species is resident. Local recoveries showed movements across the Falklands of up to 190km (120 miles), as well as regular use of winter feeding areas and the probability that pairs remain together throughout the year. Assuming that the population is resident and not augmented by migrating birds, one ringed bird photographed in Stanley about October 1984 by A Douse was between 20 and 24 years old.

DISTRIBUTION ABROAD: Circumpolar on coasts in the southern hemisphere; in South America the race *L. d. dominicanus* breeds from 6°S in Peru and 23°S in Brazil through Argentina and Chile to Tierra del Fuego. It also breeds at South Georgia, South Shetlands and the Antarctic Peninsula to about 68°S, sub-Antarctic islands in the southern Indian Ocean and in New Zealand and southern Australia. In South Africa a race *L. d. vetula* has been described as having darker eyes.

135. Franklin's Gull   *Larus pipixcan*   Not illustrated
A. Gaviota pipixcan
c. Gaviota de Franklin
Small-medium. 13–15in/33–38cm

IDENTIFICATION: Sometimes resembling a small pigeon, it is noticeably smaller than the Brown-hooded Gull (136), with shorter wings, a more rounded head and body, stouter bill and rather short tail showing a pale grey centre at all ages. *Adult* has darker, blue-grey back and wing-coverts, white trailing edge, white tips to the primaries, variable black on primary centres and another white band separating black from the blue-grey inner wing, forming a distinctive pattern in flight. In *adult non-breeding* plumage head is white in front with a half-hood of black, including the eye and reaching over the ear-coverts and white crescents above and below eye are prominent. Bill dark reddish-black with red tip; legs dark red or black. *First winter* birds are much darker above, the only white showing on the wings is a narrow trailing edge; outer primaries black, inner primaries and their coverts brownish forming a pale bar before the black base to the secondaries. Rump white, tail grey with black subterminal band, broad in centre but showing white outer edges. Head white with clear black half-hood and white collar behind; back dark blue-grey with slightly mottled brown and grey wing-coverts. Bill and legs are black. In *breeding plumage* (unlikely to occur), the head has a complete black hood with thick, prominent white eye-crescents.

STATUS & RECORDS: Vagrant from usual wintering areas on coasts of South America, recorded once; an adult in winter plumage seen by W Curtis at West Point Island on 5 April 1986 (Wolsey 1986b).

DISTRIBUTION ABROAD: Breeds inland in southern Canada and northwestern United States and migrates through southern USA and West Indies to winter on western coast of South America from Peru to Chile with smaller numbers reaching the Magellan Straits. Has also been recorded in Cordoba province, Argentina (Olrog 1979) and a few were seen at Comodoro Rivadavia, Santa Cruz province in 1975 (Devillers & Terschuren 1976).

136. Brown-hooded Gull   *Larus maculipennis*   Plate 15
A. Gaviota cabecicafé
C. Gaviota cahuil
Local name: Pink-breasted Gull
Small-medium. 14–15in/36–38cm
IDENTIFICATION: The smallest and least common Falkland gull, the *adult* has a pearly grey back and wings with a characteristic white leading edge, broadest on the primaries. Underparts white with a variable rosy suffusion on neck, breast and sometimes the wing edge and tail, probably brightest in winter. Undersides of primaries appear dark grey to black. In *breeding plumage*, acquired July/August and retained until February, the head is chocolate-brown from bill to rear crown, curving across the neck to the base of the throat; a white partial ring is noticeable around the rear of the dark eye. Bill fairly slender, dark red; legs and feet brighter crimson-red. In *winter plumage* head is white with a dark spot on ear-coverts and over the crown. *Juvenile* mottled brown on the back, wing-coverts and crown, head otherwise similar to winter adult; wings show mainly black primaries with a white spot on the outer two, white primary coverts and blackish secondaries appearing as a dark trailing edge; tail white with a thin black subterminal bar. Bill orange-red with black tip; legs light yellow-brown. In *first winter* plumage, upperparts are mainly grey while wings and tail are similar to juvenile. In *first summer* plumage, bill and legs are brighter, head has partial brown hood and the black tail bar is usually less extensive. Flight is buoyant, usually with shallow wingbeats. It can be separated from terns at long distance by the much shorter, broader wings and dark undersides to primaries. Flocks at breeding grounds, and occasionally in winter, will mob a human intruder, calling continuously.

VOICE: Usual flight-note is a short *kip*, lower-pitched than a tern's call. A harsh guttural *kwarr* is used at the nest and when mobbing.

FOOD: Favoured feeding places are offshore kelp beds, where it takes small fish and other small marine organisms. Also feeds by picking sandhoppers or krill from the surf edge and has been seen 'treading' waterlogged sand on beaches; occasionally takes meat around settlements in winter but does not occur regularly at hen-runs as do the Kelp and Dolphin Gulls.

HABITAT, STATUS & BREEDING: Resident breeding species, only locally common; often overlooked because its usual haunts in winter are offshore kelp beds. Feeding flocks, sometimes of hundreds have been seen with shags and penguins over tide-rips at the north end of Falkland Sound, in Port William and off Cape Dolphin (Bourne & Curtis 1987).
    Breeds in colonies of up to at least 100 pairs in lake rush-beds or on small islands in lakes up to 5km (3 miles) inland, on rocky ridges with stunted tussac grass or shingle points, often with a Dolphin Gull or South American Tern colony. Nests are usually close together, made of dry grasses and hold two to three, occasionally four, olive or buff eggs heavily blotched with brown. Lays later than other gulls, from the third week of December to early January.

DISTRIBUTION ABROAD: Widely distributed in southern South America, breeding on the coast and inland from about 40°S on the coast of Chile and 33°S in Uruguay through lowland Argentina to southern Tierra del Fuego. Leaves the Beagle Channel region in winter, when many migrate northwards to reach 10°S on coasts of Brazil and 18°S in northern Chile, possibly occuring north to Peru.

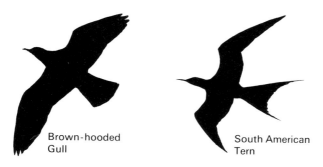

Brown-hooded Gull

South American Tern

Terns *Sternidae*

Terns are closely related to gulls but differ in their more slender build, generally smaller size, longer and narrower wings and forked tails. There is some disagreement over the number of genera, which include about 42 species. The genus Sterna *holds the majority, with about 30 species of grey-backed, white-bodied terns that have black caps in breeding plumage. They occur throughout the world, from the Arctic to the Antarctic and occur as non-breeders in coastal waters of all continents. Identification of terns is often difficult, especially at sea, where they rarely follow ships but continually fly and dive at a distance. Four species have been reported to date in Falkland waters; only the South American Tern breeds, while the Arctic and Antarctic Terns occur as non-breeding long-distance migrants. The Common Tern has been recorded once and may occur offshore. Three other tern species are described briefly below. They may visit Falkland waters but have not yet been reported.*

Trudeau's Tern   *Sterna trudeaui*
13in/33cm

Much smaller than South American Tern (140); *adult breeding* and *non-breeding* has white head with large black eye-patch extending across ear-coverts, grey underparts, pale grey upperparts, short tail streamers, fairly heavy yellow bill with black subterminal bar and reddish legs. *Juvenile* is mottled brownish above, has a dull yellowish bill and larger dark face patch. Breeds to about 50°S (Santa Cruz) on the coast of Argentina and occasionally reaches the Straits of Magellan.

Royal Tern   *Sterna maxima*
19½in/49cm

Much larger than South American Tern (140); in *breeding plumage* has heavy black cap and ragged crest at nape, very heavy dagger-shaped orange-red bill, very pale grey upperparts, white underparts and underwing with black trailing edge to primaries. *Non-breeding adult* has white head with black line through the eye and a ruff of black across nape, and a lighter red bill. *Juvenile* resembles winter adult but has a dark carpal bar, dark flecked back and upper wing-coverts, and a variable, yellowish or blackish bill. Breeds on coasts of Central America, West Indies and West Africa; also occasionally at about 45°S on the coast of Chubut, Argentina (Olrog 1979).

Cayenne Tern   *Sterna (sandvicensis) eurygnatha*
16–17in/40–43cm
Similar size to South American Tern (140) and considered by many to be a race
of the Sandwich Tern *S. sandvicensis*; *adult* in *breeding* plumage is pale grey above,
has white face and underparts with a large black cap from bill through eye to
nape and a ragged crest. Wings white below, pale grey above with blackish outer
few primaries; bill slender, all yellow or black with yellow tip; legs also vary from
yellow to black and yellow. *Non-breeding adult* has white forehead and lores, white
spotted with black on crown and retains black nape. *Juvenile* flecked brown above,
has dark carpal bar, otherwise resembles winter adult. Apparently breeds on
northern and eastern coasts of South America from Venezuela to Puerto Deseado
(47°S) on the coast of Argentina, but breeding range and winter movements are
not well known.

137. Common Tern   *Sterna hirundo*   Plate 15
A. Gaviotín golondrina
C. Gaviotín boreal
Small-medium. 12–14in/31–35cm
IDENTIFICATION: Smallest of the three migrant terns recorded and noticeably smaller than South American Tern (140), it is unlikely to be seen in breeding plumage
when adult has red bill, usually with black tip and a complete black cap. *Non-
breeding adult* has white front of head, black cap from behind eye to nape, blackish
bill sometimes with red base and white underparts. Wings above pale grey with
variable dark wedge on tips of outer primaries, showing most clearly in poor light;
underwing mostly white with diffuse blackish trailing edge to primaries; only the
inner primaries appear translucent in a close view against the light (compare with
Arctic Tern, 138); tail lacks streamers. *Immature* similar, but in first year wings
above have a dark carpal bar, blackish primaries and grey secondaries with a
noticeable broad pale grey patch on secondary coverts; tail greyish, lacks
streamers. At close range, when comparison with Arctic Tern is possible, it appears
more heavily built, longer necked and broader winged with a slightly thicker and
longer bill.

STATUS & RECORDS: Non-breeding visitor at southern limit of wintering and non-
breeding range, recorded once; one was collected at Cape Pembroke on 15 September 1945 (Cawkell & Hamilton 1961).

DISTRIBUTION ABROAD: Widely distributed in the Northern Hemisphere, through
central and northeastern United States, most of Europe and central Asia. Migrates
through northern oceans to winter as far south as Tasmania, off southern South
Africa and to the Straits of Magellan.

138. Arctic Tern   *Sterna paradisaea*   Plate 21
A. & C. Gaviotín ártico
Small-medium. 13–15in/33–38cm
IDENTIFICATION: Slightly smaller and more lightly built than Common Tern (137)

and smaller than South American Tern (140), the wings appear narrower and set further forward, the head more rounded, the bill shorter and the tail longer. In good light, when viewed from below, Arctic Terns of all ages can be recognised by the translucent appearance of most primaries. Underwing is pure white with a narrow black trailing edge to primaries. *Non-breeding adult* and *immature* over one year old are mainly grey above except for white rump and tail; grey underparts with white belly and undertail; black cap except for white forehead; blackish bill and dark red legs and feet. *First year* bird resembles non-breeding adult except for mottled grey underparts, a faint dark carpal bar on upper wing and darker outer primaries; separation from first year South American, Common and Antarctic Terns (139) may be impossible at long range. In the first and second summer after hatching, when most immatures remain in southern oceans, plumage resembles winter adult, possibly with traces of the dark carpal bar.

STATUS & RECORDS: Apparently a scarce non-breeding visitor from the Northern Hemisphere recorded offshore throughout the year (Bourne & Curtis 1985) and occasionally inshore with South American Terns (Peatfield 1981). One was seen by W Bourne in the southern approaches to Falkland Sound on 27 February 1986 (Bourne & Curtis 1987).

DISTRIBUTION ABROAD: Breeds widely in the Arctic and cold temperate Northern Hemisphere, migrating in southern oceans to the edge of the Antarctic pack ice.

139. Antarctic Tern   *Sterna vittata*   Plate 21
A. & C. Gaviotín antártico
Medium. 15–16in/38–41cm

IDENTIFICATION: Easily confused with South American Tern (140), but somewhat smaller with generally darker grey underparts and upperparts in breeding plumage. *Adult* in *breeding* plumage has bright red, fairly stout bill and dark red legs. Wings above show a faint dark wedge on outer primaries; underwing white showing only a narrow dark line along trailing edge of primaries; back dark grey contrasting with the white rump and deeply forked tail. Wing pattern similar to Arctic Tern (138) and although it closely resembles that species, most Arctic Terns would be in non-breeding plumage when present in Falkland waters. *Adult non-breeding* has extensive white front to head, black cap on nape and sides of head and white lores. Bill and legs are less bright red and underparts mainly white with a grey patch across breast. *First year* bird has dark crown, blackish bar on forewing and blackish bill and legs. *Juvenile* mottled brown and white above with black barring on back; white below with brown freckling on breast, very dark primaries and a slightly forked tail with darker outer edges.

STATUS & RECORDS: Passage migrant and probable non-breeding visitor to Falkland waters, possibly recorded in 1979 and 1980 off Cape Pembroke (Peatfield 1981) and definitely identified in Choiseul Sound by W Curtis on 31 March 1987.

DISTRIBUTION ABROAD: Four races have been described from different groups of sub-Antarctic islands in southern Atlantic and Indian Oceans. Winter movements are not well known due to identification difficulties, though it has been recorded off southern coasts of South Africa and South America.

140. South American Tern   *Sterna hirundinacea*   Plate 15
A. Gaviotín colilargo
C. Gaviotín sudamericano
Local names: Split-tail; Swallow-tailed Gull
Medium. 16–17in/40–43cm
IDENTIFICATION: The tern most likely to be seen inshore during the summer, and the only tern breeding in the Falklands, it is a slender, almost white bird with long, thin pointed wings. *Adult breeding* has a jet-black cap from bill to nape, a thin white line bordering the cap and very pale grey underparts becoming white on the belly. Upperparts pale grey with a black streak along the outer edge of the outermost primary and a narrow white trailing edge to inner wing; upper tail-coverts and rump white; tail white, deeply forked with long streamers. Bill fairly heavy, slightly drooped, bright blood-red; legs and feet blood-red. *Adult non-breeding* has a white forehead and whiter underparts; bill and legs are less bright. *Juvenile* lacks tail streamers, has blackish carpal bar and brown mottled back and wing-coverts. Head and underparts are brownish with a light forehead, dark cap and ear-coverts; bill black and legs pink. *First year* bird resembles winter adult but retains the dark carpal bar and has a blackish bill. In flight the jerky wing action, lifting the body at each stroke, and the long trailing tail are characteristic. Often seen fishing in large loose flocks over offshore kelp beds, diving vertically into water from about 7m (20 feet); it also hovers then drops to the surface to feed. When breeding it is antagonistic towards Crested Caracaras, Skuas or Kelp Gulls and may swoop close to people, sometimes striking with the feet.

VOICE: In flight often uses a short clear *kyik*, sharper and higher-pitched than the Brown-hooded Gull's call. When mobbing utters a harsh, descending scream *keeeer* or a short *ik-ik-ik*. At nesting grounds is very noisy and, when fishing offshore, calls continually.

FOOD: Small fish and crustaceans are obtained by diving into the sea surface or by picking from amongst kelp fronds.

HABITAT, STATUS & BREEDING: Common summer resident, returning to inshore waters in late September and October, leaving by late March/early April. Widespread around Falkland coasts, over kelp beds and in lower reaches of larger rivers. Breeds in colonies, often near Brown-hooded, Dolphin and Kelp Gulls in a variety of sites, mostly on shingle or rocky beaches and peninsulas or on isolated rock points sheltered by tussac grass or thrift. Nests are mere scrapes on beaches but are lined with grasses when available. Colonies also occur at freshwater ponds inland. Lays two eggs, very variable in shape and colour, ranging from buff to pale blue or rich olive-brown, variably speckled and blotched with brown and smaller than those of the Brown-hooded Gull. Eggs are laid between late November and late December; fledged young may be seen from late January.

DISTRIBUTION ABROAD: A common breeding species on both coasts of South America from about 14°S in Peru and 23°S in Brazil to Tierra del Fuego and Cape Horn. Ranges north in winter to about 5°S off Peru and 15°S off Brazil, though some are present in Falkland and Magellanic waters throughout the year.

Pigeons or Doves   *Columbidae*
*Pigeons or doves are a very varied family of landbirds, comprising 255 species in 43
genera, with a worldwide continental distribution, except in the colder northern and
southern regions. They range in size from that of a sparrow to a large goose and are
generally plump with a small head and have soft dense plumage. Wing and tail size
and shape vary tremendously, but most are strong fliers. Pigeons or doves feed on seeds,
fruit, flowers and leaves and some species eat small invertebrates. Forty-five species
occur in South America of which two have reached the Falklands as vagrants. The
Chilean Pigeon has occurred once and the Eared Dove is a frequent though irregular
visitor.*

141. Chilean Pigeon   *Columba araucana*   Plate 16
A. Paloma araucana
c. Torcaza
Small-medium. 14–15in/35–38cm
IDENTIFICATION: Heavily built and much larger than the Eared Dove (142), it has
a rich purple-chestnut head, mantle and underparts, a narrow whitish collar
across the nape with a metallic green patch below, grey wing-coverts, blackish
flight feathers and a grey tail with a black subterminal band. Bill is black and
legs dark red.

STATUS & RECORDS: Vagrant from South America recorded once; an adult male
in poor condition was shot at Teal Inlet on 19 September 1941 (Hamilton 1950).

DISTRIBUTION ABROAD: A forest species found in central and southern Chile (28°–
47°S) and andean regions of southern Argentina (37°–47°S). It was formerly very
abundant but numbers decreased considerably as the Chilean forests were
destroyed.

142. Eared Dove   *Zenaida auriculata*   Plate 16
A. Tórtola torcaza or Tórtola dorada
c. Tórtola
Small. 10–11in/25–28cm
IDENTIFICATION: The only pigeon occurring frequently in the Falklands, it is recognised by the olive-brown upperparts with several black spots on the scapulars
and wing-coverts. Crown and flanks pale grey with light pinkish-brown underparts, fading to whitish on the belly. Flight feathers are dark brown with narrow
buff edges. Two small black spots behind the eye and a metallic purple area at
the side of the neck are sometimes difficult to see. *Female* is slightly smaller than
male and more brownish beneath. *Immature* is lightly flecked buff beneath. Feeds
on the ground, typically in gardens where it takes seeds of garden weeds. When
flushed it rises rapidly with the long, graduated grey-brown tail fanned, showing
broad white edging and a narrow black subterminal band.

STATUS & RECORDS: Vagrant occurring irregularly and usually singly in gardens
or near settlements, it has been recorded about 30 times. Most birds reported in
March/April, also in February and June and once 20 September to 13 October
1961 when one survived in gardens at Stanley. Eared Doves seem to find sufficient
food around settlements and could possibly survive in the absence of feral cats.

DISTRIBUTION ABROAD: Common in open scrubland and cultivated savanna regions of South America from Venezuela and northeastern Brazil, through Paraguay and Uruguay to the Pampas of Argentina and in central and southern Chile to Tierra del Fuego. Occurs in huge flocks in central Argentina, where it feeds on grain crops and has become a serious pest.

Parrots   Psittacidae

Parrots are a distinctive family of 332 species in 82 genera, found mostly in tropical regions of the Southern Hemisphere. They have strongly curved, moveable upper mandibles which fit over their lower mandibles, enabling them to shell nuts before eating them. Parrots vary in size from about 8cm to 1m (3–39in) and show a similarly wide variation in wing and tail shape. Most have loud, raucous calls and show some green in their plumage. There are 141 species in South America, of which about 27 are found in Argentina. Two species have probably reached the Falklands as vagrants; the Austral Parakeet arrived in numbers one year and the Burrowing Parrot was almost certainly recorded once.

143. Burrowing Parrot   *Cyanoliseus patagonus*   Not illustrated
A. Loro barranquero
C. Tricahue
Medium. 17–18in/43–46cm
IDENTIFICATION: Larger and darker above than the Austral Parakeet (144), the Burrowing Parrot has dark green-brown head, mantle, wing-coverts and breast; a yellow lower back, rump and belly with a large red patch in the centre of the belly. Flight feathers are dark blue and the long pointed tail is dull brown; bill blackish; legs and feet red. In South America occurs in flocks and calls continually when flying.

STATUS & RECORDS: Vagrant, probably recorded once; a single bird flew overhead, screeching loudly, at New Island on 1 May 1959 and was later seen eating diddle-dee berries (Woods 1975). It was noted as larger than previously recorded Parakeets, grey-green above and rusty beneath with red legs.

DISTRIBUTION ABROAD: Three races are described from central Chile (30°–40°S), northwestern and central Argentina (25°–42°S). It inhabits open shrubby country with ravines, feeds on the ground and nests in sandstone cliffs. Southern breeding populations migrate northward in winter, possibly reaching Uruguay.

144. Austral Parakeet   *Enicognathus ferrugineus*   Plate 16
A. Cotorra austral
C. Cachaña
Small-medium. 13–14in/33–36cm
IDENTIFICATION: Dull green on head and upperparts and yellow-green below with a scaly pattern of black edges, most prominent on crown; forehead, lores and centre of belly dull red; pointed tail brownish-red and very long, about half the total length of the bird; wings darker green above, long and pointed with yellow-green under wing-coverts and grey undersides to flight feathers. Bill small, often concealed in facial feathers. Commonly flies in noisy flocks.

STATUS & RECORDS: Vagrant, recorded in only two years; in mid-June 1957 an apparent invasion occurred and many were seen at several places including New Island, Beaver Island, West Point Island (26), Speedwell Island, Fox Bay and at Chartres where 60 were counted on one roof (Woods 1975). In April 1959 about ten were seen at Fox Bay East, two at Barren Island and one in Stanley during the same week. No specimens were collected but several descriptions received suggested this species.

DISTRIBUTION ABROAD: Two races described; *E. f. ferrugineus* occurs in forested parts of Tierra del Fuego and the Magellanic region of Chile, where it is resident. *E. f. minor* inhabits andean regions of Southern Argentina (40°–52°S) and Chile (35°–47°S).

Cuckoos *Cuculidae*

The cuckoo family contains about 130 species in 34 genera, varying considerably in size. Some are very secretive terrestrial birds and many utter loud calls only when breeding. Species that are seen most often are long-tailed, slender birds with thin bills adapted to take insects, particularly hairy caterpillars which are shunned by other families of birds. They occur in tropical and temperate regions throughout the world. Twenty-three species occur in tropical South America; only three of these lay their eggs in the nest of other birds. Thirteen species have been recorded in Argentina but only one of these has occurred once as a vagrant in the Falkland Islands.

145. Dark-billed Cuckoo *Coccyzus melacoryphus*   Plate 16
A. Cuclillo piconegro
c. Cuclillo de pico negro
Small. 10–11in/25–28cm

IDENTIFICATION: About the size of the Falkland Thrush (178), this cuckoo has a very long tail, brown in the centre and black at the sides with large white tips. Head dark grey above with black line through the eye; throat whitish and underparts buff; back and fairly long rounded wings are pale grey-brown and bill and legs black. A very secretive bird of thick scrubland that flies with rapid wingbeats but tends to escape notice by hopping through undergrowth.

STATUS & RECORDS: Vagrant recorded once; a male in poor condition was caught in Government House garden, Stanley on 7 April 1937. It was thought to have been in the area for about three weeks (Bennett 1937).

DISTRIBUTION ABROAD: Widespread in tropical and subtropical South America west of the Andes from Venezuela to Peru (15°S) and resident on the Galapagos Islands; east of the Andes occurs through Brazil to about 35°S in central Argentina. Probably sedentary though southern populations may migrate northwards in winter.

Barn Owls *Tytonidae* and Owls *Strigidae*

All owls are soft-plumaged, mostly mottled or streaked birds with a large head, short tail and large forward-facing eyes in a facial disc. They are mainly nocturnal hunters. The bill is short and strongly hooked and the feet have long, sharp claws. There are about 124 species of typical owls (Strigidae) *in about 23 genera, varying in body-length from 12 to 73 cm (4½– 29 in). They have rounded facial discs and usually have thickly feathered legs. The Barn Owl family has ten species in two genera; their facial discs are heart-shaped and their eyes relatively smaller than those of the typical owls. Owls occur in all continents of the world except Antarctica and have colonised several oceanic islands. Most species are sedentary while some migrate irregularly, depending on the abundance of rodents on which they feed.*

Apart from the resident Short-eared Owl and possibly resident Barn Owl, records of owls in the Falklands are poorly documented. The Rufous-legged Owl seems most unlikely to be a resident though it has been claimed as such since at least 1921. Two others have occurred, probably as vagrants.

Short-eared Owl

146. Barn Owl   *Tyto alba*   Plate 17
A. Lechuza de campanarios
C. Lechuza
Local name: White Owl.
Small-medium. 14–16 in/35–41 cm
IDENTIFICATION: A very pale coloured owl that appears white when flying at dusk. All upperparts including crown, wings and tail are mottled pale grey and buff finely speckled with white; flight feathers and tail are also lightly barred brown. Heart-shaped facial disc is pure white, bordered with orange-brown; eyes black. Underparts vary from pure white, lightly flecked grey on flanks to warm buff. Long legs are covered with white feathers and claws are black. Flight is slow and wavering when hunting and legs often dangle noticeably.

VOICE: Flight call is an eerie scream; also makes hissing and snoring noises.

FOOD: No certain records available from the Falklands; abroad takes mainly small mammals caught by dropping onto them from about 3m (10 feet) and grabbing with the claws.

HABITAT, STATUS & BREEDING: Status uncertain; possibly breeding up to 1951 in Port Howard camp at Shag Cove and Mount Caroline near Port Purvis (Cawkell & Hamilton 1961). Two specimens were obtained at Port Stephens in about 1976, one apparently lived in a barn at Chartres 'for years', one inhabited a shed at Moody Brook near Stanley 'for some time', a dead bird was picked up at West Point Island in March 1983 and another was seen flying at West Point on several days that month (R Napier pers. comm.). One was shot near Johnson's Harbour before 1951 (Cawkell & Hamilton 1961) and one killed at Cape Pembroke Light on 14 September 1937 (British Museum). One was caught alive at George Island in July 1963 (Woods 1975); one, first noticed on 25 May 1976 at Carcass Island, was found dead on 28 May (K Bertrand pers. comm.). One was seen near Stanley in November 1981 and S Francis collected ten pellets containing House Mouse remains, from a possible roosting place in a house at Limpet Creek, Salvador in December 1983 (Wolsey, 1986c).

Unfortunately, no suspected or confirmed breeding records have been received. In other parts of its range, the Barn Owl nests in old buildings where entry and exit are easy and ample space around the nest is available. It also nests on exposed cliffs where buildings are not suitable. It is therefore possible that Barn Owls breed in the Falklands though the apparent weak state of several birds seen, and later found dead, suggests they were vagrants from South America.

DISTRIBUTION ABROAD: About 36 races of *Tyto alba* have been described. They occur throughout the world except in African desert regions, parts of central Asia and northern regions of Eurasia and North America. The race *T. a. tuidara* inhabits South America from the Guianas and Peru to Tierra del Fuego.

147. Great Horned Owl *Bubo virginianus* Not illustrated
A. Búho or Ñacurutú
C. Tucúquere
Medium to medium-large. 18–22in/45–56cm

IDENTIFICATION: Much larger than the resident Short-eared Owl (150), about the same size as the Red-backed Hawk (89), this very large and bulky owl is dark brown above heavily mottled with buff and grey and the flight feathers are dark brown broadly barred whitish and mottled grey. Face is cinnamon bordered narrowly with black; two prominent widely spaced 'eartufts' are black, marked buff on inner sides; eyes yellow; lower edge of face white; upper throat buff, and lower throat and foreneck white. Rest of underparts are buffy-white closely barred dark brown. Plumage varies in tone, some birds being much whiter below, marked with grey. Hunts nocturnally, usually spending the daytime motionless in a large tree.

STATUS & RECORDS: Vagrant recorded once; single bird seen in a 16 year-old plantation of Monterey and Austrian Pines *Pinus radiata* & *P. nigra* at Carcass Island in early January 1975 (K Bertrand pers. comm.).

DISTRIBUTION ABROAD: Widespread in North and South America from Canada to Tierra del Fuego, inhabiting forests and more open country with scrub. Resident in Tierra del Fuego but less common on islands south of the Beagle Channel.

148. Burrowing Owl *Athene cunicularia* Plate 17
A. Lechucita de las viscacheras
C. Pequén
Small. 8–10in/20–25cm

IDENTIFICATION: A small light brown owl, spotted on crown and mottled with white on back and wing-coverts; creamy-white below barred with brown on breast and flanks. Facial disc brown; forehead and 'eyebrow' white; throat white bordered blackish below; eyes yellow; legs are whitish and noticeably long. *Immatures* are buff-white on the breast and lack bars below. Occurs in open country away from trees, typically perching on a hummock near the nest burrow during the day. Hunts at night, though it often flies by day. Uses a soft clucking hoot when intruders approach.

STATUS & RECORDS: Status uncertain, probably a vagrant; one record of a dead bird found on West Point Island in November 1945 by G Napier. Cawkell and Hamilton (1961) reported eggs, possibly of this species, taken from short burrows in white grass at Island Harbour, East Falkland in the early 1950s and Fox Bay, West Falkland in 1955. White grass camp may provide suitable habitat but no birds have been reported since 1945.

DISTRIBUTION ABROAD: Occurs from the western United States through Central and most of South America in suitable open country to southern Argentina (50°S) and Chile to about 40°S. Three races recognised in South America; *A. c. partridgei* occurs from southern Brazil and Uruguay through most of Argentina. Formerly common in northern Tierra del Fuego but apparently exterminated by about 1920, probably following the increase in sheep which tend to destroy burrows by trampling.

149. Rufous-legged Owl   *Strix rufipes*   Plate 17
A. Lechuza bataraz
C. Concón
Small-medium. 14–15in/35–38cm
IDENTIFICATION: Slightly smaller than Short-eared Owl (150) and generally much darker in colour, the head is blackish-brown with red-brown facial disc bordered with black, white 'eyebrows', lores and throat and brown eyes. Underparts are buffy-white heavily barred with black, upperparts dark brown narrowly barred with white and buff; flight feathers barred red-brown and blackish; tail broadly barred dark brown on buff. Legs covered with reddish-buff feathers.

STATUS & RECORDS: Status uncertain, probably a vagrant; Wace (1921) stated that it bred in the Falklands and there were specimens in the local collection. Bennett (1926) stated, 'A rare bird which perhaps breeds in the Falklands. The feet of the local bird are not red but a pale brown.' Cawkell and Hamilton (1961) simply stated, 'A rare breeder on Hill Cove and Port Howard farms.' Bennett preserved the skin of an owl in September 1937, but it was wrongly labelled *Strix rufipes*. It was a Barn Owl *Tyto alba* and is in the British Museum. There have been no documented records for over 60 years. It seems unlikely that a bird of continental forests would inhabit the Falklands.

DISTRIBUTION ABROAD: Three races described from central and southern Argentina and Chile to Tierra del Fuego. Said to be the least known owl in Chile (Goodall, Johnson & Philippi 1951) and local in Argentina (Olrog 1984).

150. Short-eared Owl   *Asio flammeus*   Plate 17
A. Lechuzón campestre
C. Nuco
Local name: Owl
Small-medium. 14–15in/35–38cm
IDENTIFICATION: The only widespread and well-known owl in the Falklands, it is buff above beautifully mottled and barred with dark brown; underparts are rich buff with wide dark brown streaks on neck and breast and more lightly streaked,

paler buff flanks and belly. The head is large and rounded with a light buff facial disc, white 'eyebrows' and lores and bright orange/lemon-yellow eyes surrounded by black feathers. Small 'eartufts' are inconspicuous and only raised when the bird is excited. Legs are covered by buff feathers; claws and bill are blackish. In flight is unlike any other Falkland bird; wings are broad, long and round-ended showing a dark mark at the carpal joint below, dark barred wingtips and a buff patch at base of primaries above; the body tapers from the bulky head to the short tail; wingbeats are typically deep and slow with a wavering action. Usually flies near the ground when hunting and is most active around dusk and until at least midnight in mid-summer. It also flies by day, sometimes at considerable heights.

VOICE: Silent except during the breeding season when territorial adults use a sharp *yip-yip-yip* or a sneezing *wheechiz* as they circle over intruders near nests. In display flight the male circles high above territory, repeatedly claps the wings together and drops suddenly while uttering a repeated low *boo-boo-boo*. This song is also uttered from perches. In distraction-display, when intruders are near a nest, the adult utters a quiet squealing note.

FOOD: Apparently lives on Grey-backed Storm-Petrels, Diving Petrels and Camel-crickets on tussac islands where these species are present. Also takes large weevils found in diddle-dee, Tussac-birds and probably Thin-billed Prions. Rats and House Sparrows or other small birds may be taken around settlements in winter. It is not known how petrels are caught but it seems likely that they are captured in flight as they approach or leave nest burrows after dark.

HABITAT, STATUS & BREEDING: Breeding resident, widely distributed but only locally common on some of the larger islands and tussac islands, where it usually breeds. Occurs more widely, over open camp in winter. Nests on the ground in the shelter of thick grass or rushes and apparently lays only two rounded, white eggs, but there are few nest-records. Nestlings have been heard calling in mid-November, suggesting that eggs are laid from early October. Adults may swoop aggressively at intruders near the nest.

DISTRIBUTION ABROAD: About eight races have been described, occurring mainly in the Northern Hemisphere from temperate to arctic regions, but also in the Hawaiian and Caroline Islands and South America. The race *A. f. suinda* is fairly common in open country from Venezuela to Peru and from southern Brazil through Argentina and Chile to northern Tierra del Fuego. Falkland breeding birds have been described as a distinct race, *A. f. sanfordi*.

Swifts *Apodidae*

Swifts are the most aerial of all birds, feeding, roosting, gathering nest material and copulating on the wing. Though superficially resembling swallows, they have much longer, narrower wings particularly adapted for high-speed flight, very short legs with strong claws and very wide gapes enabling them to scoop flying insects. All are blackish or brown coloured, sometimes with white or lighter patches, and many species are very difficult to identify in the field. Most of the 82 known species inhabit tropical regions; a few species breed in northern temperate latitudes and migrate to the Southern

Hemisphere in winter. Of the 23 species recorded in South America, eight occur in northern Argentina. Two species have been recorded as long-distance vagrants in the Falklands.

151. White-collared Swift   *Streptoprocne zonaris*   Not illustrated
A. Vencejo cuelliblanco
c. Not recorded
Very small to small. 7½–9in/19–23cm
IDENTIFICATION: The largest South American swift, it is sooty black on throat, wings and tail with a prominent white collar around the neck, broader on the breast; underparts and back are deeper black and the tail is of medium length, slightly forked. *Immature* faintly flecked whitish below and almost lacking the white band on foreneck.

STATUS & RECORDS: Vagrant recorded once; a single bird was seen to fly in towards Cape Pembroke Lighthouse on 12 November 1986 and circle for at least half an hour. It was watched closely and photographed by R Martins, S Wolsey and P Dukes (Wolsey 1986d).

DISTRIBUTION ABROAD: A tropical region species occurring from Panama, Venezuela and Columbia, through Peru and in southern Brazil, Uruguay, Paraguay and Argentina to about 35°S. It inhabits the skies over open country and mountainous regions to an altitude of about 3000m (10,000 feet). A few vagrants have been recorded in the United States.

152. Ashy-tailed Swift   *Chaetura andrei*   Plate 16
A. Vencejo gargantiblanco
c. Not recorded
Tiny. 5–6in/12–15cm
IDENTIFICATION: A small swift, shiny dark brown above with a paler rump and a very short square tail with needle-like projecting feather shafts (2–4cm). Primaries and secondaries are black and slightly glossy. Underparts are sooty brown, except for a pale whitish throat. Under tail-coverts, greater under wing-coverts and upper wing-coverts sometimes show a slightly green sheen.

STATUS & RECORDS: Vagrant recorded once; a perfectly preserved mummified corpse was found in a shed at the old Naval Wireless Station, Moody Brook near Stanley on 1 March 1959 by B Withers. It had apparently entered the building through a partly open window and could not escape (Woods 1975).

DISTRIBUTION ABROAD: Two races are described from tropical South America. *C. a. andrei* occurs in Surinam, Venezuela and northern Colombia and the other, *C. a. meridionalis* inhabits eastern and southern Brazil from about 5°S through Paraguay to northern Argentina (30°S). This race is found over savanna, open woodland and along rivers. It does not normally occur within 2400km (1500 miles) of the Falklands.

Hummingbirds *Trochilidae*
Hummingbirds are a New World family of 320 mostly tiny birds, with specialised tongues and slender, usually long bills, that feed on nectar from flowers. The wings are highly modified to permit a rotary movement which allows hovering and very rapid forward and backward flight. Hummingbirds are found from Alaska to Tierra del Fuego, in all kinds of habitats, and up to the snow-line in the Andes. Of the 235 species occurring in South America, most occupy tropical regions. Thirty species inhabit Argentina and the one with the most southerly distribution has occurred several times in the Falklands.

153. Green-backed Firecrown   *Sephanoides sephanoides*   Plate 16
A. Picaflor cabeza granate
C. Picaflor
Very tiny. 4–4½in/10–11cm
Bill 0.6in/1.5cm
IDENTIFICATION: The smallest bird recorded in the Falklands, the *male* is bronzy-green above with a glittering red crown and blackish flight feathers and grey-white underparts speckled with bronze on breast. *Female* is similar above but has a black crown and whitish underparts, closely spotted with brown on the throat and upper breast.

STATUS & RECORDS: Wind-blown vagrant recorded at least four times. A male was caught on West Falkland, probably at Fox Bay before 1912 (M White & D Davidson pers. comm.) and one was picked up dead at Fox Bay East in late October 1930 (Bennett 1931). One was eaten by a cat at Government House, Stanley in 1952 (Cawkell unpublished ms.) and a female caught in Government House greenhouse on 28 March 1963 by P Peck, died the following day; this bird weighed 4.25gms, after surviving a journey of about 725km (450 miles) without food (Woods 1975).

DISTRIBUTION ABROAD: Breeds over a wide range in Chile from about 28°S to 53°S in northern Tierra del Fuego and from about 1800m (6000 feet) in the Andes to sea level. In Argentina breeds only in andean regions from 32°S to 53°S. Migrates northward to about 27°S in Chile and to the eastern lowlands of Argentina in winter while andean populations migrate to lower altitudes.

Ovenbirds *Furnariidae*
An extremely varied family of New World passerines, containing about 220 species, mostly occurring in South America. The majority are dull coloured birds of thick vegetation, particularly wooded regions in the tropics, though they occur in all habitats from andean highlands to open plains and shorelines between central Mexico and Cape Horn. In Argentina there are 74 species in 28 genera; only one species, the Tussac-bird is resident in the Falklands. Two others, the Thorn-tailed Rayadito and Austral Canastero are of doubtful status, possibly former breeding species or vagrants.

Tussac-bird

154. Thorn-tailed Rayadito   *Aphrastura spinicauda*   Plate 17
A. & C. Rayadito
Very tiny to tiny. 4–5½in/10–14cm
IDENTIFICATION: A tiny, noisy and active bird of wooded areas in southern South America, it is distinctively patterned; head is black with broad and long buff eye-stripe extending to sides of the nape; back light brown; rump and centre of tail cinnamon, centre of outer feathers black with 1cm (0.4in) long spines projecting from the central tips of each tail feather. Flight feathers blackish with buff edges to secondaries and bases of primaries, forming a double buff bar; underparts white from chin to belly becoming greyish on flanks. Bill short and thin, black; legs greenish-grey with long toes. In flight the tail looks broad and trails behind the body. When feeding it can run up or down vertical tree trunks without pressing the tail against the surface and continually bobs; notable for its habit of scolding and approaching close to an observer. The usual call is a double *tzt-tzt* often repeated and sometimes prolonged into a shrill scolding note.

STATUS & RECORDS: Uncertain, possibly vagrant or lost breeding species; one specimen said to have been collected in the Falklands by the Antarctic Expedition of 1842, was presented to the British Museum by the Admiralty in the nineteenth century (Sclater & Sharpe 1885–98). This specimen could have come from Hermite Island, west of Cape Horn which was visited by Ross's expedition in September/November 1842, between periods at Port Louis. Reports were received from C Bertrand in 1963 and 1983 of tiny birds that 'flicked about up and down tussac grass stems' around the pond on the west end of East Sea Lion Island in 1933/34. They were said to be the colour of Tussac-birds above with a most noticeable yellow eye-stripe, smaller than wrens and 'frail'. C Bertrand's description of colour and behaviour was a vivid memory recalled from 50 or more years earlier; it suggests this species but is not conclusive. A brief visit to East Sea Lion Island on 6 November 1983 produced no sightings.

DISTRIBUTION ABROAD: Common in wooded areas of central Chile (from 30°S) and Argentina (from 37°S) to Tierra del Fuego, Staten Island and the Magellanic Islands (56°S). Reynolds (1935) described it as a bird of thick scrub and forest and reported it from all Magellanic islands in any semblance of a tree; 'At Barnevelt Island it has found an excellent substitute for trees in the huge groves of tussock-grass.'

155. Tussac-bird   *Cinclodes antarcticus*   Plate 17
A. Remolinera negra
C. Churrete austral
Local name: Black Bird
Very small. 7¼–8¼in/18–21cm
IDENTIFICATION: The only small Falkland landbird with all brown plumage, black bill and legs, this tame, restless and inquisitive bird is easily recognised. *Adults and immatures* are similar; body plumage is dark brown with red-brown edges to wing-coverts and variable buff flecks on the throat. The head is rather long and the bill is stout at the base, slightly downcurved and sharp-pointed, showing variable yellow at the gape, more noticeable on juveniles. Flight is rapid with

quick beats of fairly broad black-brown wings showing a faint red-brown bar across inner primaries and secondaries. Typically flies just above the grass and shoots down slopes in long glides. On the ground, has a low stance and runs rapidly. Is so tame that it may approach someone and even perch on a foot or shoulder. If handled it has a peculiar musty odour.

VOICE: Call-notes and song are mostly high-pitched and often explosive. The usual call is a short, sharp *chip*, uttered singly or repeated with rising pitch, as a trill. In territorial chases and disputes over feeding sites, trills are persistent, with lower buzzing notes also used. The explosive and ear-piercing song is mainly used in early morning from a low perch or in song-flight reaching about 10m (33 feet) and ending in a dive to ground; it is a rhythmic sequence of staccato *chip-chip-chip-chip* notes slurred onto a very rapid, lower-pitched, trill and continuing with alternating staccato and trill sequences for several minutes. It is often accompanied by a wing-raising display which may be seen throughout the year during aggressive encounters. Information on song-period is lacking but it probably sings from early September to January.

FOOD: The diet is varied, consists mostly of animal matter and includes small marine invertebrates picked from the surf edge or amongst heaps of rotting kelp, where larvae of flies and small molluscs are also taken. Camel-crickets and the remains of regurgitated fish collected in Shag colonies are fed to the young in the nest. At settlements it will enter houses to steal butter or breadcrumbs and it also takes mutton scraps from carcasses.

HABITAT, STATUS & BREEDING: Resident, very common on outer islands that have remained free of introduced mammalian predators and rare where cats and rats are present. Uncommon on mainland East and West Falkland coasts. A terrestrial species, typical of boulder and sand-beaches where kelp accumulates, and dense tussac grass provides cover and soft ground where it can nest. It is not restricted to tussac islands however and is able to take advantage of artificial cover such as sheds and walls. Tussac-bird population density in a mixed tussac (40%) and short grazed grass (60%) coastal habitat can be twice as high as that achieved in the coastal strip of an island covered with dense mature tussac (Woods 1985). It also occurs up to at least 500m (550yds) inland and to a height of 200m (650 feet) on islands where it is abundant. Nests from early September to December with most starting to lay in October and often with second broods. The nest is a shallow cup of grasses lined with a few feathers, placed in a hole under tussac grass, beneath loose rocks on a beach, under a shed or house, in an earth bank or old burrow of Magellanic Penguin or petrel. Lays one to three slightly glossy white eggs, sometimes minutely spotted with red around the blunt end.

A small colour-ringing study on Kidney Island between 1959 and 1963 showed that pairs tended to remain in territory between October and mid-April, though adults would cross the island (300m/330yds) to collect food for nestlings from a Shag colony. Four birds reached three and a half years and two survived at least five years.

DISTRIBUTION ABROAD: Two races have been described; the race *C. a. antarcticus* is restricted to the Falklands and *C. a. maculirostris* occurs only on islands south of Tierra del Fuego and Staten Island.

156. Austral Canastero   *Thripophaga anthoides*   Plate 17
A. Canastero manchado
C. Canastero del sur
Very small. 6½in/16cm
IDENTIFICATION: A secretive little bird of dense thickets in northern Tierra del Fuego, it has dull olive-grey upperparts heavily streaked with black and red-brown wing-coverts showing as a patch on the side. The tail is fairly long, blackish with chestnut tips to outer feathers. Head is thickly streaked black with yellowish or rufous throat; rest of underparts buff-grey, finely streaked black on breast, paler on belly. Bill greyish with yellow base, short and pointed; legs dull grey. Separated from other species of Canastero, which could reach the Falklands, by the heavy black streaking above. Call-notes are said to be chirping or warbling (Crawshay 1907, Humphrey 1970).

STATUS & RECORDS: Uncertain; possibly former breeding species or vagrant apparently recorded once. Darwin collected an adult specimen in 1833 or 1834 (Sclater & Sharpe 1885–98). It was reported as originating in the Falklands. Darwin does not comment on this species (Gould & Darwin 1841) and Barlow (1963) records the series of skins, including this one, as originating in Chile.

DISTRIBUTION ABROAD: Inhabits pastures, thickets and slopes of the Andes to about 1300m (4000 feet) from 37°S in Chile and Argentina to northern Tierra del Fuego and Staten Island. Apparently resident in Tierra del Fuego though other populations migrate north to about 32°S.

Tapaculos   *Rhinocryptidae*
Tapaculos are secretive, mostly dark coloured, ground-living birds with long legs that carry their tails erect like wrens. They vary in size from about 10–25cm (4–10in), rarely fly but run rapidly through dense vegetation. Twenty-eight species in 12 genera occur only in the New World, from Costa Rica to Tierra del Fuego. They occur in andean habitats in the tropics and at lower altitudes in southern temperate regions. Ten species inhabit Argentina and one species that may have bred, was recorded in the Falklands last century.

157. Andean Tapaculo   *Scytalopus magellanicus*   Plate 17
A. Churrín común
C. Churrín del Sur
Very tiny. 4–4½in/10–11cm
IDENTIFICATION: A tiny, dark bird, resembling the House Wren (175) in shape and very difficult to see as it runs through thickets. Head, back, underparts and tail are dark slaty-grey; wings and belly tinged with brown; bill black, legs yellow-brown. Individuals vary in tone, some being almost black or having a variable amount of silvery-grey on the crown. *Juveniles* have narrow chestnut bars on the rump. Restless in search of insect food, it rarely flies and its presence is usually revealed by various loud harsh calls, repeated frequently. The song is a repeated '*pa-tras, pa-tras, pa-tras*' (Goodall *et al* 1957).

STATUS & RECORDS: Uncertain, possibly former breeding species or vagrant; Darwin collected one juvenile in 1833/34 (Sclater & Sharpe 1885–98). Bennett (1926) believed that he saw one near Stanley in 1916, but there have been no further records. Darwin's notes (Gould & Darwin 1841) suggest that he saw others and that it was a breeding species before sheep were established in numbers about 15 years later. He stated, 'It has found its way over to the Falkland Islands, where, instead of inhabiting forests, it frequents the coarse herbage and low bushes, which in most parts conceal the peaty surface of that island.' Darwin apparently only visited East Falkland. He remarked that it was difficult to observe, which may partly account for the lack of later records. There was far more ground cover in the 1830s, though unlike the thickets and forests of Tierra del Fuego.

DISTRIBUTION ABROAD: Three races described from andean regions of South America between Venezuela and Cape Horn, occurring in dense woodland and thickets, often near streams. The smaller, darker race *S. m. magellanicus* occurs between about 37°S and Cape Horn. Reynolds (1932) noted its occurrence in a 'pseudo-Falkland Island setting' in scrub and tussac-grass on Snipe Island in the Beagle Channel.

Tyrant-flycatchers *Tyrannidae*
The largest family of birds in the New World, containing about 380 species in about 90 genera, they are found from Alaska and northern Canada to Cape Horn. The majority occur in tropical regions of South America. There is great variation in size and shape due to their diverse methods of feeding. Most prey on insects, in the air or from vegetation; some eat fruit, while the larger species catch fish, amphibians and crickets. South America has over 300 species, of which about 120 are found in Argentina. One species breeds in the Falklands and eight have occurred as vagrants.

Dark-faced Ground-tyrant

158. Black-billed Shrike-tyrant *Agriornis montana*   Plate 18
A. Gaucho coliblanco
c. Mero gaucho
Small. 9–10in/23–25cm

IDENTIFICATION: Much larger than the resident Dark-faced Ground-tyrant (161), with far more white on the tail, it is dark brown above and lighter brown beneath. The head shows a narrow buff patch on the lores and the grey throat is streaked with black; belly washed chestnut, flanks and undertail creamy white. Wings dark brown with broad white edges around all secondaries and white tips to primaries;

tail brown in centre with broad white outer edges and white tips to all but the central pair. Bill black, heavy with a hooked tip; legs black. Usually tame around human habitations. Has a loud whistling call in breeding territory, used at first light, but unlikely to be heard in the Falklands.

STATUS & RECORDS: Vagrant recorded once; a single bird seen on West Point Island on 8 December 1963 by R Napier (Woods 1975).

DISTRIBUTION ABROAD: Three races occur in andean regions from Colombia and Ecuador through Chile to 40°S and Argentina to about 48°S where it is found in lowlands. The race *A. m. leucura* described above has the most southerly distribution, 32°–40°S in Chile and 30°–48°S in Argentina.

159. Fire-eyed Diucon   *Pyrope pyrope*   Plate 18
A. Monjita diucón
c. Diucón
Small. 8–8½in/19–21cm

IDENTIFICATION: The Diucón is darker and slightly larger than the Dark-faced Ground-tyrant (161), but the tail has a dark grey central stripe and broad white sides and the iris is conspicuously crimson or orange. Forehead, crown, nape, mantle and lesser wing-coverts sooty grey-brown with an olive tinge; primaries dark brown with narrow light edges; secondaries dark brown broadly edged white showing a 'V' pattern when folded; chin and throat white with a few dark streaks visible on close view; upper breast light blue-grey, darkening to light grey-brown on breast, fading to white on lower belly and under tail-coverts. There is an orange-buff patch on the flanks, usually mostly hidden when the wings are folded. Rump is slaty-grey, lighter than back; underside of wings dark slaty-grey; bill and legs are black. *Juveniles* have a brown iris. Call-note is a single very squeaky *seep* and a quiet *whit*. Feeds on the ground, taking fly larvae and other insects. Often perches on fences, bushes or trees and hovers before dropping onto prey.

STATUS & RECORDS: Vagrant or rare winter visitor, recorded at least six times. The earlier record of Vallentin (1904) quoted in the literature from Wace (1921) to Woods (1975) has been rejected; examination of Vallentin's notes shows clear reference to the resident tyrant (161). One seen at the west end of Stanley harbour on 10 July 1961 had been present since late April (Woods 1975); one at Hill Cove from April to September 1981 and one at West Point Island from March to 4 May 1984 (Wolsey 1986c); one on Weddell Island from May to at least September 1985 (A Felton pers. comm.); one in Stanley June 1985 and two at Beaver Island 15 April to 19 September 1986 (Wolsey 1986d). Most of these records show survival in or through the winter period, up to at least five months. All birds were seen at settlements or in sheltered areas near buildings. It is possible that a few individuals are drifting eastwards and wintering in the Falklands instead of migrating northward in South America.

DISTRIBUTION ABROAD: Common in valleys and andean foothills to 1400m (4500 feet) between 32°–55°S in Chile and 36°–55°S in Argentina, including wooded islands south of Tierra del Fuego. In winter, occurs north to about 27°S in Chile though some are resident in the Magellanic region.

160. White-browed Ground-tyrant   *Muscisaxicola albilora*   Plate 18
A. Dormilona nuquirrojiza
C. Dormilona de ceja blanca
Very small. 7in/17–18cm

IDENTIFICATION: Resembles the Dark-faced Ground-tyrant (161) in size and general colour and is distinguished by the long, narrow, white 'eyebrow'; forehead, crown and nape red-brown, more orange on nape though often inconspicuous; back and wing-coverts grey-brown and more red-brown on the mantle. Tail is black with white sides; secondaries dark brown edged white; underparts white, tinged pale grey on neck, breast and flanks. Bill and legs black and the iris is light brown.

STATUS & RECORDS: Vagrant recorded once; H Bennett found one injured in Stanley on 25 February 1949 (Cawkell & Hamilton 1961).

DISTRIBUTION ABROAD: Inhabits open country often near water in andean regions of Chile and Argentina between 1500 and 3000m (4500 to 9000 feet) from 32°S in Chile and 36°S in Argentina to 53°S; also recorded once at Isla Nueva, Beagle Channel (Venegas & Jory 1979). Migrates north to Peru, Bolivia and Ecuador (0°–23°S) in winter.

161. Dark-faced Ground-tyrant   *Muscisaxicola macloviana*   Plate 18
A. Dormilona cabeza parda
C. Dormilona tontita
Local names: News Bird, Blue Bird
Very small. 6½in/16cm

IDENTIFICATION: A slim sprightly bird, pale grey-brown above with a darker brown crown, black lores and around the eye, grey-white underparts, long black legs and short pointed black bill. Lower back, rump and tail black with a prominent white outer edge to tail. Flight feathers are dark brown with clear white edges. *Male* slightly larger than *female*; *Juvenile* has orange-yellow bill with dark brown tip and yellow gape. Has an upright stance; runs and hops rapidly, repeatedly flicking and fanning the tail and wings at each brief pause. Its habit of approaching people led to the name of News Bird. The flight is swift and easy with quick beats of the long wings. Always chooses the highest perch available after a flight. Sometimes darts from an elevated perch to catch flies and frequently hovers before dropping 1–2m (3–6 feet) to the ground when searching for food over long grass. Occurs singly or in pairs when breeding; in winter small loose parties are formed.

VOICE: Usual call-note, frequently uttered, is a short squeaky *tseet*. Also has a low hard note, *tu*, which may be repeated rapidly or combined with the first as *seetu*. Has a weak twittering song, rarely heard but noted in September and October when the male displays to a female on the ground, singing and raising one or both wings slowly to about 60° above horizontal then closing them and repeating the movements frequently, like a butterfly sunning itself. Also has a display flight when it climbs to about 15m (50 feet) as it sings and then drops quickly to a perch.

FOOD: Takes various small invertebrates, particularly flies, moths and their larvae on which the young are also fed.

HABITAT, STATUS & BREEDING: Resident breeding species, common throughout the islands in open country inland wherever rock outcrops or stone-runs occur, on coastal cliffs and sand-beaches. Frequents gardens in Stanley and the settlements in winter and shows no dependence on the tussac grass habitat (Woods 1985). Nests between late October and late December, laying two to three slightly glossy white eggs closely spotted with red-brown. The nest is of dry grass or root fibres well lined with wool or feathers, placed up to 60cm (2 feet) below the surface of a stone-run or in a deep rock crevice on a rocky ridge or cliff. It is probably double-brooded.

DISTRIBUTION ABROAD: Two races described; *M. m. macloviana* is restricted to the Falklands and most of the population, if not all, is resident throughout the year, though Olrog (1979) stated that the Falkland race migrated to Buenos Aires province and Uruguay. Two recent reports suggest some migration in the vicinity of the Falklands but these may be local movements of the resident race; Bourne and Curtis (1987) reported one on board a ship 71km (44 miles) south of Cape Meredith on 4 April 1984 and seven alighting on a ship at dawn on 26 March 1985, in the northern approaches to Falkland Sound. The race *M. m. mentalis* breeds in southern Chile from 42°S and Argentina from 30°S to Tierra del Fuego and Cape Horn. In winter some migrate north to 12°S in Peru and 22°S in north-western Argentina, though part of the Magellanic population is resident (Venegas & Jory 1979).

162. Rufous-backed Negrito   *Lessonia rufa*   Plate 18
A. Negrito or Sobrepuesto
c. Colegial
Very tiny. 4½–5in/11–12cm

IDENTIFICATION: In Tierra del Fuego, the Negrito is the commonest bird in open country, near beaches, in marshes and by rivers. It is familiar at settlements and easily recognised. The *male* is all black except for the back, which is a clear chestnut. The *female* is grey-brown on the head, fading to pale rufous on back and wing-coverts; wings are black with rufous edges; tail black; underparts are generally pale grey-brown, darker on the breast becoming pale chestnut on the belly. Perches on low bushes and wires and makes sorties to catch flying insects, also taking insects on the ground.

STATUS & RECORDS: Vagrant, recorded once; a male seen at West Point Island by R Napier on 28 September 1963 (Woods 1975).

DISTRIBUTION ABROAD: Two races described in South America; *L. r. rufa* the southern form, is found in Argentina and Chile from about 30°S to southern Tierra del Fuego, between sea level and about 4000m (13,000 feet). It migrates northward as far as southern Brazil, Paraguay and southern Bolivia. In Tierra del Fuego, males of this race return in mid-September, about two to three weeks before the females. After breeding, males depart about mid-January while females and juveniles leave between mid-February and late March. *L. r. oreas* breeds in north-western Argentina, northern Chile and southern Peru.

163. Fork-tailed Flycatcher *Tyrannus savana*   Plate 18
A. Tijereta
C. Cazamoscas tijereta
Small-medium overall. Body 5–6in/13–15cm
Tail 8–11in/20–28cm
IDENTIFICATION: Easily recognised, this tyrant has a body-length similar to Dark-faced Ground-tyrant (161) and an extremely long, deeply forked black tail. Head is jet-black to nape and below eyes; back pale grey; wings blackish; underparts pure white including underwing; bill and legs black. *Male* has a concealed yellow streak on the crown and longer tail streamers than the female, often showing white basal outer edges. *Immature* has shorter tail, otherwise resembles adult. In direct flight, the tail streams out like ribbons and if pausing or changing direction, opens out to a broad 'V'. Call-notes sharp, like castanets rattling.

STATUS & RECORDS: Vagrant, recorded three times; one found dead at Saunders Island in December 1930 (Kinnear 1931); one was seen at West Point Island for about a week in October 1966 (R Napier in Woods 1975) and another at New Island on 7 January 1972 (Pettingill 1974).

DISTRIBUTION ABROAD: Breeds in Uruguay, Paraguay, Bolivia, southern Brazil and northern Argentina east of the Andes to about 43°S. Migrates to Venezuela, Colombia and Central America. It has occurred once in Chile and as a vagrant to about 35°N in the United States.

164. Eastern Kingbird *Tyrannus tyrannus*   Not illustrated
A. Pitirre americano
C. Benteveo blanco y negro
Small. 8–8½in/20–21cm
IDENTIFICATION: A large tyrant, very similar in colour to the Fork-tailed Flycatcher (163) but is more heavily built and has a rounded black tail with a narrow white tip. Head is black with a rarely visible orange-red crown streak; back and wings dark grey-brown with narrow white edges to coverts; underparts white, washed grey on the breast; bill and legs black. *Immature* has dark brown-grey head and back. Uses perches such as fences from which to fly after insect prey.

STATUS & RECORDS: Vagrant, recorded once; one seen in fairly calm weather on 7 January 1978 near Beatrice Cove, Port William by R Lévêque (1978). On 2 January there had been a period of exceptionally strong northwesterly winds.

DISTRIBUTION ABROAD: Breeds commonly in Canada and the United States between 60°–25°N and migrates through Central America to winter in South America between Colombia and northwestern Argentina to about 28°S. Has occurred occasionally in Chile and once on South Georgia, on 11 November 1973 (Prince & Payne 1979).

165. Great Kiskadee *Pitangus sulphuratus*   Plate 18
A. & C. Benteveo
Small. 8–10in/20–25cm
IDENTIFICATION: A large, heavily built and very handsomely marked tyrant, with

white chin and throat and bright yellow underparts; broad black band through the eye, white band above eye and black sides to the crown which has a partly concealed lemon-yellow centre. Back, tail and wings above are dark brown tinged rufous; under wing-coverts yellow and undersides of flight feathers red-brown. The black bill is three-quarters of the head length, stout and ridged; legs also black. Uses perches from which to catch flies and also dives after fish like a king-fisher, though it does not submerge completely. A common call-note, from which the name is derived, is a slow *kis-ka-dee*. It has several other loud calls.

STATUS & RECORDS: Vagrant, recorded once, at Port Stephens settlement from 21 March to 8 April 1962 with Falkland Thrushes but was very shy and left them whenever it was disturbed. It sheltered in a small plantation of Monterey Cypress near the houses and was seen trying to catch flies (M Shaw in Woods 1975).

DISTRIBUTION ABROAD: Widespread and common throughout tropical South America mostly east of the Andes, from Venezuela and Colombia to Rio Negro province (42°S) in Argentina. It has been recorded once in central Chile and also occurs as a vagrant in the southern United States.

166. White-crested Elaenia *Elaenia albiceps* Plate 18
A. Fío-fío común

c. Fío-fío

Tiny. 5½–6in/14–15cm

IDENTIFICATION: Very small and inconspicuously coloured, this tyrant usually reveals itself in southern South America by its frequently repeated, two-toned call *fee-oo, fee-oo, fee-oo*, closely resembling the usual call of the Rufous-chested Dotterel (106). Upperparts olive-green; eye-ring yellowish; head darker above with a small white crest on the slightly peaked crown; wings blackish with two narrow jagged whitish bars on tips of median and greater coverts and whitish edges to secondaries; tail uniform dark olive-brown; underparts pale olive-grey, lighter than the back, becoming whitish with a yellow wash on the belly and under the tail. The bill is short and pointed, dark brown with a pinkish base and the legs are brown.

STATUS & RECORDS: Vagrant, recorded twice; one specimen obtained in Stanley 15 December 1934 (Cawkell & Hamilton 1961); one seen in a pine plantation at West Point Island by R Wilson in late January 1987, may have been present some time (Wolsey 1987a).

DISTRIBUTION ABROAD: Two races described in South America; *E. a. chilensis* breeds from about 25°S in Chile and Argentina to the islands south of Tierra del Fuego and inhabits densely wooded areas up to an altitude of 2500m (7500 feet). It migrates north between March and early April to winter in tropical areas as far as Colombia and northeastern Brazil. Southward migrating birds reach Tierra del Fuego in mid-October. The race *E. a. albiceps* breeds in northwestern Argentina and migrates north to Bolivia.

Plantcutters *Phytotomidae*
This family of stocky, finch-like birds contains three species which occur only in western

and southern South America. They have short, heavy conical bills, serrated on both mandibles and ideally suited to stripping buds, leaves and fruits. The wings are short and tails fairly long.

167. Rufous-tailed Plantcutter   *Phytotoma rara*   Plate 19
A. & C. Rara or Cortarramas grande
Very small. $7\frac{1}{2}$–8in/19–20cm

IDENTIFICATION: *Male* has a bright chestnut crown, throat and all underparts; black sides of head below eye with small white patch on lores; olive-brown upperparts very heavily streaked black; black wings with broad white tips on median coverts, narrow white tips on greater coverts, white edges to primaries and chestnut edged secondaries. The tail has brown central feathers, but the rest have chestnut inner webs, black outer webs and broad black tips. *Female* has light chestnut forehead and throat, buff underparts streaked brown on breast, buff back heavily streaked brown, brown flight feathers with buff tipped coverts and edges; tail similar to male. Iris of male and female bright orange; bills and legs yellowish-brown. The flight is undulating; wingbars of the male are conspicuous and both show the black-tipped tail.

STATUS & RECORDS: Vagrant, recorded once; an adult female in rather worn plumage was found at Douglas Station on 12 March 1937 skulking among bushes and being shadowed by a Falkland Thrush (Hamilton 1939).

DISTRIBUTION ABROAD: Well known to farmers and horticulturalists in central Chile (28°–43°S) from the coast to about 2000m (6000 feet) in valleys of the andean foothills. It has been seen during the breeding season at 52°S in the Magellanic region of Chile (Venegas & Jory 1979) and also occurs in western Argentina (36°–42°S). Southern and high altitude breeding populations migrate northward or to lower country in winter.

Swallows   *Hirundinidae*
Swallows and martins (a name sometimes used for shorter-tailed species) are a family of small, streamlined, long-winged and often fork-tailed birds that mostly feed on insects caught in flight. They resemble swifts but differ in their slower flight and twittering calls. There are 74 species in 17 genera with a worldwide distribution except in Antarctica. Most species occur in African regions, either as wintering migrants or when breeding. Of the 23 species found in South America, 13 occur in Argentina where nine species breed and four are wintering migrants from North America. Five swallows have

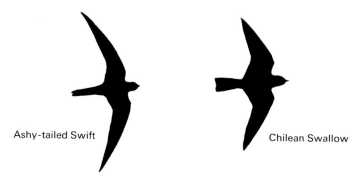

Ashy-tailed Swift   Chilean Swallow

been identified in the Falklands, three of them are South American breeding species, one of which has recently been recorded as breeding in the Falklands for the first time.

168. Chilean Swallow   *Tachycineta leucopyga*   Plate 19
A. Golondrina azul
C. Golondrina chilena
Very tiny. 4½–5¼in/11–13cm
IDENTIFICATION: This species is difficult to separate in flight from the White-rumped Swallow *T. leucorrhoa* (see below). Both are small swallows with short, slightly forked tails and white rumps, glossy blue-black upperparts and mainly white underparts from bill to tail. They have relatively short wings compared with the Barn Swallow (171) and characteristic triangular shaped wingspread. Although few specimens have been examined closely enough to determine the species, it seems likely that most small black and white swallows recorded in the Falklands are Chilean Swallows. From the limited published material, the only noticeable differences between them appear to be as follows.

Adult Chilean Swallow has a shiny purplish-black head with a very narrow white streak above the lores and the tail has a slightly deeper fork. Juvenile is said to have a more distinct white streak above the lores.

Adult White-rumped Swallow has a similar black head to below the eye, but shows a narrow white patch on the forehead, extending slightly to the lores and has a less forked tail. The difference in head pattern is only visible in a very close view and would not be seen against the sky. *Immature* birds of both species are generally dull blackish-brown above with white rumps and white underparts.

Flight silhouettes and flying action differ from those of the Barn Swallow. They fly with few wingbeats between long glides, often change direction or shoot up high in the air and appear to loiter while catching flying insects.

VOICE: Two Chilean Swallows observed closely in April 1958 in Stanley, called frequently, using a buzzy *chrimp* or *chreez* varying in pitch, as they hawked along John Street. Two, probably of this species, in Stanley on 18 February 1962 used a rapid chattering *chi-chi-chi-chi . . .* when perched on a garden fence.

FOOD: Both species feed exclusively on small day-flying insects which are relatively scarce in the Falklands, except over tussac islands or where trees have been planted and around settlements where introduced blowflies are abundant.

HABITAT, STATUS & BREEDING: Status is apparently changing. Vallentin (1904) stated that local people had seen 'occasional flocks of swallows' from time to time at Darwin and on West Falkland. The Chilean Swallow was first recorded on 6 March 1937 when a specimen was obtained from six or seven seen (Hamilton 1939). One exhausted bird arrived at Kidney Island on 24 February 1954 (Pettingill 1962). Between 1958 and 1962 up to six at a time were seen annually in the Stanley area between December and June, mostly from late March, with up to two probably surviving as long as seven weeks. Between 1976 and 1986 records have been irregular though this period produced the first six records for the spring. Two were seen at West Point Island about 18 October 1976 and two survived there for about 40 days from early March to mid-April 1977 (D Davidson pers. comm.) and 'many' were reported at Stanley and Fox Bay in February 1984

(Wolsey 1986c). At Sea Lion Island in 1985, one appeared on 24 February and the following day, three looking thin and tired, were seen hawking above a pond and along a beach over heaps of rotted kelp. Numbers increased to at least 20 and possibly 30 by 8 March, when they looked much plumper but only one was seen on 9 March (B Paul and A Spencer pers. comm.). Several were seen at Speedwell Island on 20 March 1985 (J Larsen pers. comm.).

In the 1983/84 season, a pair was noticed by P Robertson, Manager at Port Stephens, nesting on the iron struts below the metal roof of a Dutch barn about 6m (20 feet) above ground. The nest was not disturbed and three young were believed to have hatched. These birds did not return in subsequent seasons. The Chilean Swallow should now be considered a very rare breeding species and a frequent vagrant, particularly during autumn migration periods.

DISTRIBUTION ABROAD: Breeds in southern Chile and Argentina from Tierra del Fuego to about 27°S in Chile and 37°S in Argentina, where it nests in natural holes in trees or under the eaves of buildings. Southern breeding populations are migratory, arriving in the Magellanic region between the last week of September and mid-October, departing northwards between mid-February and mid-March (Venegas & Jory 1979).

The White-rumped Swallow *T. leucorrhoa* known as 'Golondrina celeste' in Argentina, breeds in Paraguay, Uruguay, southern Brazil and northern Argentina to about 40°S. It migrates northward in winter, reaching the Equator and could occur in the Falklands as a wind-drifted vagrant.

169. Southern Martin *Progne modesta* Plate 19
A. & C. Golondrina negra
Small. 8–8¾in/20–22cm

IDENTIFICATION: Immediately distinguished from other swallows recorded in the Falklands by its larger and bulkier appearance, all dark plumage and deeply forked tail without streamers. *Male* is glossy blue-black above and below with blackish wings and tail. *Female* is blackish above with some blue sheen on wing-coverts and rump; underparts grey-brown with variable paler edges, lighter on throat. *Immature* resembles female but has a less forked tail. Flight is similar to Barn Swallow (171), with rapid wingbeats followed by long glides, and more direct than the flight of Chilean Swallow (168).

STATUS & RECORDS: Vagrant, irregularly recorded; Vallentin (1904) mentioned 'a martin' near Stanley towards the end of March. Wace (1921) described it as a frequent visitor and Bennett (1926) stated that it was ' a frequent autumn visitor on migration' but neither quoted dates. Cawkell and Hamilton (1961) commented, 'they have been seen in spring' and mentioned autumn records of 12 at Cape Pembroke and three and five earlier the same week at Stanley in March 1951. The only record since 1951 is of three birds in Port William on 4 December 1984, one of which came aboard a ship in an exhausted condition, died and was examined by B Bewsher (Wolsey 1986c).

DISTRIBUTION ABROAD: Two races described in South America; *P. m. elegans* breeds from Bolivia (17°S) and Uruguay through northwestern Argentina to about 46°S (Chubut province) and has occurred in central Chile. It migrates northward as far as northern Brazil. Another smaller race inhabits coastal Peru.

170. Rough-winged Swallow   *Stelgidopteryx ruficollis*   Plate 21
A. Golondrina de ribera
c. Not recorded
Very tiny to tiny. $4\frac{1}{2}$–$5\frac{1}{4}$in/11–13cm
IDENTIFICATION: A small swallow, earth-brown on the head and above with a paler brown rump and a slightly forked tail; darker brown wings and tail; lighter underparts, cinnamon on throat, light brown on breast and at sides of body with a yellowish belly. *Adults* are glossy brown above with a darker crown; *immatures* probably appear duller brown above with pale edges to wing-coverts. Flight is erratic and fluttering with rapid wingbeats.

A related species, the Bank Swallow or Sand Martin *Riparia riparia* is similar in size and colouring above but shows a broad brown breast band across otherwise white underparts. It is a Northern Hemisphere breeding species which regularly winters to 26°S in northern Argentina; one was collected at sea 540km (335 miles) east-southeast of Stanley in November 1967 (Watson 1975). It could occur occasionally in the Falklands.

STATUS & RECORDS: Vagrant, recorded three times: one at Eliza Cove, south of Stanley on 15 October 1979 (Peatfield 1981); one over John Street with three Barn Swallows on 5 November 1981 and two seen briefly over a pond on East Sea Lion Island by S da Prato and R Woods on 6 November 1983 (Wolsey 1986c).

DISTRIBUTION ABROAD: Breeds throughout much of South America from Venezuela southward through Brazil and east of the Andes to central Argentina and Uruguay (35°S). It is apparently non-migratory, though immature birds would tend to disperse after fledging.

171. Barn Swallow   *Hirundo rustica*   Plate 19
A. Golondrina tijereta
c. Golondrina bermeja
Very small. 6–7in/15–18cm
IDENTIFICATION: Larger than the Chilean Swallow (168), the shape, colour and flying action of this species attract attention when it occurs in the Falklands. *Adult* blue-black above, including rump and tail; forehead and throat chestnut; underparts buff with a blue-black patch either side of the breast, sometimes joined as a band. Tail is deeply forked with outer feathers elongated into streamers, longer on the male, and all except the central pair show a white patch on the inner web near the tip. *Juvenile* lacks tail streamers, is duller and more brown above with paler buff on the head, brown patches either side of the breast narrowly joining and a whitish belly; buff under wing-coverts and axillaries. Tail feathers show the same pattern of white spots as the adult. Flight is rapid and graceful, showing long wings and tail. Separated from Cliff Swallow (172) by uniform dark back and deeply forked tail.

STATUS & RECORDS: Vagrant, occurring frequently in spring (October/November) and rarely in autumn (March/April). Earliest record is 20 September 1962 in Stanley; one doubtful record in January 1959; four probable records between 7 March and 15 April. Single birds and parties of up to 40 have been reported, often from widely separated places on the same date, suggesting that large numbers are drifted from the coast of South America at one time. Survival is poor;

the longest recorded period is 11 days, when five seen on 8 October had decreased to two by 19 October (Woods 1975). May occur almost anywhere over the Falklands, particularly where flying insects are more abundant.

DISTRIBUTION ABROAD: Several races are described which breed in the Northern Hemisphere between about 70°N and 25°N. The North American race *H. r. erythrogaster*, which has been identified in the Falklands, migrates southward to winter through Argentina and Chile to Tierra del Fuego. Vagrants of this race have also occurred on South Georgia and Tristan da Cunha (Watson 1975).

172. Cliff Swallow *Petrochelidon pyrrhonota*   Not illustrated
A. Golondrina roquera
C. Golondrina grande
Very tiny to tiny. 4½–5½in/11–14cm

IDENTIFICATION: Smaller than Barn Swallow (171) and recognised by pale buff forehead, blackish throat, rufous cheeks, throat and narrow collar, rufous rump and blackish square-ended tail without white spots or streamers. Upperparts of *adult* blackish with dark blue sheen on back and crown; breast is blue-black in centre with buff sides; belly white. *Immature* dull, appears dark brown above.

STATUS & RECORDS: Vagrant, recorded once; two seen flying near River Murrell, East Falkland on 6 December 1980 by P Prince and M Whitehouse (pers. comm.) who had both seen this species in North America.

DISTRIBUTION ABROAD: Breeds throughout much of North and Central America from about 65°N (Canada) to 20°N (Mexico) and winters from southern Brazil and Argentina to about 52°S, occasionally occurring in Chile and reaching Tierra del Fuego.

Pipits & Wagtails *Motacillidae*
Small, slender ground-feeding birds with long tails, thin bills and long legs, the family includes 11 species of wagtails that are conspicuously patterned black, white, yellow or green. Wagtails do not occur in South America or the Falklands. Pipits are duller in colour, generally streaked brown above and often difficult to identify by sight, though they each have distinctive flight calls and songs. They occur in all continents, and the Antarctic island of South Georgia has one resident species. Eight of the 35 species of pipits occur in South America and seven breed in parts of Argentina. One species breeds in the Falklands and is probably resident though there is some evidence of migration in autumn.

Falkland Pipit

173. Falkland Pipit *Anthus correndera*   Plate 20
A. Cachirla común
C. Bailarín chico
Local names: Skylark; Lark
Very small. 6–6½in/15–16cm

IDENTIFICATION: An inconspicuous small bird of open camp, the Falkland Pipit is heavily streaked buff and dark brown above, particularly on crown, nape and back; flight feathers are dark brown broadly edged rich buff; tail mainly dark brown with sandy centre, the two white outer feathers showing as a broad white edge, conspicuous in flight and immediately separating it from the female Black-throated Finch (182). Underparts are buff, paler on throat and streaked with dark brown, particularly on the sides of breast and flanks.

Plumage varies considerably, some birds being greyish-white beneath and buff-white streaked with dark brown above. In early winter (May) plumage is usually brighter and more prominently streaked above, with heavy black streaking on flanks. *Juveniles* are generally more buff than adults. Bill broad-based, tapering sharply, horn-coloured; legs and feet pale pink with a long, almost straight hind claw. Difficult to see on the ground as it runs through grass like a mouse, particularly when near the nest. Flight is jerky over short distances and undulating when flying further, or at heights of 30m (100 feet) or more.

VOICE: Call-notes are varied; the usual flight-call is a short and squeaky, *prits* or *skinch* or a triple *tipitip*. When agitated near the nest uses a higher-pitched, explosive *princh*. The song, a thin and rather squeaky short phrase of three or four notes followed by a harsh churring, is heard from mid-August to January and infrequently in March and early April. It is delivered in a song-flight when the bird mounts from the ground rather jerkily to about 30m (100 feet) and parachutes down with the tail held high. Sometimes stays aloft for several minutes, singing one song after another, interspersed with parachuting and churring. It also sings from the ground.

FOOD: Few records available; it feeds on the ground, probably taking small invertebrates; young birds are fed on small worms and moths.

HABITAT, STATUS & BREEDING: Resident or summer resident, it is one of the few species that is common and widespread throughout the Falklands in areas of coarse white grass during the breeding season. It also occurs on diddle-dee and grass camp, on wide sand-beaches littered with dead kelp and occasionally on rocky beaches. Unlike most other Falkland songbirds, it does not utilise dense tussac grass, preferring open camp with low vegetation. Usually seen singly or in pairs though small flocks occur in autumn. Appears to be less numerous in winter. Small parties of up to four birds have been seen flying high westward over Stanley and Kidney Island between mid-March and mid-April. These may have been local movements but the possibility of migration in autumn needs further investigation.

Nests from late September to late December and has at least two broods in a season. Two to four eggs are laid, varying in colour from creamy-grey to dirty white, variably spotted and blotched with yellow-brown and purplish-brown with black hairlines near the blunt end. The nest is of fine grasses sometimes lined with horsehair and well hidden in rough grass. Young nestlings have dark brown-black down.

DISTRIBUTION ABROAD: Breeds in southern South America from southern Peru and Bolivia in the andean region to about 4000m (13,000 feet), through Chile to Tierra del Fuego and in most of Argentina, Uruguay, Paraguay and southeastern Brazil (23°S). Five races have been described; A. c. *grayi*, the Falkland race, is somewhat larger than the race *A. c. chilensis* found in southern Argentina, Chile and Tierra del Fuego. Some of the southern breeding populations migrate northwards in winter to about 20°S, while others remain in northern Tierra del Fuego.

Wrens *Troglodytidae*

Wrens are tiny, rotund birds with very short wings. Their tails are often held erect and move vigorously in display. Plumage is generally brown above with narrow bars on wings and tail, a light eye-stripe and fine pointed bill which is used to take small invertebrates from vegetation. They usually live in low, dense cover and many have surprisingly loud and complex songs for such small birds. Wrens are a New World family with over 60 species, though one species occurs throughout the Northern Hemisphere. Thirty-nine species occur in South America, mainly in tropical parts and only three are found in Argentina. Two of these are resident and described as local races in the Falklands.

House Wren

Since about 1910, there have been several reports of wrenlike small birds from Carcass Island, West Point Island, Darwin and Walker Creek (Wace 1921) and, recently, from Pebble Island and Port Stephens. Descriptions received from K Bertrand over the past 25 years, mentioned a light eye-ring and more russet plumage, similar to that of a juvenile House or Grass Wren. Some photographs from a 1975 sighting suggested a longer tail than a House Wren. A Douse sent a more detailed description of similar birds at Pebble Island and Port Stephens in April 1987. Both birds had indistinct whitish eye-rings and much longer tails than a House Wren, giving them a very different appearance. One bird used its tail for balancing when feeding on a hanging mutton carcass. Further careful observations are needed to identify these birds.

174. Grass Wren/Short-billed Marsh Wren   *Cistothorus platensis*   Plate 19

A. Ratona aperdizada or Ratona sabanera
C. Chercán de las vegas
Local name: Tomtit
Very tiny. $4\frac{1}{2}$–5in/11–12cm

IDENTIFICATION: Slightly smaller and generally lighter in colour than the House Wren (175), with a noticeably shorter, straighter bill; upperparts are heavily streaked buff and black, the tail barred black and red-brown; head buff closely streaked black on crown and sides with a small buff stripe mainly behind the eye; underparts whitish on cheeks and throat, otherwise creamy-buff. *Juvenile* darker, with reddish-buff underparts and a less obvious eye-stripe. Bill light brown and legs pale pink. More shy than the House Wren, it is very active and adept at vanishing through thick vegetation. Flight is weak and slow with rapid whirring wingbeats, usually just above grass or rushes; reluctant to fly and prefers to creep away when disturbed. It is also inquisitive and will sidle up grass stems with the tail cocked and bob at a stationary observer while craning its head and neck and scolding.

VOICE: Usual call-note is a clear hard *tak-tak* or *ti-ti-ti*, frequently repeated and often run together as a harsh trill *trrrr*. The song is much longer than that of the House Wren, usually with a slower delivery and less powerful; it is composed of a repetition of different clear notes, *sioo-sioo-sioo*, *chiwi-chiwi-chiwi* and *clee-clee-clee*, separated by low trills. The whole song is often sustained for a minute or more with a few brief intervals. Sings from the tops or sides of grass clumps; often takes flight and whirrs away horizontally to another perch, sometimes singing continuously. Song has been heard from early September to mid-March; high winds do not seem to decrease song output in the early breeding season.

FOOD: Takes small invertebrates, probably including flies, moths and their larvae, small worms and spiders from dense vegetation.

HABITAT, STATUS & BREEDING: Resident, widespread through the Falklands from sea level to at least 200m (650 feet), but only locally numerous in damp areas with thick rush patches, long white grass and diddle-dee, or marram grass. In dense tussac, population density is higher than elsewhere and all feeding appears to take place above ground level. It can survive on islands with introduced cats, rats and mice (Woods 1985). The nest, built in rushes, marram grass or tussac 30 to 70cm (1–2½ feet) above ground, is a ball of grasses 10 to 20cm (4–8 in) diameter, lined with wool or feathers, sometimes with a short grass tunnel leading to the small round entrance. Five to seven pure white eggs are laid between early October and mid-November; there is no evidence for more than one brood in a season. A few adults were ringed on Kidney Island between 1958 and 1963; two were retrapped, almost exactly where they were ringed, after intervals of a year.

DISTRIBUTION ABROAD: Widely distributed in the Americas from the northeastern United States and Canada through Venezuela, Colombia, Peru, southeastern Brazil, most of Argentina and Chile to Tierra del Fuego and Cape Horn. Several races have been described; the Falkland race is separated as *C. p. falklandicus*.

175. House Wren   *Troglodytes aedon*   Plate 19
A. Ratona común or Chochin común
C. Chercán común
Local names: Rock Wren; Cobb's Wren
Very tiny to tiny. 4¾–5¼in/12–13cm

IDENTIFICATION: More robust and slightly larger than the Grass Wren (174), it is identified by the dull grey-brown head, longer, slightly curved blackish bill and uniform red-brown back and wing-coverts. The chestnut primaries, secondaries and tail are all finely barred dark brown. Underparts whitish, variably suffused with buff. *Juveniles* are more richly coloured than adults, with buff underparts.

Birds showing partial albinism have been seen on Kidney Island and Carcass Island. Some Kidney Island birds had variable white or grey patches above the eye and one with symmetrical rectangular white flank patches was caught in March 1963 (Woods 1975); on Carcass Island in 1983 one adult had several white flight feathers in each wing, scattered white feathers elsewhere and white claws. These slight plumage aberrations are probably due to genetic factors in small isolated populations.

Much tamer than the Grass Wren, it will feed close to an observer on a beach and will slip between or under boulders like a mouse; in tussac it also vanishes silently when disturbed in preference to flying.

VOICE: The usual call-notes are harsher and buzzing, *chiz*, *chiz-iz* or a higher *cheez*, quite different from Grass Wren calls. When excited, the calls become very loud and explosive. The song is louder and lower-pitched than the Grass Wren's song, consisting of a mixed phrase of quick trills and whistles with harsh notes, rapidly delivered and lasting about two seconds. The same song is frequently repeated after short intervals. Different males have distinctive songs, mostly of similar length but varying in pattern; slow trills repeated at ten second intervals or contiuous warbling lasting 20 seconds have been noted on Kidney Island. Song has been heard from late August to February and, occasionally, in mid-April.

FOOD: Feeds on small invertebrates, including insects and lice (amphipods) on beaches. It also takes crickets and feeds nestlings on moth larvae.

HABITAT, STATUS & BREEDING: Resident, widespread on offshore islands, particularly where tussac grass is abundant, and probably restricted to those without introduced mammalian predators. Distribution is poorly recorded but the optimum habitat for this wren appears to be dense tussac growing from high water mark behind a boulder beach with accumulated dead kelp in which invertebrates thrive. Two similar open tussac paddocks on islands off West Falkland were censused in 1983; no House Wrens were found on West Point Island, which has cats, rats and mice but a high density was recorded on Carcass Island, which is free of these predators (Woods 1985). The nest is a domed ball with an entrance hole 6 to 8cm (2½–3in) wide near the top, made of grasses and thickly lined with available feathers of geese, Turkey Vulture or other species. Nests are well hidden and have been found in a tussac pedestal cavity, in gaps amongst tussac stems and in a rock crevice, from ground level to about 60cm (2 feet) above ground. Three to four pinkish eggs, covered with many tiny spots of red or light brown are laid between early October and December; two broods are probably reared in a season. A nest from Kidney Island was dismantled in January 1963, after the young had fledged. It was lined with tussac root fibres and 255 feathers of at least seven species, including Short-eared Owl, Turkey Vulture, Grey-backed Storm-Petrel, Diving Petrel and Falkland Thrush but surprisingly, none of the Tussac-bird, which is numerous on the island.

DISTRIBUTION ABROAD: Widespread from about 60°N in Canada through the United States and all of South America to Tierra del Fuego. Several races have been described; the Falkland birds are separated as *T. aedon cobbi*.

Mocking-thrushes *Mimidae*

This is a New World family of 33 species in ten genera, including Catbirds and Thrashers. Thirteen in the genus Mimus, known as Mockingbirds, are fairly slender, long-tailed birds with rounded wings and strong, slightly curved bills. Most are greyish above with white markings on wings and tail. In their breeding areas, Mockingbirds are well known for their powerful songs and some are famous for their ability to mimic other songbirds. Nine species of Mocking-Thrushes occur in South America, of which four breed in parts of northern Argentina. One Fuegian species has reached the Falklands occasionally.

176. Patagonian Mockingbird *Mimus patagonicus* Plate 16
A. Calandria gris
C. Tenca patagónica
Small. 8½–9½in/21–24cm
IDENTIFICATION: Smaller than the Falkland Thrush (178), with a longer black tail, edged and tipped with white, this mockingbird is brownish-grey above becoming slightly chestnut on lower back and rump. Wings are blackish with broad white tips to coverts and secondaries, forming two white bars in flight. Head is brownish-grey on crown and sides with a narrow white eye-stripe and throat is white slightly streaked with brown; underparts paler grey-brown than the back, belly whitish and flanks tinged with cinnamon. Bill and legs are black.

STATUS & RECORDS: Vagrant, probably recorded twice; three survived at Port Louis for some days in April 1970 and even fed from the hand, until they were killed by cats (L and M Grant pers. comm.). A photograph of one perched on pines is almost certainly of this species. On about 3 October 1974 a mockingbird was seen at Carcass Island by C and K Bertrand and another was possibly present. These were probably also of the Patagonian species.

DISTRIBUTION ABROAD: Breeds in Argentina from 40°S to northern Tierra del Fuego and is rare in central Chile. Migrates northwards to about 22°S in northern Argentina.

Thrushes *Turdidae*
There are about 300 species in this family, which are found in all parts of the world except Antarctica. Thrushes are mostly medium-sized songbirds, often brown in colour or patterned in black and white. They have slender bills and strong legs and they fly rapidly, many migrating long distances. In the genus Turdus, the true thrushes, there are about 63 species including the European Blackbird T. merula and the American Robin T. migratorius. South America has about 30 species of thrush, 20 of them in this genus. Eight Turdus thrushes and four from other genera occur in Argentina. One true thrush is resident in the Falklands and a species from North America has occurred once.

Falkland Thrush

177. Wood Thrush *Hylocichla mustelina* Not illustrated
A. Zorzalito rojizo
C. Not recorded
Very small. 7–7¾in/17.5–20cm
IDENTIFICATION: The Wood Thrush is plump, much smaller than a Falkland Thrush (178), and about the size of a Tussac-bird (155). It is recognised by the

rich red-brown crown and nape, prominent white eye-ring, black and white streaked ear-coverts and white underparts heavily spotted from throat to belly with black. Mantle is red-brown; back and wings dark brown, washed with red-brown on wing-coverts; rump and tail dark olive-brown. Bill is blackish, legs and feet pink.

STATUS & RECORDS: Vagrant, recorded once; a single bird was collected at Stanley in February 1970 (Daciuk 1975, Olrog 1979).

DISTRIBUTION ABROAD: A bird of deciduous and damp woodlands, it breeds in the eastern half of North America between 30°N and 50°N, from the Atlantic coast to 100°W. Migrates southward to winter in Central America and in the extreme north of South America.

178. Falkland Thrush *Turdus falcklandii*   Plate 19
A. Zorzal patagónico
c. Zorzal
Small. 10–10½in/25–26cm
Local name: Thrush; American name: Falkland Robin
IDENTIFICATION: Plump, robust, long-legged and noisy, this brown bird is familiar around all settlements. Male and female usually differ slightly. *Male* has black crown, nape, lores and around eye with grey ear-coverts; *female* is usually reddish-brown on head with no black on nape, but some pairs show little difference in head colour. *Adult* olive-brown on back, sides of neck and wing-coverts with dark brown flight feathers, black tail and contrasting yellow-grey rump, conspicuous in flight. Underparts rich buff from breast to vent; throat of *male* white, with widely spaced large dark brown streaks, sometimes extending onto upper breast; on *female*, throat is buff with narrow mid-brown streaks. These differences are not easily seen. Plumage of adult fades considerably between October and December. Both sexes have a yellow eye-ring and a stout, pointed, bright orange-yellow bill, variably streaked brown; in *autumn* the bill is mainly yellow-brown. *Juvenile* olive-brown above lightly flecked with buff; underparts buff heavily spotted black on breast and flanks; buff rapidly fades to whitish and moult of breast feathers starts by January. In February juveniles have irregular patchy underparts, part buff and part spotted; some spotted feathers are retained until April and buff-tipped median wing-coverts are often retained until the following November. Bill mainly brown, legs dull yellow-brown.

Inquisitive but wary of people; the stance is alert and upright, often with wings held loosely and tips drooping well below sides of the tail. Usually hops or bounds over ground and sometimes runs fast. The tail is flicked up once or twice each time the bird stops or alights on a perch. Strongly territorial when breeding, it defends territory by silent chasing on the ground or in flight, or by perching and calling intermittently. Can be aggressive towards smaller birds and other intruders when it has young. Uses prominent high perches. Occurs singly or in pairs and, from January, immature birds gather in parties, later with adults. These parties, roosting socially in winter, are maintained until about August when territories are established.

VOICE: Has various call-notes, mostly loud and harsh, ranging from a thin vibratory *sreep* to a strong *choyz-choyz-choyz* used as an alarm call. In courtship chases utters a low buzzing *chiz-chiz* and, when breeding, adults will perch and utter a deep, harsh *skwuk* at intruders in their territories. Song is heard between late August and early December, rarely in mid-July and occasionally between January and March. It varies greatly in quality but is usually a plaintive, slowly delivered succession of whistles and harsh chuckles, with a loud *peeoo* or *tee* often repeated and alternating with low churring notes. Song is uttered from any high perch including bushes, tussac clumps, treetops, roofs of buildings and even from the ground. Quiet subsong, a continuous warble produced with the bill closed, has been heard in winter and spring (May–October). Full song does not appear important in maintaining territories and is usually noticeable only in the dawn and dusk periods, though a few males sing during the day, apparently when attempting to attract a mate.

FOOD: Takes many earthworms, insect larvae and pupae and Amphipods (sand-hoppers). In autumn and winter takes berries, particularly those of pigvine which are abundant and available till spring; also eats diddle-dee berries, cultivated currants and strawberries where available and will readily eat bread and mutton fat, especially during frosty weather.

HABITAT, STATUS & BREEDING: Resident, common and widespread in a variety of habitats, particularly on tussac islands and in settlements where bushes, trees and sheds provide shelter. It also occurs amongst rocky outcrops and on open slopes with ferns and diddle-dee. Few early records give an indication of habitat though it was obviously present on coasts and rocky areas with shrubby cover. Thrushes were using sheds at Port Louis in 1833, adapting quickly to changes in the environment (Gould & Darwin 1841).

Field work on Kidney Island between 1958 and 1963 indicated that the thrush was very successful in this mature tussac grass habitat (Woods 1970a). Census work in 1983 showed that it could achieve greatest population density (4 males per hectare) in mature tussac adjoining a boulder beach with accumulated dead kelp. On two islands, in paddocks of replanted tussac and short turf, thrush density was 2.6 males per hectare where there were no introduced predators and 0.38 males per hectare where cats, rats and mice were present (Woods 1984).

Nests between late August and December, though in a mild winter nest-building may start in mid-July. The nest, built by the female, is a large structure of dry grass stems and root fibres, sometimes including pieces of wool or string. The deep cup usually has an inner lining of mud or cattle dung, itself lined with grass and sometimes horsehair. Nests examined on Kidney Island lacked an inner mud lining. Nest-sites can be sheltered crevices amongst rocks or on top of a bank sheltered by grass or fern, in cypress and gorse bushes, on beams inside peat or wool sheds or on top of large tussac pedestals, sheltered by the growing leaves and height varies from ground-level to 5 to 6m (15–20 feet), but most are 1 to 2m (3–7 feet) above ground. Lays two to three blue-green eggs, closely marked with brown and purple and may rear three or more broods in a season. Incubation period is 14 to 16 days from laying the last egg and fledging takes 16 to 18 days; the interval to the next brood has been recorded as only 12 to 14 days (Woods 1975).

About 200 were ringed and 136 colour-ringed between 1957 and 1963, mostly in Stanley and at Kidney Island. The longest movement recorded was 3.6km ($2\frac{1}{4}$ miles) in $6\frac{1}{2}$ months. The greatest longevity was $4\frac{1}{2}$ years. Thrushes suffer a high mortality rate in Stanley and at other settlements from the large number of domestic and feral cats.

DISTRIBUTION ABROAD: Two races described; *T. f. magellanicus* is resident in damp woodland and shrubby ravines in Chile from 27°S and Argentina from 37°S to Tierra del Fuego, Staten Island and islands south of the Beagle Channel. The Falkland race *T. f. falcklandii* is somewhat larger.

Sparrows   *Passeridae*
This family includes about 30 species in three genera, the true sparrows, rock sparrows and snow finches. They are small and similar in appearance to the finches but have generally brown or grey plumage and various harsh chirping calls but no true song. The majority are birds of open country that feed on seeds. Most species of true sparrows inhabit African tropical regions while some occur widely in Europe and Asia. One species, the House Sparrow, is almost always found in association with man and is established throughout the world except in Japan and China. It was deliberately introduced into North America and has spread throughout America reaching the Falklands over 60 years ago.

179. House Sparrow   *Passer domesticus*   Plate 20
A. & C. Gorrión
Local name: English Sparrow
Very small. $6-6\frac{1}{2}$in/$15-16.5$cm
IDENTIFICATION: A plump, perky little bird with dull grey and brown plumage; it is bold and noisy though also wary. *Male* in *breeding* plumage has a dark grey crown, dark chestnut sides and back of the neck, a variable black bib and white cheeks. Back chestnut-brown with black streaks, median wing-coverts chestnut broadly edged white, showing as a bar in flight; rump grey and tail brown. In *winter plumage* the head pattern and lower part of the black bib are obscured by buff tips. *Female and juvenile* are alike; dull brown above streaked darker and pale grey-brown below, paler on belly with a faint buff eye-stripe. Separated from the Black-throated Finch (182) at all ages by unstreaked underparts and complete lack of yellow in wings or tail. The heavy conical bill of *females, juveniles* and *winter males* is yellow-brown, but in *summer* the *male* has a black bill. Legs are yellow-brown.

VOICE: Has several loud twittering and chirping calls, particularly a penetrating *cheep* which the male extends in summer to form a poor quality song *chissip, chissip* which is repeated monotonously.

FOOD: Takes many kinds of food, particularly seeds of grass, garden weeds and cultivated vegetables. It is partial to whole corn (maize) which it can break easily. Feeds on insects such as moth larvae from grass in spring and summer and readily scavenges domestic scraps including bread crumbs or grain scattered for hens.

HABITAT, STATUS & BREEDING: Introduced resident, established at several settlements but only numerous in Stanley, where about 20 arrived in 1919 on one or more whaling ships from Montevideo, Uruguay (Hamilton 1944). Possibly more came at other times. It has since spread, perhaps on coasting vessels, to several widely scattered settlements and islands. Three pairs reached Carcass Island in October 1959 and a small colony was established on West Point Island at about the same time. By 1963, West Point had about six birds which thrived and numbers increased to about 50 birds by 1980. During the absence of the islanders in September 1980, sparrow numbers declined sharply and they were thought to have died out until an occupied nest-site under a roof and three birds, including a pair, were seen in September 1983. Records of House Sparrows were obtained for the current Breeding Birds Survey (1983 onwards) in 12 Grid Squares. Apart from Stanley, it was present at Goose Green, Paragon House (north of Darwin), Fitzroy, North Arm and Johnson's Harbour, Speedwell Island, Sea Lion Island, Carcass and West Point Islands and Port Howard.

Breeds colonially, making a large untidy nest of grasses under roofs or in any available hole high on a building. On Carcass, the small colony bred socially in a large cypress tree. Eggs are probably laid from September onwards though little is known of breeding biology in the Falklands. In England lays three to five, occasionally seven grey-white eggs, finely spotted with brown and grey; clutch-size in the Falklands may be smaller.

DISTRIBUTION ABROAD: The House Sparrow was originally confined to Europe, North Africa and Asia and has spread to most parts of the world. It remains closely associated with human habitation and very rarely migrates.

Finches *Fringillidae*

About 125 species are classified as true finches. Of these about 122 are in the subfamily Carduelinae *and three European and Asian species in the subfamily* Fringillinae. *The* Carduelinae *are widespread in the Americas, Africa and Europe and have been introduced to Australasia. They occur in many kinds of habitat where they feed on seeds and some insects.*

Cardueline finches are small ($11–19cm/4\frac{1}{2}–7\frac{1}{2}in$), vary in colour but usually have prominent markings on wings and tail. They all have strong conical bills, variously modified for extracting and shelling seeds. Many species have melodious songs; they tend to nest colonially and often feed in flocks. Only 13 Cardueline finches occur in South America, of which five inhabit various parts of Argentina. One species is resident in the Falklands.

180. Black-chinned Siskin   *Carduelis barbatus*   Plate 20

A. Sizerín de corbata
C. Jilguero
Local names: Siskin; Canary
Very tiny. $4\frac{3}{4}–5in/12–13cm$
IDENTIFICATION: *The prominent bright yellow wingbar, yellow rump and smaller size distinguish the siskin from the Black-throated Finch (182), as does the preference for perches above ground level.* Male has a black crown and throat, greygreen ear-coverts, yellow sides to the neck, a bright lemon-yellow breast and white belly; olive-yellow nape and back are streaked blackish; brown wings have broad

yellow edges to the secondary coverts, a yellow bar halfway down the secondaries and yellow tipped lesser coverts which show as two or three bars when folded. The slightly forked tail is dark brown with yellow basal sides. Bill blackish above and horn-coloured below; legs black. *Female* is less bright yellow below with a broad curving, pale yellow facial stripe, grey-green cheeks and crown and the back is dull olive-yellow streaked with brown. Tail and wings are similar to the male, though yellow bars are paler; bill brown on ridge, otherwise flesh-pink. A very active bird, it is usually seen in small parties, especially in winter. It frequently perches on large bushes, trees, or in the tops of tussac grass. Flocks are often first detected in winter by their almost continuous twittering.

VOICE: Has several call-notes, including a shrill, rising *tsooeet* and a House Sparrow-like short *chit* or *ti-tip* and a very quiet *tsi-tsi-tsi* used when feeding. This note is very similar to the feeding call of the Black-throated Finch. The flight-note is a short *chup*. The song is loud and attractive, a hurried mixture of several repeated notes and trills, which may be sustained for up to ten minutes, almost unbroken. The male sings from a perch, sometimes high in a tree. Song has been noted from May to July and from late September to December.

FOOD: Feeds mainly on seeds, obtained from grasses including tussac, wild celery, dandelion and possibly from diddle-dee berries. On tussac, small flocks can be seen swaying on the long stems as they extract the seeds which, when available, appear to be the preferred diet.

HABITAT, STATUS & BREEDING: Resident and locally numerous. The status of this species appears to have altered with the changes in vegetation in the past two centuries. In 1764, Pernety (1771) noted the presence of 'Siskins' around Port Louis, when shrubs such as fachine and christmas bush were thriving. In 1774 Clayton remarked on a 'beautyfull little bird like a goldfinch with its pretty notes, but very troublesome in the seed time', on Saunders Island off West Falkland. Abbott (1861) killed one from a flock of five in a garden near Stanley in August 1860. This was the only occurrence known to him in East Falkland, but it was said to be very common on Keppel Island, adjacent to Saunders Island. Bennett (1926) stated that it was seldom seen on East Falkland except in winter, though it bred on West Falkland. Cawkell and Hamilton (1961) considered that the siskin only nested in bushes and that its distribution, before introduced trees and shrubs became established at settlements, was governed by the natural distribution of the native Box *Hebe elliptica* (said to be confined to West Falkland and adjacent islands). In 1952, Cawkell saw a pair of siskins on Kidney Island (Cawkell & Hamilton 1961) and speculated that this could indicate an extension of breeding range. Pettingill (1974) saw several flocks of 10 to 12 birds on Kidney Island in November 1953. Between 1960 and 1962, about ten birds were breeding there and one nest was found in tussac (Woods 1970a). These observations suggest that this grass, which attains the greatest height of any Falkland plant, is a natural habitat for siskins. Recent field work indicates that while the tussac planted in paddocks provides food, for which the birds are ready to fly up to 1.6km (1 mile) during the breeding season, trees and bushes are favoured for nesting. Nests examined on Carcass Island around the settlement averaged 2m (6½ feet) above the ground, twice the height of the nests of other passerines in the tussac (Woods

1984). Nevertheless, observations at Beauchêne Island in December 1980, '16 individuals seen, mostly in pairs' confirmed that siskins can survive in a tussac-dominated habitat (Smith & Prince 1985).

The nest is a neat, well-formed cup of fine grass roots lined with hair, wool or grass root fibres, often placed in a fork of a large bush. One nest in a very large tussac plant was about 1.8m (6 feet) above ground in growing leaves about halfway in towards the centre from the leaf tips. Three to five pinkish-white eggs, spotted or stippled with red-brown, are laid between early September and December; up to three broods may be attempted in a season.

DISTRIBUTION ABROAD: The Black-chinned Siskin is common and widespread in wooded country from Tierra del Fuego and the Magellanic islands to 27°S in the Andes of Argentina and Chile. A taxonomic investigation of the Falklands population may show it to be a distinct geographical race.

Buntings *Emberizidae*

The Emberizidae are a large varied family of mainly ground-feeding small birds, usually found in open country and often known as sparrows or finches in North and South America. Their bills are short and conical, tails fairly long and their feet relatively large. Plumage colours vary greatly, often being streaked or multi-coloured. Emberizidae inhabit most parts of the world and 42 species occur in Europe, Asia and tropical Africa. Many more species are found in the Americas; although a few species have been studied closely, their relationships are uncertain. About 140 species occur in South America, of which 80 species breed in Argentina. Four species have been identified in the Falklands; one is a common breeding species, two are vagrants and one may be a lost breeding species.

Black-throated Finch

181. Mourning Sierra-finch *Phrygilus fruticeti*   Not illustrated
A. Yal negro
C. Yal
Very small. 7–8in/18–20cm
IDENTIFICATION: Noticeably larger than the resident Black-throated Finch (182), the male and female of this species also differ considerably. The *female* is difficult to separate from the female Yellow-bridled Finch (183). *Male* is generally very dark grey, heavily streaked black on head, sides of neck and mantle; throat and centre of the breast are black variably edged whitish, remainder of underparts light grey; wings blackish with prominent white edges to median and secondary coverts forming conspicuous bars; tail fairly long, blackish, with a prominent white outer edge; bill yellow and legs yellowish-brown. *Female* is much duller; upperparts grey-brown streaked dark brown; head grey-brown with narrow white streak curving from behind eye to ear-coverts, lores and ear-coverts light red-brown; underparts pale grey-white streaked brown on breast, flanks light

chestnut; wings dark brown with two white bars like the male; tail brown with a less noticeable white outer edge. Bill and legs are dull yellow. *Immature male* has browner upperparts and heavier whitish edges to dark breast feathers.

STATUS & RECORDS: Vagrant; a male in fresh plumage found dead on Carcass Island, 19 September 1931 by Hamilton is in the British Museum (W Bourne pers. comm.). One probable female or immature was seen near Ajax Bay on 25 July 1984 by W Bourne (Wolsey 1986c). A female was seen and described at Beaver Island settlement on 9 September 1986 by S Wolsey; A Felton first saw this bird with another, possibly male, at Beaver Island on 15 April 1986. He saw the second bird, again with the female, on 19 September 1986 (S Wolsey pers. comm.).

DISTRIBUTION ABROAD: Found in western South America from about 7°S in coastal Peru through western Bolivia and Chile to about 47°S; also occurs in thickets on hillsides up to 2700m (8000 feet) in western Argentina from the north to about 47°S. One was seen in eastern Tierra del Fuego in 1929 (Humphrey 1970).

182. Black-throated Finch   *Melanodera melanodera*   Plate 20
A. Yal grisiamarillo
c. Yal austral
Local name: Sparrow
Tiny. 5½–6in/14–15cm

IDENTIFICATION: An inconspicuous, though locally well known, ground-feeding small finch, male and female are very differently coloured. *Adult male* is handsomely patterned; head, mantle and sides of the breast blue-grey; lores, around eye and throat black, bordered with white above the eye, below the black bib and at sides of the throat where the white area is broadest; centre of breast bright yellow extending to belly and becoming white under the tail; back grey tinged with olive-green becoming olive on rump; tail blackish in centre with bright yellow sides, broadest at base; primaries and secondaries blackish bordered with bright yellow on edges of secondaries; coverts olive broadly edged yellow on lesser coverts. Bill short and conical, blue-grey below and darker above; legs dark brown. Males vary in the amount of yellow on wing and olive on back. *Immature male* has less extensive white on the face, a duller grey head narrowly streaked black, heavy black streaks on flanks and some black on centres of lesser coverts. *Female* is drab; head and upperparts streaked brown and grey-buff, sometimes tinged with red-brown; lores brown, faint buff eye-stripe and dark streak on throat; flight feathers dark brown edged broadly white, with variable yellow on edges and on coverts; underparts buff variably tinged with yellow, heavily streaked dark brown on sides from neck to flanks; tail similar to male, showing less extensive yellow sides. Bill horn, legs brown. *Juvenile* resembles female. Yellow-edged tail immediately separates this species from the pipit (173) in flight; lack of wingbar separates it from the siskin (180). The male is separated from male Yellow-bridled Finch (183) by white facial stripes but both female and young are indistinguishable in the field. Flight is rapid and jerky but more direct in territorial chases. Usually seen singly or in pairs when breeding, but from early December mixed flocks of 20 or more young and old birds are formed; largest number recorded was a gathering of about 1000 spread along dunes by Yorke Bay on 30 May 1957 (Woods 1975).

VOICE: Usual call-note is a very high-pitched short *si*, often repeated as a rapid *si-si-si* especially by birds feeding in a flock on the ground. Male has loud explosive and buzzing call-notes in territorial chases. The song is a plaintive repetition of two or three phrases *peeoo-payoo-payoo*, with variations and sometimes extended slightly. Song has been recorded between the end of May and late January though it is most frequent between September and December. Song-perches are usually low, such as a rock, grass tussock or diddle-dee bush; fence posts and wires are also used.

FOOD: Feeds on seeds of grasses including tussac, sorrel, chickweed, sand cabbage and diddle-dee; also takes grass flowers and will eat breadcrumbs.

HABITAT, STATUS & BREEDING: Resident, common and widespread on inland and coastal heathland with dwarf shrubs, on greens by beaches, in dunes with marram grass and in open tussac grassland with short grazed turf. Occurs to at least 150m (500 feet) above sea level but does not inhabit dense tussac. Pairs are formed from at least mid-July and nesting occurs between mid-September and late December. Nests are usually well-hidden in white grass or a crevice between stones; one was found at a height of 1.1m (3½ feet) in tussac, showing that sites above ground are sometimes used. The nest is constructed of fine grasses, lined with horsehair, goose down or other feathers, the material being collected by the female accompanied by the male. One nest with four eggs, found 17 November 1958 on Stanley Common was partly lined with yellow Black-throated Finch tail feathers; when flushed, the female was seen to be tail-less. Lays a clutch of three to four light blue-grey or grey-green eggs, with purple-brown markings concentrated around the blunt end. Probably rears at least two broods in a season; flocks have been observed in December when other pairs have been incubating eggs. Young nestlings are separated from nestling Falkland Pipits by their crimson mouth linings and silver-grey down.

DISTRIBUTION ABROAD: Restricted to extreme southern South America. Two races have been described; *M. m. melanodera* is the Falkland race and *M. m. princetoniana* is resident from about 47°S in Chile and Argentina through the Magellanic islands to the northern unforested parts of Tierra del Fuego.

183. Yellow-bridled Finch   *Melanodera xanthogramma*   Plate 20
A. Yal verde
C. Yal cordillerano austral
Very small. 6–6¾in/15–17cm
IDENTIFICATION: Similar to the Black-throated Finch (182) though slightly larger, the *male* is recognised by yellow, rather than white, facial stripes around the black lores and bib. There are two *colour phases of males*; one has crown, nape and back clear blue-grey, variably marked with yellow-green and sometimes flecked with brown; underparts blue-grey on breast and flanks, greenish-yellow on belly and whitish under tail; wing-coverts and primaries edged yellow-green. The other males are olive-green above, dark yellow-green on upper breast and flanks and yellow on belly and under tail. Males of both colour phases usually have more yellow on the breast and belly than the male Black-throated. The tail is dark brown broadly edged yellow (southern race *xanthogramma*) or white (northern race *bar-*

rosi). *Female* very variable, closely resembling the female Black-throated but larger; probably indistinguishable unless seen together or with a male; usually more heavily streaked below with more yellow on the breast and belly though some have no yellow on the underparts. Primaries brown; only the outer three are edged with yellow-green.

STATUS & RECORDS: Uncertain, possibly a former breeding species lost through changes in the vegetation or a very rare vagrant. First recorded by Darwin (1841) who remarked that it '. . . is common at the Falkland Islands and often occurs mingled in the same flock with the last one' (Black-throated Finch), which he stated was '. . . extremely abundant in large scattered flocks . . .'. Darwin also commented that these two species 'have a very close general resemblance' and gave good descriptions of the differences between males of both species. He suspected that the Yellow-bridled '. . . more commonly frequents higher parts of the hills.' In the British Museum collection are a female taken during the Antarctic Expedition of 1842, which also visited Hermite Island south of Tierra del Fuego and a male from MacGillivray in 1850, who did not visit South America. Surprisingly, Abbott, a resident from 1858–60, stated that he knew nothing of the 'second so-called species of this genus, *Phrygilus xanthogrammus*' and did not believe that it was different from the Black-throated Finch (Abbott 1861). The only other Falkland specimen was an immature taken by Brooks in February 1916 at Port Stephens and named (wrongly) as a new species *Phrygilus malvinarum* apparently because it had 'no yellow in the plumage' (Brooks 1916). This was later stated to be a Black-chinned Siskin (Cawkell & Hamilton 1961) but the wing measurement given by Brooks is at least 20mm longer than that of the siskin. Wace (1921) and Bennett (1926) both listed the Yellow-bridled Finch as an accidental visitor while Hamilton thought he saw one in a flock of Black-throated Finches (Cawkell & Hamilton 1961). There have been no further records. Darwin's comment that it frequented higher parts than the Black-throated Finch may indicate a difference in diet and possible dependence on a food source that was eliminated by over-grazing.

DISTRIBUTION ABROAD: Two races have been described in southern South America; *M. x. barrosi* inhabits andean regions to 3000m (10,000 feet) from about 33°S in Chile and Argentina to the Magellan Straits (53°S). *M. x. xanthogramma* occurs in the mountainous southern part of Tierra del Fuego, above the tree-line and in the islands of the Beagle Channel.

184. Rufous-collared Sparrow *Junco capensis*   Plate 20
A. Chingolo
c. Chincol
Tiny to very small. $5\frac{1}{2}$–$6\frac{1}{2}$in/14–16cm
IDENTIFICATION: A slender, fairly long-tailed finch, that has associated with House Sparrows (179) in the Falklands, it is easily recognised in *adult plumage* by the broad chestnut collar across the hindneck, extending below the white throat and ending in a small black spot or patch. Head grey, slightly crested or peaked in the male, with a very variable pattern of black stripes (see * below). Underparts grey-white on the breast and white on the belly; flanks light grey-brown and under

tail-coverts white flecked brown. Mantle is grey-buff heavily streaked with dark brown, back is brown-grey becoming browner on the rump. Wings are darkish brown broadly edged buff with median and secondary coverts tipped white showing as narrow bars. Tail is brown, with faint whitish edges and is noticeably forked. Bill slate-grey above, lighter below; legs pale brown. *Juvenile* is brown above, heavily streaked dark brown and buff streaked dark brown on the breast; belly and under tail whitish. Call-note a sharp *tseep*, often repeated intermittently and at a higher pitch than House Sparrow calls.

* At least eight races have been described from southern South America. They all have a grey head; some are darker on the nape, others have very narrow black stripes on the crown and dark flecks on the nape or broad black stripes either side of the crown from bill to nape. The extent of black behind the eye, white or grey eye-stripe and black below ear-coverts also varies. Some races can be recognised in the field by the head pattern (*eg* the southern race *J. c. australis* has no crown stripes) but others show intergradation and their separation in breeding areas is not fully understood. Body size also varies; the races *australis*, *choraules* and *chilensis* are all larger than northern races.

STATUS & RECORDS: Vagrant, recorded several times since 1951. There are nine records, all from West Falkland, probably of the southern race *australis* drifting eastward on migration. Three were seen at West Point Island in the summer of 1951, one of which was in song; a dead bird was found on New Island about April 1953 (Cawkell & Hamilton 1961); one seen at Port Stephens, early April 1962, had no crown stripes (M Shaw pers. comm.); two survived at West Point Island from mid-April to at least mid-August 1973 and one at Carcass Island for a week to 28 May 1976 (K Bertrand pers. comm.); one seen at New Island on 23 July 1984 by G Clark and one seen at 52°48′S 60°21′W, 48km (30 miles) southeast of Cape Meredith on 12 March 1985 by W Bourne (Wolsey 1986c); one, possibly two at Beaver Island 13 October to mid-November 1986 described by A Felton as having no crown stripes and one at Beaver Island 20 March 1987 (S Wolsey pers. comm.).

There have been three possible records of the race *subtorquata*; one arrived in Stanley on board RRS *John Biscoe* a few years before 1958 and was seen to fly ashore (Cawkell & Hamilton); a male was seen in Stanley from 11–16 October 1960. It was trapped, ringed and photographed and a detailed description was taken. The crown had broad continuous stripes either side indicating that it was not *australis* while weight, wing, tarsus, tail and body lengths all suggested one of the smaller races of northern Argentina. Another bird with very similar plumage was first seen 11 May 1962 in a Stanley garden; it was trapped and ringed on 23 September 1962 and seen over 20 times between May and 31 December 1962. It is probable that the 1960 and 1962 birds travelled from Montevideo on RMS *Darwin*. This species can certainly survive the Falkland winter and could possibly become a breeding species.

DISTRIBUTION ABROAD: Widely distributed from southern Mexico throughout South America to Tierra del Fuego and the islands near Cape Horn. It is a bird of scrub and open country, not dense forests, and occurs up to 3000m (10,000 feet). Twenty or more races have been described, including seven from Argentina. *J. c. australis* , which occurs from about 43°S to Cape Horn is the only migratory race, some moving northward to about 20°S in winter. Others remain in the Magellanic region, moving north-eastward in Tierra del Fuego in winter and returning south-westward in spring.

American Orioles   *Icteridae*
This family has about 90 very varied species, including oropendolas, caciques, grackles, American blackbirds, cowbirds, troupials, orioles and meadowlarks. They inhabit the New World from the Canadian Arctic to the southern shores of Tierra del Fuego. Size varies between 15 to 53cm (6–21in) and plumage is often mainly black, sometimes glossy and in several species contrasted with red, orange or yellow. The most obvious family characteristic is the conical, pointed bill which all species can open against pressure, allowing them to reach hidden food items not available to other species. In general they occur in habitats disturbed by human activity such as farming, which has allowed several species to increase their populations tremendously. Sixty-three species occur in South America, of which 23 are found in Argentina. Only one species, a local race of the Long-tailed Meadowlark, is resident in the Falklands. One other species, the Austral Blackbird Curaeus curaeus *may have occurred at least once, though insufficient plumage notes were received.*

Long-tailed
Meadowlark

185. Long-tailed Meadowlark   *Sturnella loyca*   Plate 20
A. Pecho-colorado grande
C. Loica
Local names: Robin, Military Starling
Small. 9½–10in/24–25cm
IDENTIFICATION: Easily recognised by the bright red breast, heavy, conical and sharply pointed pale bill and loud calls, the Long-tailed Meadowlark is familiar around settlements. *Male* in *breeding* plumage, assumed by July, is brilliant, glowing red from chin to lower breast. Sides of the breast and belly are black with a scaly pattern of buff tips. The head is blackish-brown streaked buff, with a broad curving white eye-stripe extending to the nape, black ear-coverts and side of the neck and a red spot above the lores. Mantle, back and wing-coverts are heavily mottled black on buff; flight feathers blackish broadly edged buff and the carpal joint and leading edge of the wing are red; tail barred light brown and blackish, outer tail feathers are dark brown with a narrow white outer edge. In *autumn and early winter*, the red colouring is partly obscured by buff tips. *Female* has similar upperparts to male but has an orange-pink throat, a less extensive and paler red breast, a narrower eye-stripe and a darker bill. *Juvenile* resembles female but has only a narrow pink streak in the centre of the underparts and a shorter bill.
   Easily recognised in flight by the pure white under wing-coverts. On the ground or a perch it has a characteristic crouching attitude with the legs almost hidden.

It runs with an ungainly action and sometimes moves with powerful bounds. The method of taking flight is also characteristic; the male closely followed by the female, will suddenly shoot up from the ground almost vertically to about 15m (50 feet) with rapid wingbeats, before flying away.

VOICE: The usual flight-note is a loud explosive *cheeoo*, uttered frequently. A quieter *chook* or *chink* is used mainly when feeding. Both sexes sing; the male has a harsh powerful song of about seven notes, which falls, rises to a higher note and then falls to a much lower note. Sings from the ground, a fence post, a tree top or as high as 15m (50 feet) from an aerial mast. It also sings in gliding song-flight over territory and the song is sometimes lengthened and elaborated. The female's song is weaker, more squeaky and shorter; it often sings from the ground while the male sings nearby from a perch. Song from both male and female is heard during most of the year though more frequently between August and November.

FOOD: Feeds mainly on invertebrates, including earthworms, moth larvae and fly grubs taken from turf; also takes grain from horse droppings and has acquired the habit of digging into potatoes in the ground. Food is taken by prodding and opening the bill wide, thus exposing prey amongst grass stems or breaking up earth or dung.

HABITAT, STATUS & BREEDING: Resident, widely distributed and apparently most common on white grass camp near shores and short turf around settlements. It also inhabits mixed tussac and short grazed grass paddocks where population density may be higher than on adjacent heathland (Woods 1984). Nests from late August to late November, laying two to four blue-white eggs blotched and streaked with purple and black, mainly around the blunt end. Two broods are probably reared in a season. The nest is constructed of dry grasses; it may be well-hidden on the ground in thick white grass sheltered by a clump or, up to 1m (3 feet) above ground on a tussac grass pedestal. Nests on the ground have a noticeable pathway of up to 1m leading to the nest and those in tussac have a flattened side platform. The female apparently does all building and incubation. Recently fledged young disperse and hide beneath grass clumps where they are fed by both parents. Flocks of up to 60 are formed from January and persist until about July.

DISTRIBUTION ABROAD: Four races are described from southern South America where it occurs from about 27°S in Argentina and Chile to southern Tierra del Fuego and up to 3000m (10,000 feet) in northern parts of its range. Some migrate northward to about 23°S in winter though the southern race *S. l. loyca* is resident in the Magellanic region. The Falkland race *S. l. falklandica* is somewhat larger than the continental races.

Bibliography

Abbott, C C (1861) Notes on the birds of the Falkland Islands. *Ibis* 1; 149–167.

Anon. (1882) The cruise of HMS *'Dwarf'* amongst the Falkland Islands. *The Falkland Islands Journal* 1971, eds. J A & J I C B Jones, 36–40.

Atkinson, I A E (1985) The spread of commensal species of *Rattus* to oceanic islands and their effects on Island Avifaunas, pp35–81, in *Conservation of Island Birds*, ed. P J Moors, ICBP Cambridge.

Barlow, N (1963) Darwin's Ornithological Notes. *Bull. British Museum (Natural History)*, Historical Series 2: 203–278.

Beck, R H (1918) Photographs of Falkland Island bird life. *Bird Lore* 20: 1–8.

Bennett, A G (1926) A list of the Birds of the Falkland Islands and Dependencies. *Ibis* 12th series, No.2: 306–333.

—(1930) Nesting of the Grey-backed Storm Petrel *Garrodia nereis* Chubb. *Oologists Record* 10(4): 79.

—(1931a) Additional notes on the birds of the Falkland Islands and Dependencies. *Ibis* 13th series, No.1: 12–13.

—(1931b) First record of a Humming-bird in the Falkland Islands. *Ibis* 13th series, 1: 348–349.

—(1935) Two records from the Falkland Islands *Ibis* 13th series, 5(2): 436.

—(1937) *Coccyzus melanocoryphus* in the Falkland Islands. *Ibis* 14th series, 1(4): 868.

—(1938) Bartram's Sandpiper on the Falkland Islands. *Ibis* 14th series, 2: 764.

Bernsee, F (1855) Letter from Captain F Bernsee of the ship *'Courier'* wrecked on the SW point of East Falkland, in April 1854, *Proc. Acad. Nat. Sci. Philadelphia* 7: 287–288.

Bertrand, K (1968) Carcass Island 1765–1967, in *The Falkland Islands Journal*, ed. W H Thompson, 1968: 48–51.

—(1981) Conservation on Carcass Island, in *The Warrah*, ed. J Peatfield, No.1: 5–6.

Blake, E R (1977) *Manual of Neotropical Birds*, Vol.1. The University of Chicago Press, Chicago & London.

Bourne, W R P (1981) Rats as avian predators. *Atoll Research Bulletin* 255: 69–72.

—(1987) Falkland Farming and Fishing. Editorial in *Marine Pollution Bulletin* 18(1): 1–2.

—& Curtis, W F (1985) South Atlantic Seabirds. *Sea Swallow* 34: 18–28.

—& Curtis, W F (1987) Birds seen in Falkland waters 1982–87. (in litt.).

—& Warham, J (1966) Geographical variation in the Giant Petrels of the genus *Macronectes*. *Ardea* 54: 45–67.

Brooks, W S (1916) Two undescribed birds from the Falkland Islands. *Proc. New England Zool. Club* Vol.VI: 25–27.

—(1917) Notes on some Falkland Islands birds. *Bull. Mus. Comp. Zool. Harvard College* 61(7): 135–160.

Byron, J (1765) Letter to the Earl of Egmont at Port Famine, in *The Falkland Islands Journal*, eds. S Miller, J Smith & J Abbott, 1975: 18–22.

Campbell, B & Lack, E (eds) (1985) *A Dictionary of Birds*. Poyser, Calton & Buteo, Vermillion.

Carins, M (1974a) The Blue Petrel *Halobaena caerulea* in the Falkland Islands. *Ardea* 62: 239–241.

—(1974b) Garnot's Cormorant and the 'Brown Booby' in the Falkland Islands. *Ardea* 62: 242–245.

Cawkell, E M & Hamilton, J E (1961) The Birds of the Falkland Islands. *Ibis* 103a: 1–27.

Cawkell, E M B R Maling, D H and Cawkell, E M (1960) *The Falkland Islands*. Macmillan, London.

Clark, G S (1985) SRV *Totorora* Expedition to Chile 1983. *Expedition Yearbook* 1983: 161–162 eds N & S Winser, Expedition Advisory Centre, London.

Clayton, S W (1774) A Short Description of Falklands Islands . . . Letter to P Stephens Esq. Public Record Office Adm 7/704.

Clutton-Brock, J (1977) Man-made Dogs. *Science* 197: 1340–1342.

Cobb, A F (1910) *Wild Life in the Falkland Islands*. Gowans's Nature Books No.26, Gowans & Grey, London & Glasgow.

—(1933) *Birds of the Falkland Islands*. Witherby, London.

Colony of the Falkland Islands (1964) The Wild Animals and Birds Protection Ordinance, 1964, No.8.

—(1964) The Nature Reserves Ordinance, 1964 No.15.

Cramp, S & Simmons, K E L (eds) (1977–85) *The Birds of the Western Palearctic*, Vol. I to IV. Oxford University Press, Oxford.

Crawshay, R (1907) *The Birds of Tierra del Fuego*, Bernard Quaritch, London.

Croxall, J P et al (1984) The status and conservation of seabirds at the Falkland Islands, in *Status and Conservation of the World's Seabirds* eds. J P Croxall, P G H Evans & R W Schreiber, ICBP Cambridge.

—& Prince, P A (1980) The food of Gentoo Penguins *Pygoscelis papua* and Macaroni Penguins *Eudyptes chrysolophus* at South Georgia. *Ibis* 122: 245–253.

—Prince, P A & Baird, P (1985) The diet of the Southern Rockhopper Penguin *Eudyptes chrysocome* at Beauchêne Island, Falkland Islands. *J. Zool. Soc. London* (A) (1985) 206: 485–496.

Daciuk, J (1975) La fauna silvestre de las Islas Malvinas, in Campaña Cientifica en las islas Malvinas, 1974. *An. de la Soc Cient. Arg.* Vol.199, (4–6): 153–176.

Dallimore, W (1919) The Falkland Islands. Forestry. Tussock Grass. *Bull. Misc. Inf. Royal Bot. Gdn. Kew* No.5: 209–221.

Darwin, C R (1845) *Journal of Researches into the Natural History and Geology of countries visited during the voyage of HMS 'Beagle' round the world.* John Murray, London.

Davies, T H, Dickson, I A, McCrea, C T. Mead, H & Williams, W W (1971) *The sheep and cattle industries of the Falkland Islands.* Foreign & Commonwealth Office, Overseas Development Administration, London.

Davies, W (1939) *The grasslands of the Falkland Islands.* Government Printer, Stanley & Crown Agents, 86pp.

Devillers, P (1978) Distribution & Relationships of South American Skuas. *Le Gerfaut*, 68: 374–417.

—& Terschuren, J A (1976) Some distributional records of migrant North American Charadriiformes in coastal South America. *Le Gerfaut* 66: 107–125.

—& Terschuren, J A (1980) Les pétrels géants Macronectes de îles Falkland et du sud de l'amérique du sud. *Le Gerfaut* 70: 447–454.

Douse, A F G (1986) The 1986 Penguin Wreck: A Summary, in *Falkland Islands Trust News* No.2, ed. S Wolsey, August 1986.

Dunning, J S (1982) *South American Land Birds.* Harrowood Books, Pennsylvania.

Falla, R A, Sibson, R B and Turbott, E G (1966) *A Field Guide to the Birds of New Zealand.* Collins, London.

Felton, H (1886) Quoted in *Falkland Islands Monthly Review*, 6 May 1963 & Woods 1975: 28.

Garnot, P (1826) Remarques sur la Zoologie des îles Malouines. *Annales de Sciences Naturelles* 7: 39–59.

Gilliard, E T (1958) *Living Birds of the World.* Hamish Hamilton, London.

Goodall, J D, Johnson, A W & Philippi, R A (1951 & 1957) *Las Aves de Chile.* Vol.1 & Supplement; Vol.2. Platt Establecimientos Gráficos, Buenos Aires.

Gorham, S W (1972) History of the so-called Falkland Islands 'Wolf' *Dusicyon australis*, in *The Falkland Islands Journal* eds. J A & J I C B Jones 1972: 27–39.

Gould, J (1859) List of birds from the Falkland Islands. *Proc. Zool. Soc. London* 27: 93–99.

—& Darwin, C R (1841) *The Zoology of the voyage of HMS 'Beagle'.* Part 3 Birds: 8–145.

Gower, E (1803) The Loss of the *'Swift'*. *The Falkland Islands Journal*, ed. W H Thompson, 1970: 24–29.

Grant, J (1803) *The Narrative of a Voyage of Discovery . . in 'The Lady Nelson'.* Extracts in *The Falkland Islands Journal*, eds. S Miller, J Smith & J Abbott, 1974: 37–40.

Grey, G (1836–7) *The diary of Admiral the Hon. George Grey*, Extracts in *The Falkland Islands Journal*, ed. W H Thompson 1969: 54–68.

Hamilton, J E (1937) The Chilean Skua in the Falkland Islands. *Ibis* 14th series, 1: 177–178.

—(1939) Additions to the Falkland Islands List. *Ibis* 14th series, 3: 139–140.

—(1944) The House Sparrow in the Falkland Islands. *Ibis* 86: 553–554.

—(1945a) [Note on South Polar Skua at Stanley]. *Ibis* 87: 103.

—(1945b) First record of *Pterodroma mollis* (Gould) in the Falkland Islands. *Ibis* 87: 569–570.

244

—(1950) Addition to the Falkland Islands List. *Ibis* 92: 146.

—(1951) The breeding place of *Pachyptila belcheri* Mathews. *Ibis* 93: 139–140.

—(1954) The Emperor Penguin in the Falklands. *Ibis* 96(2): 315.

Hancock, J & Kushlan, J (1984) *The Herons Handbook*. Croom Helm. London.

Harper, P C & Kinsky, F C (1978) *Southern Albatrosses and Petrels*. Price Milburn, Wellington.

Harradine, J (1976) Geese in the Falkland Islands. *The Falkland Islands Journal*, eds. S Miller, J Smith & J Abbott, 1976: 9–20.

Harrison, P (1983) *Seabirds: An Identification Guide*. Croom Helm, London.

Hooker, J D (1847) *Botany of the Antarctic voyage, Vol.1 Flora Antarctica, part 2, The Botany of Fuegia, the Falklands etc. . .* Reeve, London.

Hubbard, C E (1937) Sand-binding grasses in the Falkland Islands. *Bull. Misc. Inf. Royal Bot. Gdn. Kew*, p274.

Hudson, W H (1920) *Birds of La Plata*. Two vols. London.

Humphrey, P S, Bridge, D, Reynolds, P W & Peterson, R T (1970) *Birds of Isla Grande (Tierra del Fuego)*. Smithsonian Institution, Washington DC.

—& Livezey, B C (1983) Giant Petrel (*Macronectes giganteus*), nesting in Chubut, Argentina. *Le Gerfaut* 73: 3–8.

—& Thompson, M C (1981) A new species of steamer-duck (*Tachyeres*) from Argentina. *Univ. Kansas Mus. Nat. Hist., Occas. Papers* 95: 1–12.

Huxley, L (1918) *Life and Letters of Sir J D Hooker*, Two vols, John Murray, London.

Jehl, J R (1975) *Pluvianellus socialis*: Biology, ecology and relationships of an enigmatic Patagonian shorebird. *Trans. San Diego Soc. of Nat, Hist.* 18(3): 25–74.

—(1978) A new hybrid Oystercatcher from South America *Haematopus leucopodus x H ater*. *Condor* 80: 344–346.

Johnsgard, P A (1968) *Waterfowl*. University of Nebraska Press, Lincoln.

Kinnear, N B (1931) Swallow-tailed Flycatcher in the Falkland Islands. *Ibis* 13th series, 1(3): 578.

Lévêque, R (1978) Première observation du Tyran tritri *Tyrannus tyrannus* aux îles Falkland. *Alauda* 46(4): 362.

Lowcay, R (1838) Lieutenant Lowcay & HM Ketch 'Sparrow', 1837, in *The Falkland Islands Journal* eds. S Miller, J Smith & J Abbott, 1977: 10–20.

Maling, D H (1960) Climate, in *The Falkland Islands*, M B R Cawkell, D H Maling & E M Cawkell. Macmillan, London.

Marchant, J, Prater, T & Hayman, P (1986) *Shorebirds: An Identification Guide to the waders of the world*. Croom Helm, London.

McBride, J (1767) letter to Mr Stephens from 'Jason', in *The Falkland Islands Journal* eds. S Miller, J Smith & J Abbott, 1978: 32–35.

McCormick, R (1884) *Voyages of Discovery in the Arctic and Antarctic seas and round the world*. Two vols. London.

Meyer de Schaunsee, R (1971) *A Guide to the Birds of South America*, Oliver & Boyd, Edinburgh.

Miller, S (1975) Patagonian Missionary Society Keppel Island, 1855–1911, in *The Falkland Islands Journal* 1975: 9–17.

Mödinger, B A & Holman, G M (1986) *Guia de campo de las aves de Chile*. Editorial Universitaria, Santiago de Chile.

Moody, R C (1842) Despatch from Lieutenant Governor Moody to Lord Stanley, in *The Falkland Islands Journal*, ed. W H Thompson 1969: 4–33.

Moore, D M (1968) The Vascular Flora of the Falkland Islands. *British Antarctic Survey Scientific Reports* No.60. NERC.

Mowat, J T (1896) Letter from the *Marlborough Express*, in *The Falkland Islands Journal*, ed. W H Thompson 1970: 33–35.

Munro, H (1924) *Report of an investigation into the conditions and practice of sheep farming in the Falkland Islands*, Waterlow & Sons, London.

Murphy, R C (1936) *Oceanic Birds of South America*, Two vols. The Macmillan Company & American Museum of Natural History, New York.

Murton, R H *et al* (1974) The ecology of the Eared Dove *Zenaida auriculata* in Argentina. *Condor* 76: 80–88.

Napier, R B (1968) Erect-crested and Rockhopper Penguins interbreeding in the Falkland Islands. *Bulletin British Antarctic Survey* 16: 71–72.

Nores, M & Yzurieta, D (1981) Nuevas localidades para aves argentinas. *Historia Natural* Vol.2, No.5: 33–34.

Olrog, C C (1959) *Las Aves Argentinas, Una Guia de Campo*, Universidad Nacional de Tucuman, Instituto 'Miguel Lillo'.

—(1979) Nueva Lista de la Avifauna Argentina. *Opera Lilloana* 27: 1–324.

—(1984) *Las Aves Argentinas, Una Nueva Guia de Campo*. Administracion de Parques Nacionales, Buenos Aires.

Peatfield, J (1981) Birds and Sea-mammals Report. *The Warrah* 1: 7–15.

—(1981) 'Sterna' Terns in the Falklands. *The Warrah* 1: 16–18.

Pernety, A J (1771) *The history of a voyage to the Malouine (or Falkland) Islands* . . . Translated for T Jeffreys, London.

Pettingill, E R (1962) *Penguin Summer*. Cassell, London.

Pettingill, O S jr (1960a) The effects of climate and weather on the birds of the Falkland Islands. *Procs. XIIth Int. Ornith. Congress, Helsinki* 1958: 604–614.

—(1960b) Crèche behaviour and individual recognition in a colony of Rockhopper Penguins. *The Wilson Bulletin*, Vol.72(3): 213–221.

—(1964) Penguins ashore at the Falkland Islands. *The Living Bird* 3: 45–64, Cornell Laboratory of Ornithology.

—(1965) Kelp Geese and Flightless Steamer Ducks in the Falkland Islands. *The Living Bird* 4: 65–79.

—(1974) Passerine birds of the Falkland Islands: their behaviour & ecology; *The Living Bird* 12: 95–136.

—(1975) *Another Penguin Summer*. Charles Scribner's Sons, New York.

Phillips, B (1983) *A selected bibliography of Falkland Islands birds*. ICBP for the Falkland Islands Foundation, Cambridge.

Prince, P A (1982) The Black-browed Albatross *Diomedea melanophris* population at Beauchêne Island, Falkland Islands. *Comité Nat. Franc. de Recherches Antarctiques*, 51: 111–117.

—& Payne, M R (1979) Current status of birds at South Georgia. *British Antarctic Survey Bulletin* 48: 103–118.

Ramsay, LN G (1913) Ornithology of the Scottish National Antarctic Expedition in, *Sci. Res. Scot. Nat. Ant. Exped.* 4: Sect.II: 207–209.

Reynolds. P W (1932) Notes on the birds of Snipe and the Woodcock Islands in the Beagle Channel. *Ibis* 13th series, 1: 34–39.

—(1935) Notes on the birds of Cape Horn. *Ibis* 13th series, Vol.5(1): 65–101.

Ross, A K (1986) Seaborne observations of Peregrine Falcon behaviour. *Sea Swallow* 35: 66–67.

Ross, J C (1847) *A voyage of discovery and research in the southern and antarctic regions during the years 1839–43*, London.

Sclater, P L (1860) Catalogue of the birds of the Falkland Islands. *Proc. Zool. Soc. London* Part 28: 382–391.

—(1861) Additions and corrections to the List of Birds of the Falkland Islands. *Proc. Zool. Soc. London*, February 1861: 45–47.

—(1868) Extract from: The Secretary on additions to the menagerie, November 12, 1868. *Proc. Zool. Soc. London*, 527–529.

—& Sharpe, R B (1885–98) Catalogue of Birds in the British Museum, Vols. X-XV and XXIII-XXVII, London.

Shackleton, The Rt Hon Lord (1976) *Economic Survey of the Falkland Islands*. Two vols, HMSO, London.

Skottsberg, C (1913) A Botanical Survey of the Falkland Islands. *K. svenska Vetensk Akad. Handl.* 50, No.3: 1–129.

Sladen, W J L (1952) Arctic Skua in the Antarctic. *Ibis* 94: 543.

Smith, R I L & Clymo, R S (1984) An extraordinary peat-forming community on the Falkland Islands. *Nature* vol. 309: 617–620.

—& Prince, P A (1985) The natural history of Beauchêne Island. *Biol. J. of the Linnean Society* 24: 233–283.

Soames, B (1980) *Keeping Domestic Geese.* Blandford Press, Poole.

Spafford. R N (1987) Trees in the Falklands. *Falkland Islands Association Newsletter*, No.31: 9.

Standring, K T (1982) *Falkland Islands Draft Nature Conservation Legislation.* Unpublished report, 28 April 1982.

Stewart, P J (1982) Trees for the Falkland Islands. *Commonwealth Forestry Review* 61(3): 219–225.

Strange, I J (1968) A breeding colony of *Pachyptila turtur* in the Falkland Islands. *Ibis* 110: 358–359.

—(1979) Distribution of Cattle Egrets *Bubulcus ibis* to the Falkland Islands. *Le Gerfaut* 69: 397–401.

—(1980) The Thin-billed Prion *Pachyptila belcheri* at New Island, Falkland Islands. *Le Gerfaut* 70: 411–445.

—(1982) Breeding Ecology of the Rockhopper Penguin in the Falkland Islands. *Le Gerfaut* 72: 137–188.

—(1985) Nature Reserves and the Law – Time for a change. *Falkland Islands Foundation Newsletter* January 1985, No.3: 2–3.

Summers, R W (1982) The absence of flightless moult in the Ruddy-headed Goose in Argentina and Chile. *Wildfowl* 33: 5–6.

—(1983a) Moult-skipping by Upland Geese *Chloephaga picta* in the Falkland Islands. *Ibis* 125: 262–266.

—(1983b) The life cycle of the Upland Goose *Chloephaga picta* in the Falkland Islands. *Ibis* 125: 524–544.

—(1985) The size and composition of Sheld-geese populations and their food consumption on different vegetation types in the Falkland Islands. *J. Appl. Ecol.* 22: 1–17.

—& Crocker, J (1983) A wild goose chase. *Wildlife* March 1983: 86.

—& Dunnet, G M (1984) Sheld-Geese and Man in the Falkland Islands. *Biol. Cons.* 30: 319–340.

—& Grieve, A (1982) Diet, feeding behaviour and food intake of the Upland Goose and the Ruddy-headed Goose in the Falkland Islands. *J. Appl. Ecol.* 19: 783–804.

Tickell, W L N (1967) Movements of Black-browed and Grey-headed Albatrosses in the South Atlantic. *Emu* Vol. 66(4): 357–367.

—& Woods, R W (1972) Ornithological observations at sea in the South Atlantic Ocean, 1954–64. *British Antarctic Survey Bulletin* No.31: 63–84.

Tuck, G & Heinzel, H (1978) *A Field Guide to the Seabirds of Britain and the World.* Collins, London.

Vallentin, R (1904) Notes on the Falkland Islands. *Manchester Memoirs* Vol. XLVIII, No.23: 1–51.

—(1924) Birds, pp 285–335 in *The Falkland Islands*, V F Boyson, Clarendon Press, Oxford.

Venegas, C & Jory, J (1979) *Guia de Campo para las Aves de Magallanes.* Instituto de la Patagonia, Punta Arenas.

Wace, N M (1960) The botany of the southern oceanic islands. *Proc. Royal Society*, Series B, 152: 475–490.

Wace, R H (1921) Lista de aves de las islas Falkland. *El Hornero* II: 194–204.

Wallace, D I M (1986) Muggers of the ocean. *Bird Watching* November 1986: 34–35.

Waterhouse, G R & Darwin, C R (1839) Zoology of the voyage of HMS '*Beagle*', Part II Mammalia.

Watson, G E (1975) *Birds of the Antarctic and Sub-Antarctic.* American Geophysical Union, Washington.

Weller, M W (1967) Notes on some marsh birds of Cape San Antonio, Argentina. *Ibis* 109: 391–411.

—(1972) Ecological studies of Falkland Islands' waterfowl. *Wildfowl* 23: 25–44.

Wetmore, A (1965 & 1968) *The Birds of the Republic of Panama.* Parts 1 & 2. Smithsonian Institution, Washington DC.

Whitington, G T (1840) *The Climate, Soil, Natural Productions and Sundry Advantages of the Falkland Islands* . . . in, *The Falkland Islands Journal* ed. W H Thompson 1967: 16–20.

Witherby, H F *et al* (1940–41) *The Handbook of British Birds.* Five vols. H F & G Witherby, London.

Wolsey, R P S (1986a) ed. *Falkland Islands Trust News* No.1, May 1986.

—(1986b) ed. *Falkland Islands Trust News* No.2, August 1986.

—(1986c) ed. *Warrah*, Annual Report 1985 of the Falkland Islands Trust: Falkland Bird Report, pp 21–31.

—(1986d) ed. *Falkland Islands Trust News* No.3, November 1986.

—(1987a) ed. *Falkland Islands Trust News* No.4, February 1987.

—(1987b) ed. *Falkland Islands Trust News* No.5, May 1987.

Woods R W (1970a) The avian ecology of a tussock island in the Falkland Islands. *Ibis* 112: 15–24.

—(1970b) Great Shearwater *Puffinus gravis* breeding in the Falkland Islands. *Ibis* 112: 259–260.

—(1975) *The Birds of the Falkland Islands*. Anthony Nelson, Oswestry.

—(1982) *Falkland Islands Birds*. Anthony Nelson, Oswestry.

—(1984) A Census of Breeding Falkland Islands Passerine Birds in Tussac Grass: pp 132. (Unpublished, copy in Stanley Library).

—(1985) Falkland Islands Avian Ecology Expedition 1983, in *Expedition Yearbook 1983*, eds. N & S Winser, Expedition Advisory Centre, London.

—(1986) How many islands in the Falkland Islands? in *Falkland Islands Foundation Newsletter*, July 1986, No.5: 8–9.

Zotta, A R (1944) *Lista Sistematica de las Aves Argentinas*, 236 pp. Mus. Arg. de Cienc. Nat., Buenos Aires.

Index of birds and places

Plate numbers are shown in **bold** type; other references are to the main text.